Huguccio

STUDIES IN MEDIEVAL AND EARLY
MODERN CANON LAW

KENNETH PENNINGTON,
GENERAL EDITOR

STUDIES IN MEDIEVAL AND EARLY
MODERN CANON LAW

VOLUME 3

Huguccio

THE LIFE, WORKS, AND THOUGHT
OF A TWELFTH-CENTURY JURIST

WOLFGANG P. MÜLLER

THE CATHOLIC UNIVERSITY OF AMERICA PRESS
WASHINGTON, D.C.

The paper used in this publication meets the minimum requirements
of American National Standards for Information Sciences—
Permanence of Paper for Printed Library materials,
ANSI Z39.48-1984.

∞

LIBRARY OF CONGRESS CATALOGING-IN-PUBLICATION DATA
Müller, Wolfgang P., 1960–
Huguccio, the life, works, and thought of a twelfth-century jurist
/ by Wolfgang P. Müller.
    p.   cm. — (Studies in medieval and early modern canon law ;
v. 3)
Includes bibliographical references and index.
    1. Uguccione, da Pisa, Bishop of Ferrara, d. 1210.   2. Canonists—
Italy—Biography.   I. Title.   II. Series.
LAW
282'.092—dc20
[B]
93-1896
ISBN 0-8132-0787-8 (alk. paper)

CONTENTS

ACKNOWLEDGMENTS

The core of the present book originally formed part of my PhD dissertation, which was submitted to the Graduate School of Syracuse University in the spring of 1991. I have supplied the original format with a new Introduction and an Epilogue, and thoroughly revised Chapter II and the Appendices I and II. The rest of the text was retouched to a lesser extent. An earlier version of Chapter I appeared in *Viator* 22 (1991), 121–52, published by the Institute of Medieval and Renaissance Studies in Los Angeles, California. The Bibliography has been kept until the end of 1992.

I completed most of the work on *Huguccio* during my graduate and post-doctoral years at Syracuse University, between the fall of 1987 and the spring of 1992. The project was not performed in a vacuum, so that I owe thanks to many people and institutions. I am particularly grateful for the financial support I received from the Graduate School of Syracuse University, which granted me a three-year University Fellowship (1987–90), plus a Graduate Assistantship for 1990/91. I also obtained a Research Assistantship from Syracuse Law School (Fall 1991) and two stipends from the Roscoe Martin Fund, which allowed me to obtain important medieval manuscript material on microfilm. Since much of *Huguccio* is worked from manuscripts, the collaboration of various European and American libraries proved indispensable. Their names appear in the first section of the Bibliography. My special thanks go to the Bayerische Staatsbibliothek in Munich, whose staff has always treated me with exceptional kindness. The same applies to the people working at Syracuse University's Interlibrary Loan.

In the course of my research, I had many stimulating discussions with scholars and colleagues. Whenever possible, I included appropriate references to their contributions in the text and the notes. The task of these critics was made especially difficult due to the deficiencies of my English. Almost unaffected by any number of revisions, it would still retain a peculiar, non-native flavor. As a result, the stylistic outcome of *Huguccio* depends more on the idiomatic skills of others than I would like to admit. However, I must mention, with gratitude, Professor James Powell (Syracuse University), my colleague Brendan J. McManus, the readers for The Catholic University of America Press, and the patient copyeditor, Susan Needham.

This final paragraph is dedicated to Kenneth Pennington. As my graduate advisor, he supported the work on *Huguccio* in many ways. I do not need to describe his role in great detail, as long as there may be a single word to capture its essence. I think the Germans are right when they call someone like him a good *Doktorvater*.

WOLFGANG P. MÜLLER
Munich, Germany

Note: The abbreviations used for modern journals, series, and standard works follow the format and style of the *Bulletin of medieval canon law*, published by "The Institute of medieval canon law" in Berkeley, California.

LEGAL CITATIONS

a.c.	*Dictum* of Gratian before chapter
C.	Causa (division of the second part of Gratian's *Decretum*)
c.	chapter
Cod.	Code of Justinian
1 Comp	*Compilatio prima*
2 Comp etc.	*Compilatio secunda* etc.
D.	*Distinctio* (division of the first and third parts of Gratian's *Decretum*)
De cons.	*De consecratione* (part III of Gratian's *Decretum*)
De pen.	*De penitentia* (C.33 q.3 of Gratian's *Decretum*)
Dig.	Digest of Justinian
Inst.	Institutes of Justinian
Nov.	Novellae of Justinian
p.c.	*Dictum* of Gratian after chapter
q.	*quaestio* (division of Causa of Gratian's *Decretum*)
s.v.	*sub verbo*, gloss to a phrase in a law, canon, etc.
X	*Liber Extra* or Decretals of Gregory IX

Introduction

BY THE BEGINNING OF the last quarter of the twelfth century, Bologna was well on its way toward establishing a reputation as the capital of jurisprudence on the European continent. Less than a hundred years had gone by since the Bolognese jurist Pepo and his student Wernerius had begun reassembling the four parts of Justinian's *Corpus iuris civilis* in order to provide a basis for their lectures on the Roman law. They had been followed by two generations of teachers who systematically explored the complexities of the Institutes, the Code, the Novellae, and, most importantly, the Digest. Their success turned out to be permanent. By 1175, it had become routine for the Bolognese to see large numbers of students from all over Latin Europe arriving at their city.[1] The Bolognese example, moreover, had encouraged the growth of similar schools of law else-

---

1. For bibliographical information about the Bolognese law schools, see G. Zanella, *Bibliografia per la storia dell'Università di Bologna* (Studi e memorie per la storia dell'Università di Bologna, Nuova Serie 5; Bologna, 1985). A comprehensive account of the early teachers, their teaching methods, and the literary production has been given by P. Weimar, "Die legistische Literatur der Glossatorenzeit," *Handbuch der Quellen und Literatur zur neueren europäischen Privatrechtsgeschichte I: Mittelalter, 1100–1500,* ed. H. Coing (Munich, 1973), 129–60; more recent works on the origins of the Bolognese schools and their legal textbooks include S. Kuttner, "The revival of jurisprudence," in *Renaissance and renewal in the twelfth century,* ed. R. Benson and G. Constable (Cambridge, Mass., 1982; reprint Toronto, 1991), 299–323, also published, with "Retractationes iii," in S. Kuttner, *Studies in the history of medieval canon law* (Aldershot, 1990); on Pepo and Wernerius (Irnerius): C. Dolcini, *Velut aurora surgente: Pepo, il vescovo Pietro e le origini dello Studium Bolognese* (Rome, 1987); idem, "Pepo, Irnerio, Graziano: Alle origini dello 'Studium' di Bologna," in *L'Università di Bologna: personaggi, momenti e luoghi dalle origini al xvi secolo,* ed. O. Capitani (Bologna, 1987), 17–27.

where. Southern French jurists brought the Bolognese method and teachings home as early as during the lifetime of Wernerius (ca. 1125), and the jurist Vacarius composed an affordable textbook, the *Liber pauperum* (ca. 1170), for the study of Roman law in England.[2] These developments, however, never seriously challenged the importance of Bologna, which retained its leading status until the end of the Middle Ages.

The emergence of legal science at Bologna was part of a larger intellectual phenomenon, the rise of medieval scholasticism. The twelfth century witnessed the formation of curricula for each of the new academic disciplines, which included the arts (philosophy), medicine, law, and theology. They all based their courses on a corpus of authoritative writings, in what became the main characteristic of the medieval scholastic method.[3] In Justinian's legislation the lawyers had the most suitable source at their disposal. It was the principal testimony to Roman legal culture, which they considered superior to their own; it bore the authoritative stamp of a Roman emperor, which at least in theory gave it binding force; and it was comprehensive, which made it an appropriate focus of scholarly reflection.[4]

With the legal studies already thriving, it is hardly surprising that Bologna also became the focal point of the scholastic interpretation of the ecclesiastical law. It was there that, around 1140, Gratian composed his *Decretum,* which was immediately acknowledged as an academic textbook and the foundation of canon law as a scientific discipline. Obviously, time and place favored Gratian's undertaking. He skillfully applied to his work current scholastic standards and half

2. The attribution and the chronology of the oldest southern French treatises have long been disputed, cf. A. Gouron, *La science juridique française aux xie et xiie siècles: Diffusion du droit de Justinien et influences canoniques jusqu'à Gratien* (IRMAe I, 4 d–e; Milan, 1978). On Vacarius and the influence of his *Liber pauperum* (ed. F. de Zulueta [London, 1927]) on early English legal studies, L. Boyle, "The beginning of legal studies at Oxford," *Viator* 14 (1983), 107–31; F. de Zulueta and P. Stein, *The teaching of Roman law in England around 1200* (London, 1990), xiii–liii.

3. An overview of twelfth-century scholasticism and culture is provided in the collections of essays edited by R. Benson and G. Constable, *Renaissance and renewal,* and P. Weimar, *Die Renaissance der Wissenschaften im 12. Jahrhundert* (Zurich, 1981).

4. Today's standard edition of Justinian's compilation is by P. Krüger, T. Mommsen, R. Schöll, and W. Kroll, *Corpus iuris civilis I–III: Institutiones, Digesta, Codex, Novellae* (Berlin, 1872–95).

a century of Bolognese legal experience. As a result, the *Decretum* not only offered a comprehensive compilation of authoritative statements concerning the laws of the Church, but also presented them in an arrangement suited for scholarly reflection. Gratian distributed the canonical material according to subject matter, assembled contradictory evidence, and finally reconciled it in comments (*dicta*) of his own.[5]

In the following decades, scholarship on the *Decretum* advanced steadily. The canonists applied the same techniques as their civilian colleagues and contributed greatly to Bologna's fame.[6] As early as in the 1160s, a French decretist school followed in the footsteps of the Bolognese, and an Anglo-Norman branch developed not much later.[7] Simultaneously, Rufin of Bologna (ca. 1164) and Stephan of Tournai (ca. 1166) produced their *Summe* on the *Decretum,* which offered the first major syntheses of early decretist doctrine. Their influence was only increased, when, at the beginning of his career (ca. 1171), Johannes Faventinus combined both texts into a *Summa* of his own.[8]

5. Recent studies surveying the vast literature on Gratian's biography and his chief accomplishment, the *Decretum* (ed. E. Friedberg, *Corpus iuris canonici,* I [Leipzig, 1879]), are: J. Noonan, "Gratian slept here: The changing identity of the father of the systematic study of canon law," *Traditio* 35 (1979), 145–72; P. Landau, "Quellen und Bedeutung des gratianischen Dekrets," SDHI 52 (1986), 218–35; idem, "Gratian (von Bologna)," TRE 14 (1986), 124–30.
6. For the writings of the decretist period (1140–1215), S. Kuttner, *Repertorium der Kanonistik (1140–1234)* (Studi e testi 71; Vatican City, 1937) is still fundamental; bibliographical updates are provided by K. Nörr, "Die kanonistische Literatur," in H. Coing, *Handbuch,* 365–75; S. Kuttner, *Gratian and the schools of canon law (1140–1234)* (London, 1983), and the annual *Bulletin,* published by the Institute of Medieval Canon Law, in *Traditio* 11 (1955)–26 (1970), then separately as the BMCL 1– (1971–). A new reference work is meanwhile in preparation: *History of medieval canon law,* ed. W. Hartmann and K. Pennington, to be published by The Catholic University of America Press, Washington, D.C.
7. See A. Gouron, "Une école ou des écoles? Sur les canonistes français (vers 1150–vers 1210)," *Proceedings Berkeley* (Vatican City, 1985), 223–40; S. Kuttner and E. Rathbone, "Anglo-Norman canonists of the twelfth century," *Traditio* 7 (1949–51), 279–358, reprinted in S. Kuttner, *Gratian,* with "Retractationes viii"; R. Weigand, "Die anglo-normannische Kanonistik in den letzten Jahrzehnten des 12. Jahrhunderts," *Proceedings Cambridge* (Vatican City, 1988), 249–63.
8. H. Singer (ed.), *Rufinus von Bologna, Summa Decretorum* (Paderborn, 1902; reprinted Aalen, 1965); J. F. v. Schulte (ed.), *Die Summa des Stephanus Tornacensis über das Decretum Gratiani* (Giessen, 1891); a new edition of Stephanus's prologue and critical remarks on Schulte's edition is H. Kalb, *Studiem zur Summa Stephans von Tournai* (Innsbruck, 1983), 12–13, 113–20; regarding the chronology of both *Sum-*

After composing this largely derivative work, Johannes went on to prove that he was a legal thinker in his own right. He produced numerous glosses on the *Decretum*, which made him the most often quoted decretist of the 1170s and 1180s.[9]

By 1175, Johannes had left Bologna. His students turned to other *magistri* to continue their studies. It is likely that Huguccio was already among these teachers, despite the fact that, for this period, direct evidence of his canonistic activities is lacking. He appears, however, as the principal contributor to the first recension of *Ordinaturus magister*, the oldest gloss-apparatus to the *Decretum* (ca. 1180). His share in the drafting of the work indicates that he must have held a leading position among the Bolognese canonists as early as in the 1170s.[10] A decade later, Huguccio's prominence was uncontested. He was again collaborating in a revision of *Ordinaturus magister* (1190), yet his attention was chiefly directed toward the

---

mae, cf. also A. Gouron, "Sur les sources civilistes et la datation des sommes de Rufin et d'Étienne de Tournai," BMCL 16 (1986), 55–70. The *Summa* of Johannes Faventinus remains unedited; MSS are listed by S. Kuttner, *Repertorium*, 143–45; and idem, "Retractationes vii," in *Gratian*, 9.

9. For biographical information, see N. Höhl, "Wer war Johannes Faventinus? Neue Erkenntnisse zu Leben und Werk eines der bedeutendsten Dekretisten des 12. Jahrhunderts," *Proceedings San Diego* (Vatican City, 1992), 189–203; K. Borchard, "Archbishop Gerard of Ravenna and Bishop John of Faenza," ibid., 572–92, at 584–92; on Johannes's glosses, see N. Höhl, *Die Glossen des Johannes Faventinus zur Pars I des Decretum Gratiani: Eine literargeschichtliche Untersuchung* (thesis; Würzburg, 1987); R. Weigand, "Die Glossen des Johannes Faventinus zur Causa 1 des Dekrets und ihr Vorkommen in späteren Glossenapparaten," AKKR 157 (1988), 73–107.

10. *Ordinaturus magister* has been identified as the earliest decretist apparatus, to be distinguished from various older, rather loosely arranged gloss-compositions: R. Weigand, "Huguccio und der Apparat 'Ordinaturus Magister,'" AKKR 154 (1985), 490–520; idem, "Paleae und andere Zusätze in Dekrethandschriften mit dem Glossenapparat 'Ordinaturus Magister,'" AKKR 159 (1990), 448–63; idem, *Die Glossen zum Dekret Gratians. Studien zu den frühen Glossen und Glossenkompositionen* (SG 25–26; Rome, 1992), 451–563. Some modern biographers of Huguccio have held that he was teaching at Bologna by 1178, citing as proof M. Sarti (and M. Fattorini), *De claris archigymnasii Bononiensis professoribus* 1 (Bologna, 1769; ed. by C. Albicinius and C. Malagola, Bologna, 1888), 297 (371). Sarti, however, had misread a date that occurs in a passage of Huguccio's commentary (to C.2 q.8 p.c.5 s.v. *libellorum*) as "1178" instead of "1188." The mistake was corrected by F. Gillmann, "Die Abfassungszeit der Dekretsumme Huguccios," AKKR 94 (1914), 233–51, at 241 n.2, yet has reappeared since C. Leonardi, "La vita e l'opera di Uguccione da Pisa decretista," SG 4 (1956–57), 54, 87 n.174.

completion of his own, massive commentary on the *Decretum*, the *Summa decretorum*. This work forms the main subject of the present volume.

There is little personal information about the Bolognese canonist Huguccio. All we know derives from the succinct and technical language of official documents and his professional writings. By the time he was composing the *Summa*, in the late 1180s, he was most likely a priest. There are also indications that he was living in a community of secular clergy, perhaps attached to the household of the Bolognese bishop.[11] The *Summa* further reveals that Huguccio wrote two minor theological and etymological treatises, both of which have survived.[12] Yet aside from these rare glimpses, direct biographical evidence has not been found.

Modern scholarship since Mauro Sarti (1769) has resorted to indirect clues to supply additional data on Huguccio's life.[13] It is commonly accepted that his academic career at Bologna ended abruptly in 1190, when he became bishop of Ferrara. There he proved an able administrator of the diocese, until his death on 30 April 1210.[14]

11. This can be inferred from *Summa* C.16 q.1 c.41 s.v. *De his vero*, where Huguccio speaks of "his fraternity" (*nostra fraternitas*) in a way ruling out any identification with a community of monks or canons or membership in a military order: C. Leonardi, "La vita," 55–57.

12. Those are the *Hagiographia*, ed. G. Cremascoli, *Uguccione da Pisa: Liber de dubio accentu. Agiographia. Expositio de symbolo apostolorum* (Spoleto, 1978), 137–74, which Huguccio identifies as his work at *Summa*, De cons. D.3 c.19 s.v. *in predicto die kalendarum* (cf. chap. I, n.80 below); and the *Expositio de symbolo apostolorum*, ed. G. Cremascoli, *Uguccione*, 227–55; N. Häring, "Zwei Kommentare von Huguccio, Bischof von Ferrara," SG 19 (1976), 365–416, also cited by the *Summa*, De cons. D.4 c.73 s.v. *sic credatur in ecclesiam catholicam* (see chap. I, n.109 below).

13. M. Sarti and M. Fattorini, *De professoribus*, 1.296–301 (1.370–76). Most important among the later biographical studies are J. F. v. Schulte, *Geschichte der Quellen und Literatur des canonischen Rechts von Gratian bis auf die Gegenwart* 1 (Stuttgart, 1875), 156–70; F. Gillmann, "Die Abfassungszeit," 233–51, repr. in R. Weigand (ed.), *Gesammelte Schriften zur klassischen Kanonistik von Franz Gillmann 1: Schriften zum Dekret Gratians und den Dekretisten* (Würzburg, 1988), n.8; C. Leonardi, "La vita," 37–120; G. Catalano, "Contributo alla biografia di Uguccione da Pisa," *Il diritto ecclesiastico* 65 (1954), 3–67; A. Stickler, "Uguccio de Pise," DDC 7 (1965), 1355–62; R. Weigand, "Huguccio," LMA 5 (1990), 181–82.

14. The documentary evidence of Huguccio's episcopal career has been discussed in detail by C. Leonardi, "La vita," 62–77; G. Catalano, "Contributo," 11–43. The date of Huguccio's death is reported in the chronicle of Salimbene da Parma (1283); cf. chap. I, n.40 below.

As to the earliest stages of Huguccio's career, biographers further assert that he had started out as a first-rate grammarian during the 1160s. He is said to have produced an etymological dictionary, the *Derivationes,* which became the most widely circulating work of its kind in the later Middle Ages.[15] The author of the *Derivationes* also made reference to his birthplace, Pisa, and to other grammatical treatises of his, some of which have been identified and edited.[16]

Chapter I of this volume (Huguccio: Canonist, Bishop, and Grammarian?) reexamines the biographical evidence bearing on Huguccio's life. After all, the data assembled thus far delineate an unusual, though not entirely impossible, career in terms of length and success. Few medieval intellectuals could claim lasting fame in two different scholastic disciplines, as Huguccio apparently did in grammar and canon law.

Huguccio was, on the other hand, a man of truly exceptional talent. The *Summa* attests to his skills in summarizing and analyzing fifty years of decretist discussion in the most comprehensive fashion. While eclipsing all of his decretist successors, Huguccio's influence on later medieval canonists was lasting. Johannes Teutonicus made ample use of his doctrine in the *Glossa ordinaria* (1215), and he was still remembered when Guido of Baysio put together the *Rosarium,* a collection of supplements to the *ordinaria,* in 1300. Manuscripts of the *Summa,* moreover, continued to be produced until the fifteenth century.[17]

---

15. Cf. G. Schizzerotto, "Uguccione da Pisa," *Enciclopedia dantesca* 5 (1976), 800–802; MSS of the *Derivationes* have been listed by A. Marigo, *I codici manoscritti delle Derivationes di Uguccione Pisano* (Rome, 1936), 1–29, including incipits and explicits; G. Bursill-Hall, *A census of medieval latin grammatical manuscripts* (Stuttgart, 1981), 308 (index).

16. The lexicographer mentions his native city twice, in the prologue, ed. A. Marigo, "De Huguccionis Pisani Derivationum latinitate earumque prologo," *Archivum Romanicum* 11 (1927), 97–106, at 101–6; idem, *I codici* xiii–xiv; and under the lemma "PIS" of the dictionary. The *Derivationes* also refers to other treatises by the same author, the *Liber de dubio accentu,* ed. G. Cremascoli, *Uguccione,* 65–87, and the *Rosarium:* MSS in G. Bursill-Hall, *A census,* 349. For further details, see chap. I, nn.44–45 below.

17. A copy of the *Summa,* now preserved at Florence, Bibl. Laur. Fes. 125–26, was produced at the request of Cosimo de Medici (d. 1464): K. Pennington, *Pope and bishops. The theory of papal monarchy in the twelfth and thirteenth centuries* (Phil-

Legal historians since Friedrich Maassen (1857) and Johann Friedrich von Schulte (1875) have compiled a rather exhaustive list of the copies of the *Summa* surviving in today's libraries. They have also established the fragmentary nature of Huguccio's work (he never commented on C.23 q.4 c.34–C.26 of Gratian's *Decretum*). There is further agreement that Huguccio occasionally departed from the order of Gratian's text, thus leaving Causa 1, the so-called *Cause hereticorum* (C.23–26), *De penitentia,* and *De consecratione* for later treatment.[18] This not only resulted in a manuscript tradition displaying different stages of completeness but also led to the inclusion of other decretist comments supplying the gaps. Chapter II of this volume summarizes these findings and elaborates particularly on the aspect of the supplements. Most of them cover the fragmentary portion from C.23 q.4 c.34 onward, and the text added most frequently is the *Summa Casinensis* (or *Continuatio prima*). Due to its regular appearance as part of Huguccio's work, some scholars have concluded that it had been written by a student of Huguccio, with the sole purpose of completing the *Summa* (hence *Continuatio*). Others believed that the *Continuatio* was a collection of notes based on Huguccio's lectures. Still others argued that it represented an interpolation, taken from one of the contemporary decretist comments

---

adelphia, 1984), 81 n.21. The *Glossa ordinaria* of Johannes Teutonicus, revised by Bartholomeus Brixiensis (ca. 1245), became the standard marginal comment to Gratian's *Decretum* in medieval MSS and early modern printed editions. Like Guido's *Rosarium,* it identifies Huguccio's opinions by the sigla "h." and "hug."; for bibliography, cf. S. Kuttner, "Johannes Teutonicus," NDB 10 (1974), 571–73; K. Pennington, "Johannes Teutonicus (Semeca, Zemeke)," DMA 7 (1986), 121–22; F. Liotta, "Baisio, Guido da," DBI 5 (1963), 294–97; H. Van de Wouw, "Guido de Baysio," LMA 4 (1989), 1774. Later canonists with firsthand knowledge of the *Summa* include, for example, Johannes Andreae, who died in 1348 (see chap. I, n.8 below).

18. The various stages of composition have been discussed most extensively by L. Prosdocimi, "La 'Summa Decretorum' di Uguccione da Pisa," SG 3 (1955), 349–74. Modern scholarship on the *Summa* begins with F. Maassen, "Beiträge zur Geschichte der juristischen Literatur des Mittelalters, insbesondere der Decretisten-Literatur des 12. Jahrhunderts," SB Vienna 24 (1857), 35–46; comprehensive manuscript surveys have appeared in J. F. v. Schulte, *Geschichte,* 1.157 n.6; S. Kuttner, *Repertorium,* 155–60; idem, "An interim checklist of manuscripts," Traditio 11 (1955), 441–44; C. Leonardi, "La vita," 80–98.

available to the copyist. Only a close inspection of the work, however, can determine the precise nature of the *Continuatio*.[19]

Huguccio's enduring fame rested, of course, on his contribution to legal doctrine. This aspect has consequently received much more of the attention of medieval jurists and modern legal historians than the preliminary questions of his personality and the original format of his work. Despite the lack of a printed edition and the difficulties of access to the *Summa,* scholars have frequently consulted it in manuscript form. Since the groundbreaking studies of Maassen and Schulte, dozens of monographs have dealt with Huguccio's legal doctrine and revealed the encyclopedic dimension of his work.[20] The *Summa* forms a dense and continuous gloss on the *Decretum,* which Gratian himself had designed as a comprehensive statement of ecclesiastical law. In addition, Huguccio gave an elaborate evaluation of fifty years of ensuing scholastic discussion. His expertise not only extended to the essentials of previous canonistic debate but also covered important theological issues. Unlike most of his colleagues, Huguccio produced, for example, full comments to Gratian's sections on penance and confession. The result was a commentary of all-encompassing scope, which modern scholars have characterized as "a moment of synthesis."[21]

Huguccio in fact owed much of his importance to this synthetical approach, which often allowed him to spell out the hitherto un-

19. Cf. S. Kuttner, *Repertorium,* 158–60; idem, "Bernardus Compostellanus Antiquus: A study in the glossators of the canon law," *Traditio* 1 (1943), 277–340, at 283, repr. in idem, *Gratian,* with "Retractationes vii," 11–12; A. Stickler, "Der Schwerterbegriff bei Huguccio," *Ephemerides iuris canonici* 3 (1947), 201–42, at 206–7; L. Prosdocimi, "La Summa," 364–74; T. Lehnherr, *Die Exkommunikationsgewalt der Häretiker bei Gratian und den Dekretisten bis zur Glossa Ordinaria des Johannes Teutonicus* (St. Ottilien, 1987), 226–28.

20. The most complete guide to the older literature (until 1961) is by A. M. Stickler, DDC 7 (1965), 1359–62; see also G. Cremascoli, "Uguccione da Pisa: saggio bibliografico," *Aevum* 42 (1968), 123–68. Later publications appear in the bibliographical sections of *Traditio* and the BMCL (n.6 above).

21. S. Mochi Onory, *Fonti canonistiche dell'idea moderna dello stato* (Milan, 1951), 141–77, first introduced Huguccio and his *Summa* as "un momento di sintesi." For Huguccio's contributions to theology, see A. Landgraf, "Diritto canonico e teologia nel secolo dodicesimo," SG 1 (1953), 373–407; idem, *Dogmengeschichte der Frühscholastik* 1–4 (Regensburg, 1952–56), passim; for moral theology, J. Baldwin, *Masters, merchants, and princes: The social views of Peter Chanter and his circle* (2 vols.; Princeton, 1970), passim.

noticed implications of older decretist doctrine. A case in point is his theory of the political aspects of ecclesiastical government. Forming one of the best-studied areas of Huguccionian thought, it includes remarks on the proper functioning of the church hierarchy (ecclesiology) and on the relationship between the temporal and spiritual powers. To begin with, modern studies have established, after some controversy, that Huguccio's view of the two realms, clerical and lay, was essentially "dualist."[22] Each, the imperial and the sacerdotal (papal) power, had been divinely instituted in autonomous spheres. Yet at the same time, each depended on the other's assistance. Huguccio attributed to the emperor the power to govern all laymen and reduced the multiplicity of medieval kings, princes, and communes to an inferior status of delegated authority. He also analyzed the right to confer imperial power, which for him rested solely with the princes participating in imperial elections. The customary papal coronation of the emperor did not add any substantive right to the elect. Huguccio instead argued that the pope could depose a secular ruler only if called upon to do so by the electing princes.[23]

In this fashion, the *Summa* clearly delineates an area of self-standing imperial competence. But Huguccio made sure, too, that his

---

22. G. Catalano, *Impero, regni e sacerdozio nel pensiero di Uguccio da Pisa* (Milan, 1959), has offered a careful analysis of Huguccio's argument and has edited the pertinent passages from the *Summa*. This work summarized a decade of scholarly debate about Huguccio's political ideas, begun by S. Mochi Onory, *Fonti*, 141–77.

23. On the divine origin of the spiritual and the temporal powers, see *Summa* D.96 c.6 and D.96 c.10 s.v. *principaliter*: G. Catalano, *Impero*, 52–57, 64–68 (ed.); A. Stickler, "Schwertbegriff," 208–15; the subordination of kings and communes, *Summa* C.6 q.3 c.2, C.7 q.1 c.41: G. Catalano, *Impero*, 15–34, 69–71 (ed.), 75–76 (ed.); cf. also the recent discussion by A. Rigaudière, "Regnum et civitas chez les décrétistes et les premiers décrétalistes (1150 env.–1250 env.)," *Théologie et droit dans la science politique de l'état moderne* (Collection de l'Ecole française de Rome, 147; Rome, 1991), 117–53; the direct bestowal of imperial authority through princely election, *Summa* D.93 c.24 s.v. *quomodo*, D.96 c.6 s.v. *officiis*: F. Kempf, *Papsttum und Kaisertum bei Innocenz III. Die geistigen und rechtlichen Grundlagen seiner Thronstreitpolitik* (Miscellanea historiae pontificiae 19; Rome, 1954), 213–18; the deposition of the emperor, *Summa* C.7 q.1 c.1, C.15 q.6 c.3: F. Kempf, *Papsttum*, 219–23; G. Catalano, *Impero*, 35–41, 75–78 (ed.); O. Hageneder, "Das päpstliche Recht der Fürstenabsetzung: Seine kanonistische Grundlegung (1150–1250)," AHP 1 (1963), 53–95, at 63; E. Peters, *The shadow king. Rex inutilis in medieval law and literature*, 754–1327 (New Haven/London, 1970), 120–31; L. Fowler, "Innocent uselessness in civilian and canonist thought," ZRG Kan. Abt. 58 (1972), 107–65, at 159–61.

dualist framework was complemented by all the central demands of
Libertas Ecclesie. Since the beginning of papal reform more than a
century earlier, great advances had been made in asserting the general
principle that laymen, and particularly emperors, should not interfere
in ecclesiastical affairs.[24] By the time Huguccio came on the scene,
there was still reason to repeat these claims. Chapter III shows that,
under the impact of Frederick Barbarossa's aggressive policy toward
the Church during the 1160s, canonistic discussion had modified the
boundaries separating the legislative spheres of the Church and the
empire. Against certain pro-imperial arguments, Huguccio forcefully
restated that the Church enjoyed complete legislative autonomy. Applying the same principle elsewhere, he also insisted that laymen be
barred from acting as ordinary judges of clerics or usurping ecclesiastical rights. A sole exception he made for laymen who held rights
of patronage. As a matter of fact, Huguccio treated them with more
respect than other decretists did, conceding, for example, the right
to participate in canonical elections. Yet he otherwise denied any direct, secular interference in cases involving church property.[25]

24. A convenient summary of the historiography on the "Gregorian" reform gives
U. Blumenthal, *The investiture controversy: Church and monarchy from the ninth to
the twelfth century* (Philadelphia, 1988); for the impact of reform ideas on Gratian's
Decretum, see S. Chodorow, *Christian political theory and church politics in the midtwelfth century: The ecclesiology of Gratian's Decretum* (Berkeley/Los Angeles/Lon-
don, 1972) and the critical review by R. Benson, *Speculum* 50 (1975), 97–106.
25. A study dealing with Huguccio's views regarding the ecclesiastical autonomy
in legislative matters is: C. Munier, "Droit canonique et droit romain d'après Gratien
et les décrétistes," *Études dediées à Gabriel Le Bras* (Paris, 1965), 2.943–54, citing
Summa D.10 c.1 s.v. *iudicio* (cf. chap. III n.27 below); the procedural privileges of
the clergy are treated at *Summa* C.11 q.1 a.c.1 s.v. *Quod clericus*, cf. R. Génestal, *Le
privilegium fori en France du Décret de Gratien à la fin du XIVe siècle* (2 vols.; Paris,
1921–24), passim; on the Church as holder of temporal authority: *Summa* C.9 q.3
c.18 (G. Catalano, "Contributo," 57 n.145 [ed.]), C.33 q.2 c.6 s.v. *non habet* (T.
Lehnherr, "Der Begriff 'executio' in der Summa Decretorum des Huguccio," AKKR
150 [1981], 5–44, 361–420, at 420 [ed.]); G. Catalano, *Impero*, 44–49; its execution
by secular agents: *Summa* C.22 s.v. *patriciatus dignitatem* (T. Lehnherr, "Der
Begriff," 397 [ed.]), c.23 s.v. *ultimis suppliciis*: A. Stickler, "Schwerterbegriff," 215–
23; T. Lehnherr, "Der Begriff," 387–89. On patronage, see *Summa* C.16 q.7 c.26 s.v.
pie mentis, discussed by P. Landau, *Ius patronatus. Studien zur Entwicklung des Patronats im Dekretalenrecht und der Kanonistik des 12. und 13. Jahrhunderts* (Cologne/
Vienna, 1975), passim; the participation of laypatrons in canonical elections, *Summa*
D.63 c.1 s.v. *Nullus clericorum*: K. Ganzer, "Zur Beschränkung der Bischofswahl auf

It might be argued that Huguccio's dualism regarding *imperium* and *sacerdotium* was essentially moderate, conservative, and perhaps even defensively oriented. Any account of his dualist system would, however, remain inaccurate without a mention of the hierocratic elements in his thought. In fact, the *Summa* provided most of the legal instruments that soon afterward, during the pontificates from Innocent III (1198–1216) to Boniface VIII (1294–1302), would be employed to tip the balance between the two powers decidedly in favor of the papacy.[26] Above all, Huguccio and his contemporaries applied their conceptual skills to increase the effectiveness of excommunication. They were little hesitant to form this sanction into a formidable instrument of political control, allowing the spiritual authorities to overstep the jurisdictional borderlines "ratione peccati," in order to prevent sinful behavior.[27] Canonists soon discussed, for example, the particular effects of excommunication on the feudal ties between the (imperial) lord and his vassal. Huguccio, moreover, extended the threat of excommunication to almost any type of contumacious re-

---

die Domkapitel in Theorie und Praxis des 12. und 13. Jahrhunderts," ZRG Kan. Abt. 57 (1971), 22–82, at 46–54; H. Müller, *Der Anteil der Laien an der Bischofswahl. Ein Beitrag zur Geschichte der Kanonistik von Gratian bis Gregor IX.* (Amsterdam, 1977), 109–16.

26. The integrity of each—the spiritual and the temporal—sphere in Huguccio's thought has been emphasized by A. Stickler, "Sacerdotium et Regnum nei decretisti e primi decretalisti. Considerazioni metodologiche di ricerca e testi," *Salesianum* 15 (1953), 575–612; idem, "Imperator vicarius papae. Die Lehren der französisch-deutschen Dekretistenschule des 12. und beginnenden 13. Jahrhunderts," MIÖG 62 (1954), 165–212; and again in idem, "Die Ekklesiologie des Dekretisten Huguccio von Pisa," *Proceedings Berkeley* (Vatican City, 1985), 333–49, at 346–47. The hierocratic connotations have been pointed out by F. Kempf, *Papsttum*, 219–23; G. Catalano, *Impero*, 51–58. They anticipated most of the thirteenth-century doctrinal and political developments: see J. Watt, *The theory of papal monarchy in the thirteenth century* (New York, 1965; reprinted from *Traditio* 20 [1964], 179–317), 12–33, 81–84, 93–94; J. Muldoon, "Extra ecclesiam non est imperium. The canonists and the legitimacy of secular power," SG 9 (1966), 551–80, at 557–62.

27. For a general treatment of excommunication, see *Summa* C.11 q.3 c.15 s.v. *Si inimicus* (ed. J. Zeliauskas, *De excommunicatione vitiata apud glossatores [1140–1350]* [Zurich, 1967], 73*–75*); cf. also E. Vodola, *Excommunication in the Middle Ages* (Berkeley/Los Angeles/London, 1986); P. Huizing, "The earliest development of excommunication latae sententiae by Gratian and the earliest decretists," SG 3 (1955), 277–320. Ecclesiastical competence over laymen "ratione peccati" is discussed at *Summa* D.63 c.3, D.96 c.6 s.v. *officiis*, D.96 c.10–11: A. Stickler, "Schwerterbegriff," 211–15.

sistance against the papal will. Simultaneously, he did not attempt to limit the applicability of the sanction. The *Summa* attests to Huguccio's resolve to demand obedience to unjust and illicit sentences as well. Excommunication thus offered the Church an extraordinary means to draw before its court almost any case ordinarily subject to secular jurisdiction.[28]

Huguccio's treatment of excommunication questions the sincerity of his dualist notions, and there are other elements in his doctrine that reveal similar, hierocratic tendencies. They are often expressed by way of a reference to *equitas canonica,* with its concern for the sake of the Christian soul. Huguccio frequently used the concept in order to reserve certain legal cases to ecclesiastical jurisdiction alone, or to promote the application of canonical rules in secular courts as well.[29] Whereas this was rather conventional among contemporaries with regard to usury and the sacrament of marriage, Huguccio showed an unusual insistence when dealing with other, often typically secular, legal institutions. He thus tried to conform the theory of con-

28. The effects of excommunication on feudal obligations are expounded at *Summa* C.11 q.3 c.94 s.v. *obediebant* (ed. J. Zeliauskas, *De excommunicatione,* 83*), C.15 q.6 c.4 s.v. *absolvimus*: T. Lehnherr, "Der Begriff," 15–20, 34–36 (ed.); E. Hehl, *Kirche und Krieg im 12. Jahrhundert. Studien zu kanonischem Recht und politischer Wirklichkeit* (Stuttgart, 1980), 265 (ed.); G. Catalano, *Impero,* 35–44, 79–80 (ed.); an ordinary appeal was the only remedy against unjust or illicit sentences, *Summa* C.11 q.3 pr. s.v. *Sed ponatur* usque *queritur*: J. Zeliauskas, *De excommunicatione,* 270, 276, 63*–85* (ed.); secular assistance could be enlisted to punish contumacious excommunicates, *Summa* C.11 q.1 c.3 and c.18; C.23 q.3 c.4: R. Génestal, *Le privilegium,* 2.27–30.

29. A case in point is the question of the validity of imperial laws in de facto independent kingdoms. The *Summa* D.1 c.12 s.v. *in eos solos* (cf. chap. III, n.28 below), suggests that they apply only insofar as they have received papal approval, "ratione pontificis": F. Kempf, *Papsttum,* 231–37; G. Catalano, *Impero,* 30–34, 61–62 (ed.). Concerning Huguccio's understanding of *equitas canonica,* L. Scavo Lombardo, *Il concetto di buona fede nel diritto canonico* (Rome, 1944), 65–70, has presented a good sketch. An equitable sentence was always constituted of both, the principles of "iusticia" (justice) and "misericordia" (mercy), *Summa* D.45 c.10 s.v. *temperat penam*: L. Mayali, "The concept of discretionary punishment in medieval jurisprudence," *Studia in honorem eminentissimi cardinalis Alphonsi M. Stickler,* ed. R. Card. Castillo Lara (Rome, 1992), 299–315, at 311–12. The general accounts of *equitas canonica* in twelfth- and early thirteenth-century terminology by C. Lefebvre, "L' 'Aequitas canonica,' " *Histoire du droit et des institutions de l'église en Occident vii: L'âge classique, 1140–1378. Sources et théorie du droit,* ed. G. Le Bras (Paris, 1965), 406–20; P. Caron, "*Aequitas Romana,*" "*misericordia patristica*" ed "*epicheia Aristotelica*" *nella dottrina dell' "aequitas canonica"* (Milan, 1971) fail to recognize this; further details, chap. III, nn.35–36 below.

tracts by adding new elements to its Roman foundations. His interpretation of prescription and usucaption offers another striking
example. As chapter III demonstrates, he included an open criticism
of teachings of the Roman jurists, which unduly disregarded the demands of *equitas canonica*. Obviously, Hugucccio was little hesitant
to add to the list of spiritual offenses at the expense of secular jurisdictional competence.[30]

Turning to the internal structure of the Church, Huguccio's views
again attest to his adherence to the ideas of ecclesiastical reform, and
in particular to the main ecclesiological tenet of papal monarchy. Huguccio devoted all of his interpretive skills to specifying the legal implications of this principle. For him and his colleagues, the pope had
received his extraordinary powers directly from God, with the chief
goal of ensuring the unity of the Church.[31] To secure this purpose,
Huguccio gave a detailed account of the elevated position of the pope
as the supreme judge and legislator of the Church. His list of the papal
prerogatives included the right to transfer and depose bishops, to
ratify their resignations, and to accept appeals from all over Christendom. He could also summon to his court every case of litigation
within ecclesiastical jurisdiction. As a legislator, the pope alone could

---

30. Concerning ecclesiastical competence in cases involving usury (cf. chap. III,
n.30 below), see *Summa* C.14 q.4 c.11 (invoking *equitas canonica* against Roman
law!): T. P. McLaughlin, "The teachings of the canonists on usury (xii, xiii, and xiv
centuries)," *Mediaeval studies* 1 (1939), 81–147, 2 (1940), 1–22, at 1.84, 2.18; K.
Weinzierl, "Das Zinsproblem im Dekret Gratians und in den Summen zum Dekret,"
SG 1 (1953), 549–76, at 572–75; for *equitas* in canonical marriage, see G. Minnucci,
*La capacità della donna nel processo canonistico classico. Da Graziano a Uguccione
da Pisa* (Milan, 1989), 107–20, quoting *Summa* C.32 q.1 c.10 §1 s.v. *reos facere* (ed.
ibid., 117, also app. III, n.9 below). Huguccio's interpretation of prescription and
usucaption, *Summa* C.16 q.3 pr. s.v. *Quod autem prescriptione*, is discussed in chap.
III, n.36; *equitas* and contracts, *Summa* C.2 q.1 c.19, C.12 q.2 c.66, in the Epilogue,
n.14 below.

31. *Summa* D.19 c.7, D.22 c.1 and c.2 *non ab apostolis*. A monograph dealing
with Huguccio's doctrine of papal primacy is M. Ríos Fernández, "El primado del
romano pontífice en el pensamiento de Huguccio de Pisa decretista," *Compostellanum*
6 (1961), 47–97, 7 (1962), 97–149, 8 (1963), 65–99, 11 (1966), 29–67; cf. esp.
6.67–85. Huguccio was among the first to include the denial of papal primacy in his
list of heretical offenses, *Summa* D.19 c.5: P. Huizing, "Excommunication latae sententiae," 289–91; M. Ríos Fernández, "El primado," 8.65–67; O. Hageneder, "Der
Häresiebegriff bei den Juristen des 12. und 13. Jahrhunderts," in *The concept of heresy
in the Middle Ages*, ed. W. Lourdaux and D. Verhelst (Louvain/The Hague, 1976),
42–102, at 65–67.

issue statutes that bind the Church as a whole or resolve a question of faith. At the same time, he might revoke the constitutions of his apostolic predecessors, provided they did not affect the "general state of the Church," or the "articles of faith" central to Christian religion.[32] Formal constitutional safeguards against any abuse of these wide-ranging powers were, on the other hand, rather undeveloped in Huguccio's scheme. With the majority of the twelfth-century thinkers, he did not attempt to form episcopal government into an instrument that might effectively counterbalance papal initiative. Conciliar legislation remained entirely dependent on papal approval, and the college of cardinals was restricted to merely advisory functions in papal government. This was a rather limited role, considering that Huguccio's theory not only made the cardinals the exclusive participants in papal election but also allowed them to take over much of the administration every time the Apostolic See fell vacant.[33]

32. The *Summa* D.17 c.3 s.v. *concessa*, treats comprehensively the jurisdictional prerogatives of the papacy; cf. M. Ríos Fernández, "El primado," 7.121–49, 8.73–99; ; K. Pennington, *Pope and bishops*, 81–110. On papal legislative authority, *Summa* D.4 p.c.3 s.v. *abrogate*, D.17 p.c.6 s.v. *iussione domini*: M. Ríos Fernández, "El primado," 6.90, 11.42–52, 62–67; A. Stickler, "La 'sollicitudo omnium ecclesiarum' nella canonistica classica," in *Communione interecclesiale: collegialità-primato-ecumenismo*, ed. G. D'Ercole and A. Stickler (Communio, 13; Rome, 1972), 2.547–86, at 554–55; his exclusive right to revoke apostolic statutes, see Epilogue, n.28 below; to issue general laws and privileges impairing the rights of others, *Summa* D.11 c.2 s.v. *plena auctoritate* (ed. G. Catalano, *Impero*, 63), C.9 q.3 c.18: D. Lindner, *Die Lehre vom Privileg nach Gratian und den Glossatoren des CIC* (Altötting, 1917), 56–57; papal privileges should receive the broadest possible interpretation, *Summa* C.16 q.1 c.52 s.v. *aliquid iurisdictionis*: K. Pennington, *Pope and bishops,* 160–62; but could not go against the articles of faith and the general state of the Church, *Summa* D.15 c.2 s.v. *integerrima approbatione*, D.40 c.6 s.v. *a fide devius* (cf. n.35 below): G. Post, "Copyists' errors and the problem of papal dispensations 'contra statutum generale ecclesiae' or 'contra statum generalem ecclesiae' according to the decretists and decretalists, ca. 1150–1234," SG 9 (1966), 359–405, at 371–74.

33. It is uncertain if Huguccio thought of the episcopacy as instituted independently from the papacy, as his treatment of episcopal elections, D.63 c.10 s.v. *subscripta relatio*, would suggest: R. Benson, *The bishop-elect. A study in medieval ecclesiastical office* (Princeton, 1968), 116–33, 397–402 (ed.); T. Lehnherr, "Der Begriff," 382–87, 393–96 (ed.). Huguccio also taught, on the other hand, that the pope could allow a bishop to appoint his successor, *Summa* C.8 q.1 a.c.1 s.v. *Quod autem*: M. Ríos Fernández, "El primado," 8.67–73; episcopal election, moreover, required confirmation, given by a prelate from the supra-episcopal level, whose rights rested on custom and papal privilege: *Summa* C.2 q.1 c.5 s.v. *vel sententiam*, C.3 q.6 c.7 s.v. *ab apostolis*, C.9 q.3 c.8 s.v. *prisca consuetudo*: M. Ríos Fernández, "El primado," 8.73–78; P. Erdö, *L'ufficio del primate nella canonistica da Graziano ad Uguccione*

As a result, Huguccio seems to have done everything possible to enhance papal monarchy. The canonical tradition, to be sure, was rarely ever used to make an alternative argument. During his days, the centralization of church government was still a novelty many contemporaries appreciated for its efficiency. Yet even when, two centuries after Huguccio, the system came under the attack of the conciliarist movement, monarchical notions of Church government did not lose much of their appeal. Twelfth-century decretists were all the more indebted to the principle, as they found in the *Decretum* the almost proverbial statement about the pope who "is to be judged by no one." Still, Gratian's compilation also contained material reporting the case of Pope Anastasius, who had fallen into heresy and was condemned for it.[34] Huguccio speculated extensively on the possibilities for reconciling this instance with the principle of papal immunity from judgment. He tentatively outlined a procedure, according to which an obstinately and openly heretical pope could act as his own accuser and be brought to trial before the college of cardinals. Despite operating on a flimsy legal basis, Huguccio's argument proved that he was seriously concerned about possible

---

da Pisa (Rome, 1986; reprinted from *Apollinaris* 54 [1981] 357–98, 55 [1982] 165–93, at 178–90), 71–84. As to the cardinals and their electoral rights, see *Summa* C.8 q.1 a.c.1 s.v. *Quod autem*; the validity of simoniacal papal elections, *Summa* D.79 c.9 s.v. *quasi sit inthronizatus*; the invalidity of papal designations, *Summa* D.79 c.10 s.v. *si transitus* usque *decernere*; the cardinals as judges over a criminal or heretical pope, n.35 below; as administrators in case of a vacancy, *Summa* D.79 c.4 s.v. *Nullus* and c.7 s.v. *nisi tertio die depositionis eius*; their advisory role in regular government, *Summa* C.9 q.1 a.c.1 s.v. *Quod ordinatio*: M. Ríos Fernández, "El primado," 11.29–42; also F. Gillmann, "Die simonistische Papstwahl nach Huguccio," AKKR 89 (1909), 606–11; idem, "Die Designation des Nachfolgers durch den Papst nach dem Urteil der Dekretglossatoren des zwölften Jahrhunderts," AKKR 90 (1910), 407–17, at 414–16.

34. The maxim "papa a nemine iudicatur" echoes repeatedly through the *Decretum*, at D.17 p.c.6, D.21 c.4 and c.7, D.79 p.c.10, C.9 q.3 c.10–18, C.17 q.4 c.30, and, most importantly, D.40 c.6 (cf. next note); the case of Pope Anastasius is presented at D.19 c.8–9. The standard treatment of the origins of medieval conciliarist doctrine is by B. Tierney, *Foundations of the conciliar theory. The contribution of the medieval canonists from Gratian to the Great Schism* (Cambridge, 1955, repr. 1968); also idem, "Pope and council: Some new decretist texts," *Medieval studies* 19 (1957), 197–218 (repr. in idem, *Church law and constitutional thought in the Middle Ages* [London, 1979], n.ii); an update provides K. Pennington, "Law, legislative authority, and theory of government, 1150–1300," in *The Cambridge history of medieval political thought, c.350–c.1450*, ed. J. Burns (Cambridge, 1988), 424–53.

transgressions against the "articles of faith" or the "general status of the Church." Unlike most of his colleagues, he made the pope liable not only for persistent heresy but also for notorious crimes.[35]

Modern studies sometimes suggest that these debates on papal heresy were essentially academic and should not obscure the fact that twelfth-century legal thought did everything to foster papal absolutism. Decretist theory, it is true, never worked out an ecclesiastical system of formal checks and balances in the modern sense. But it would be anachronistic and too positivistic to conclude, therefore, that they disregarded constitutional elements altogether. As a matter of fact, some of the crucial concepts of decretist thought rest on informal, moral and theological principles. Most important among them is, of course, the idea of infallibility. Huguccio and other twelfth-century canonists had little doubt as to the enduring nature of the ecclesiological structure, which, after all, was guaranteed by the divine promise that the Church of St. Peter "shall not fail." Their belief in the indefectibility of the community of the faithful also assured them that God would not permit the Church to act permanently against its divinely instituted function.[36] Accordingly, heretical acts and laws might occur, yet were not to prevail among the faithful.

35. Huguccio deals with the question at D.40 c.6 s.v. *a fide devius*, probably the most famous and often discussed passage of the *Summa*; cf. B. Tierney, *Foundations*, 58–63, 248–50 (ed.); J. Moynihan, *Papal immunity and liability in the writings of the medieval canonists* (Analecta Gregoriana, 120; Rome, 1961), 75–82; M. Ríos Fernández, "El primado," 7.140–44, 11.61–67. Elsewhere, Huguccio mentions in passing the cardinals as the judges of a heretical or criminal pope, *Summa* D.63 c.23 s.v. *exceptis*; in all other cases, the pope can only submit voluntarily to judgment, C.2 q.7 c.41 s.v. *vestro iudicio*: M. Ríos Fernández, "El primado," 7.135–37; and follows his conscience, *Summa* C.16 q.1 c.52 s.v. *ventiletur*; as in abdication, *Summa* C.7 q.1 c.8 s.v. *periculosum* and c.12 s.v. *incolumi*; or in order to fulfill his marital duties, *Summa* D.79 c.9 s.v. *sine*, C.27 q.2 c.21 s.v. *tonsuratus*: M. Bertram, "Die Abdankung Papst Coelestins V. (1294) und die Kanonisten," ZRG Kan. Abt. 56 (1970), 1–101, at 15–22, 79–81 (ed.), 88 (ed.).

36. Luke 22.32: "I have prayed for you, Peter, that your faith shall not fail," is quoted by Gratian at D.21 a.c.1; regarding the indefectibility of Peter's church, cf. also Matt. 16.18 = D.19 c.7 and the pertinent comment of the *Summa*, treated by F. Gillmann, "Zur scholastischen Auslegung von Mt. 16.18," AKKR 104 (1924), 41–53, at 44–45; and B. Tierney, *The origins of papal infallibility, 1150–1350* (Leiden/London, 1972, repr. 1988), who has correctly pointed out that Huguccio and his colleagues applied the concept of infallibility only to the Church as a whole, not, however, to specific papal pronouncements. Tierney has summarized the criticism of his interpretation in a Postscript to the second edition (1988) of *Origins*, 299–327, at 299 n.1, 308–14.

It was in fact a matter of routine among medieval legal commentators to emphasize the intrinsic qualities of ecclesiastical law. Regardless of formal validity, authoritative pronouncements could not command lasting obedience if they failed to conform with justice and reason. In an important article, Brian Tierney has aptly summed up the implications of this mentality: "[The canonists] were expressing a serene assurance that in actual fact, in the ongoing life of the church, the truth always would come to be accepted by the church as a whole (whatever its immediate source) and would eventually be proclaimed through the church's institutions."[37] Medieval canonistic discussions leave little doubt that these considerations meant more to the participants than just a rhetorical exercise. The spiritual goals of the Church not only colored most of their concepts and arguments, but also shaped its institutions decisively. This is evident from Huguccio's *Summa* as well. It once offers a commentary on the legislative authority of the pope and the council that illustrates how real the tensions were between the formal, monarchical structure of the Church and the informal controls of ecclesiastical rule:[38]

But behold, a council has been summoned from all over Christendom! A doubt emerges. One opinion is proposed by the pope, another by everybody else. Whose is to be preferred? The argument here says, the pope's. I, however, distinguish and say: If either one contains an iniquity it is overruled;

37. B. Tierney, " 'Only the truth has authority': The problem of 'reception' in the decretists and in Johannes de Turrecremata," in *Law, church, and society. Essays in honor of Stephan Kuttner,* ed. K. Pennington and R. Somerville (Philadelphia, 1977), 69–96, at 89; repr. in B. Tierney, *Church law,* n.xiv.

38. "Sed ecce congregatum est concilium de toto orbe; oritur dubitatio. Fertur una sententia a solo papa, alia ab omnibus aliis. Que ergo cui est preponenda? Ar. hic quod sententia pape. Distinguo tamen et dico: si altera contineat iniquitatem illi preiudicatur; si vero neutra videtur continere iniquitatem et dubium est que veritatem contineat, pares debent esse et ambe teneri. Et hec vel illa pro voluntate potest eligi, quia paris sunt auctoritatis, cum hinc sit maior auctoritas, inde maior numerus, ar. di. xviiii In canonicis [c.6]; xxxi Quoniam [c.13], Aliter [c.14]. Si tamen papa precipiat ut sua sentientia teneatur et non teneatur sententia concilii, obediendum est ei et sua sententia est tenenda et non illa, ar. hic et d.xi Nolite [c.3]": *Summa* C.9 q.3 c.17 s.v. *semper valebit,* ed. M. Ríos Fernández, "El primado," 11.48 n.14; cf. also *Summa* D.19 a.c.1 s.v. *De epistolis*: ibid., 50–52. R. Weigand, "Die Rechtslehre der Scholastik bei den Dekretisten und Dekretalisten," *Ius canonicum* 16 (1976), 61–90, at 84 = *Persona y derecho* 4 (1977), 339–70, at 363–64; B. Tierney, "Only the truth," 75–76; and K. Pennington, *Pope and bishops,* 21–22, further quote *Summa* D.4 p.c.3 s.v. *abrogate* as a similar instance. Legislation consequently involved sin, if the pope acted without cause, *Summa* C.16 q.1 c.52 s.v. *ventiletur,* ibid., 23–24.

but if none seems to contain any iniquity and there is doubt as to which states the truth, both are equal and to be upheld. Then, either one can be chosen freely, because they are of equal authority. On the one hand, there is greater authority, on the other, there is a greater number, as is argued in D.19 c.6; D.31 c.13 and c.14. If, however, the pope demands that his opinion be held and not that of the council, one ought to obey him. His, not the other opinion is to be held, as is argued here and in D.11 c.3.

The quotation proves the extent to which Huguccio's ecclesiological ideas center on the substantive content of ecclesiastical legislation. The supreme authority of the pope may overrule any conciliar enactment, but only if the papal act is not nullified by its own iniquity. There is no doubt about Huguccio's resolve to enforce this standard. The *Summa* contains numerous remarks on recent papal decretals, which have surprised modern scholars because of Huguccio's sharp and rather irreverent criticism.[39]

Interestingly, the text continues by posing yet another limit to papal action:[40]

I consider this to be true when the articles of faith are involved, or something that does not depend on the will of others. But if it is something that does depend on it, it has no validity without their willing consent, even if the council agrees. So if, for example, the pope wanted to impose continence on exorcists and acolytes, he could not. There would be no validity without their consent, if he passed such a law, as is argued in D.31 c.1.

This reference to the "will of others" invokes a set of principles that obviously cannot be omitted from a complete account of Huguccio's ecclesiological vision: the rules governing Christian conscience. They

39. It has found a strong expression in *Summa* C.27 q.1 pr., where Huguccio rejects outright a doctrinal position held by "the pope (i.e. Alexander III in his letters, JL 13162 as well as another, unidentified decretal, GRATUM [see app. I, below]), and almost the entire Church": "Alexander in suis decretalibus utitur distinctione voti solempnis et simplicis . . . et fere tota ecclesia. Dico quod Alexander ibi loquitur non ut papa sed ut magister secundum suam opinionem," quoted after A. Scharnagl, *Das feierliche Gelübde als Ehehindernis* (Freiburg, 1908), 153–56; further examples of his intransigence have been given by J. F. v. Schulte, *Geschichte*, 1.164–65 n.25–26; cf. also Epilogue, n.6 below.

40. "Hoc intelligo verum esse si de articulis fidei vel de aliis que non pendent de arbitrio aliorum. Si autem est de eo quod pendet de arbitrio aliorum, non valet sine voluntate illorum, etiam si concilium consentiat. Puta vult indicere continentiam exorcistis vel acolitis, non potest nec valet sine eorum voluntate si hoc statuit, ar. di. xxxi Ante [c.1]." *Summa* loc. cit. (n.38 above).

complement Huguccio's informal obstacles to papal absolutism with an ingredient sufficiently powerful to warrant the straightforward assertion that the pope, with or without the council, cannot legislate against them. Speaking of the "will," Huguccio has, of course, no intention of promoting boundless individualism. As his reference to Gratian's Distinction 31 makes clear, the concept is strictly confined to the specific case of clergy in the lower orders, who cannot be forced by a papal decree to take a vow of chastity.[41]

Studies analyzing the pope's legislative powers have established that twelfth-century canonists denied to him the right to modify certain precepts of divine and natural law. Although legal commentaries did not specify them in great detail, the vows attached to the clerical orders or the monastic habit were undoubtedly included.[42] Huguccio's concern about individual promises, however, went much further than that. Medieval and modern readers of the *Summa* have noticed his peculiar treatment of voluntary acts and their legal effects and have often characterized it as "rigorous." The final chapter of this volume discusses the underlying assumptions of this rigor, which

---

41. The rubric to D.31 c.1 (*Ante*) reads: "Qui castitatem non promisit ab uxore sua separari non cogatur."

42. On vows in general, see *Summa* C.17 q.1 a.c.1 s.v. *Quod a voto*, C.22 q.1 pr. *Quod iuramentum*, C.35 q.1 c.1 s.v. *Cum igitur*: J. Brundage, *Medieval canon law and the crusader* (Madison/Milwaukee/London, 1969), 52–53. The limits of papal dispensatory power in decretist thought have been treated by J. Brys, *De dispensatione in iure canonico, praesertim apud decretistas et decretalistas usque ad saeculum decimum quartum* (Bruges/Wetteren, 1925), 121–34, 195–226; on natural law, see most recently B. Tierney, "Origins of natural rights language: Texts and contexts, 1150–1250," *History of Political Thought* 10 (1989), 615–46, at 629–38; concerning dispensation from natural law, cf. *Summa* D.85 c.1 s.v. *si tactis sacrosanctis*, C.15 q.6 c.2 s.v. *direpte*; in specific cases: R. Weigand, *Die Naturrechtslehre der Legisten und Dekretisten von Irnerius bis Accursius und von Gratian bis Johannes Teutonicus* (Munich, 1967), passim, who cites *Summa* D.1 c.7 s.v. *omnium una libertas* and c.9 s.v. *servitutes*, C.12 q.2 c.68 s.v. *natura protulit liberos* (concerning slavery), D.1 c.7 *viri et femine coniunctio* (marriage), Prologue and D.1 c.7 *communis omnium possessio*, D.8 c.1 *divinum ius* (property; see also Epilogue, n.18–21), C.14 q.5 c.2 *nec Israelite*, C.32 q.4 c.3 *pretexuit* (divine modification of natural law); also idem, "Rechtslehre," 72–73 (351–52); further, P. Landau, "Die 'Duae leges' im kanonischen Recht des 12. Jahrhunderts," in idem, *Officium und libertas Christiana* (Munich, 1991), 55–96, at 83–91, who discusses *Summa* C.19 q.2 c.2 (on private natural law); F. Gillmann, "Abfassungszeit," 238 n.1, quoting C.22 q.4 pr. *Quod autem*; C.32 q.8 c.1 *sine ulla conditione* (on vows); regarding vows of clerical continence, *Summa* D.27 pr. *Quod autem*, D.28 c.1 *approbata*: F. Liotta, *La continenza dei chierici nel pensiero canonistico classico da Graziano a Gregorio IX* (Milan, 1971), 114–25.

seems to rest on certain theological notions concerning Man's freedom to choose between virtue and sin. The chapter may also indicate that, compared to its merits of synthesis, the *Summa* is even more original as an attempt to integrate extremely voluntaristic views into canon law doctrine. Huguccio may in fact have been more thorough than any other medieval canonist in applying the guidelines of Christian conscience to the external forum of the Church as well.

Huguccio: Canonist, Bishop, and Grammarian?

A MONG THE MANY studies devoted to Huguccio, some have attempted to reconstruct the major stages of his career.[1] They have distinguished a threefold pattern, according to which Huguccio, born in Pisa, moved to Bologna early in his life and began to study the liberal arts. He produced a variety of writings on grammar, which established his great reputation in that discipline. Most prominent among those works was the *Derivationes,* a Latin etymological dictionary that was more comprehensive than any other of the period. Two hundred manuscripts and fragments still illustrate its enormous success in shaping the Latinity of subsequent generations, right down to the humanists. Later, Huguccio seems to have turned to legal studies. By the 1180s, he was a celebrated professor of canon law at Bologna. Toward the end of the same decade (1188/90), he forged his lecture material on Gratian's *Decretum* into a massive commentary, the *Summa decretorum,* in which he summarized the juristic thought handed down by his predecessors and pushed legal learning and doctrines in new directions.[2] The *Summa* circulated

1. An earlier version of this chapter has appeared in *Viator* 22 (1991), 121–52; cf. also above, Introduction nn.11–16.
2. Which "justly honors the author as the greatest of all decretists"; A. M. Stickler, "Hugh (Huguccio)," NCE 7 (1967), 200; concerning the exact date of the *Summa,* see below, chap. II.1.

widely, so that more than forty copies survive in libraries to the present day.[3] Finally, while still working on the last portions of his *Summa,* Huguccio in 1190 was appointed bishop of Ferrara.[4] He ruled the diocese until his death on 30 April 1210.

The account of Huguccio of Pisa, grammarian, canonist, and bishop, was first put together by Mauro Sarti and was published posthumously, in 1769. Following the method he had used for the biographies of many other medieval jurists, this Camaldolese monk first gathered systematically all available evidence for the life of Huguccio. Subsequent generations of researchers added no more than footnotes to his work, carrying on the method of accumulating source material in a rather mechanical way.[5] Only recently has the method been criticized.[6] Sarti did solid groundwork, but certain aspects of his biographical information remain questionable and open to challenge.[7] The chief purpose of the present chapter is to continue the process of reexamination and to evaluate, in particular, all the evidence suggesting Huguccio's triple identity. It is therefore appropriate to discuss one by one the respective links between canonist, bishop, and grammarian. Eventually, a picture will emerge that differs from that presented by Sarti. On the one hand, the traditional identification of

3. The commentary remains unprinted; for modifications of the most recent lists of manuscripts (cf. Introduction, n.18 above), see further *Traditio* 12 (1956), 563; 13 (1957), 469; 17 (1961), 534; 19 (1963), 534; BMCL 1 (1971), 71–72.

4. That this turn in his career came suddenly is suggested by the fragmentary state of the *Summa,* which breaks inadvertently at C.23 q.4 c.33 s.v. *quod sibi iubetur,* leaving the commentary on the *Decretum* until the end of C.26 unfinished. Regarding the gradual completion of the *Summa,* cf. chap. II.2 below; literature discussing particular aspects of the manuscript tradition is cited chap. II.3 below.

5. M. Sarti, *De professoribus,* 1.296–301 (1.370–76). Since then, G. Catalano, "Contributo," 11–43, has collected new evidence regarding Bishop Huguccio's administrative activities at Ferrara, Pomposa, and Nonantola; C. Leonardi, "La vita," 62–77, instead focuses on papal correspondence touching the Ferrarese episcopate during the years 1190–1210.

6. See J. Noonan, "Gratian slept here: The changing identity of the father of the systematic study of canon law," *Traditio* 35 (1979), 145–72, who has offered a model for further biographical work on medieval canonists, including this study.

7. Such as the claims of a direct teacher-pupil relationship between Huguccio and Innocent III: K. Pennington, "The legal education of Pope Innocent III," BMCL 4 (1974), 70–77; see also n.38 below; likewise, most scholars have abandoned Sarti's date of composition for the *Derivationes;* the first to do so was A. M. Stickler, "Huguccio," LThK 5 (1960), 521–22.

the canonist and the bishop is confirmed, but on the other, the hitherto unquestioned common authorship of the *Derivationes* and the *Summa* will turn out to warrant less credit than it is usually given. Although a possible connection between the two works cannot be denied, the ensuing argument amply demonstrates its problematical nature. This in turn may affect our understanding and future interpretations of these two works.

I. CANONIST AND BISHOP?

Shortly before 1348, Johannes Andreae summarized what he and his fellow teachers knew about their predecessor Huguccio. While earlier canonists had written about him in scattered glosses, Johannes composed a single comprehensive account:[8]

It is certain that he saw *Compilatio I* and *II*. However, in his *Summa* he rarely refers to decretals, and if he does so, . . . he does not refer to them by citing the respective *Compilatio* and the title; the reason, I believe, is that these [compilations] were not papal. That he saw them is evident, because two decretals, IN QUADAM [X 3.41.8], and QUANTO [X 4.19.7], were directed to him, then bishop of Ferrara, as I said there.

Johannes's passage includes the essential reasons that have induced scholars to identify the canonist and the bishop. Appropriately, he chose as his point of departure Huguccio's *Summa*. Gleaning its scant material bearing on the author's life, he was baffled by what appeared as contradictory evidence: Why did the work not cite papal rescripts after *Compilatio prima* (1191) and *Compilatio secunda* (1211)? He endeavored in vain to reconcile this circumstance with the conclusions to be drawn from two papal letters, IN QUADAM and QUANTO, which clearly established that Huguccio, "then bishop," had resided in Ferrara as late as 1209.[9] During March 1209, Huguccio received

---

8. *Adnotationes super speculum Durantis*, Praefatio (Lyons, 1521, fol. 2va): "Hugo: Certum est quod vidit primam et secundam compilationem. In sua tamen summa rarissime decretales allegat, et si allegat . . . non tamen allegat sub compilatione vel sub rubrica, motus ut puto quia non fuerint papales. Quod illas viderit patet, quia decretalis In quadam, De celebr. miss., et decretalis Quanto, De divor., directe fuerint ad ipsum tunc Ferrariensem episcopum, ut ibi dixi."

9. Johannes refers to (a) Po.684 QUANTO TE MAGIS (1 May 1199) = Register 2.48

IN QUADAM, a response by Innocent III to a previous inquiry of his. The pope began by referring to CUM MARTHE, a decretal he had issued more than seven years earlier:[10]

In a certain letter of mine you say that you read it would be against divine law if someone repeats the opinion of those who presumptuously maintain that in the Eucharist the sacramental water is turned into bodily liquid [*phlegma*]; for they falsely claim that no water, but a watery substance, had flowed from the wound Christ had suffered in his side.

Having thus sharply rejected the opposite doctrine, the same letter then turned directly against Huguccio:[11]

Although you note that to this many famous and authoritative persons have agreed whose opinion you have previously accepted in teachings and writings, nonetheless you will be compelled to adhere to our position, since we think the contrary.

Obviously, the bishop had openly challenged a judgment passed and published by Innocent. But for Johannes Andreae this was of minor importance. He gave the reference to this letter because of the

---

(50) = 3 Comp 4.14.1 = X 4.19.7; (b) Po. 3684 IN QUADAM NOSTRA (5 March 1209) = Reg. 12.7 = 3 Comp 3.33.7 = X 3.41.8. Decretals that bear somehow on Huguccio's biographical tradition at canon law school and that will be mentioned below are listed here: (c) Po. 2749 VENIENS AD APOSTOLICAM (13 April 1206) = Reg. 9.54 = 3 Comp 5.22.1 = X 3.43.3; (d) Po. 3666 RESPONSO NOSTRO POSTULAS (February 1208) = Reg. 11.267 = 3 Comp 5.21.6 = X 5.39.43, both also directed to the bishop. Again, (e) Po. 88 CUM M. FERRARIENSIS (20 April 1198) = Reg. 1.98 = 3 Comp 1.1.5 = X 1.2.9; (f) Po. 575 INTER CORPORALIA (21 January 1199) = Reg. 1.534 = 3 Comp 1.5.2 = X 1.7.2; (g) Po. 1327 LITTERAS VESTRAS (March/April 1201) = Reg. – = 3 Comp 1.9.5 = X 1.11.13; (h) Po. 1337 CORAM DILECTO FILIO (March/April 1201) = Reg. – = 3 Comp 3.22.1 = X 1.29.34; (i) Po. 1779 CUM MARTHE (29 November 1201) = Reg. 5.121 = 3 Comp 3.33.5 = X 3.41.6.

10. "In quadam nostra littera decretali asseris te legisse illud nefarium esse opinari quod quidam dicere presumpserunt in sacramento videlicet eucharistie aquam in phlegma converti. Nam de latere Christi non aquam sed humorem aquaticum mentiuntur exisse." The text (cf. above n.9 b) has been taken from 3 Comp 3.33.7 = MS Florence, Bibl. Naz. Convv. sopp. da ord.: Vallombrosa 36 (325) = Reg. 12.7 = PL 216.16. CUM MARTHE dates 29 November 1201 (cf. above n.9 i). K. Pennington, ZRG Kan. Abt. 72 (1986), 420, has wondered why it took the bishop of Ferrara more than seven years to express his criticism, if he was identical with the canonist.

11. Ibid.: "Licet autem hoc magnos et authenticos viros sensisse recenseas quorum opinionem dictis et scriptis hactenus es secutus, ex quo tamen in contrarium nos sentimus, nostre compelleris sententie consentire."

explicit mention made in it of Huguccio's former "teachings and writings."

Even more convincingly, however, the second papal rescript cited by Johannes Andreae, QUANTO, suited the purpose of relating the Ferrarese prelate to the canonist. Writing on a similar occasion a decade earlier (1199), the pope had furnished the decretal with a full introductory flourish:[12]

> The more we know you as an expert in canon law, the more we recommend you, bishop, to our Lord for turning to the Apostolic See when confronted with dubious and questionable [legal] matters; to the Apostolic See which, according to His plan, is mother of all the faithful and their teacher. Thus the opinion you once held in these matters when you taught others the doctrine of canon law can be either corrected or approved by the Apostolic See.

These flattering words leave little room for doubt. The bishop was familiar with canon law and had formerly taught, facts that strongly recommend the idea that he and his celebrated namesake at Bologna were one and the same. Not only Johannes Andreae and his medieval colleagues, but also later historians, therefore, have accepted an identification of the bishop and the canonist.

Yet despite such seemingly compelling proof, Huguccio, the teacher of canon law and bishop of Ferrara, still could have been a different person from the author of the *Summa*. After all, Innocent's words offer no direct clue as to whether or not they were intended to address the great Bolognese decretist of the 1180s. There were other bishops who had been canonists of lesser rank. Innocent praised them in similar formulations.[13] Mere coincidence of names and professional interest cannot establish truth beyond any further question.[14]

---

12. "Quanto te magis novimus in canonico iure peritum, tanto fraternitatem tuam amplius in Domino commendamus quod in dubiis questionum articulis ad apostolicam sedem recurris que disponente Domino cunctorum fidelium mater est et magistra; ut opinio quam in eis quondam habueras dum alios canonici iuris periciam edoceres vel corrigatur per sedem apostolicam vel probetur." See letter n.9a above = Reg. 2.48 (50), ed. O. Hageneder, W. Maleczek, and A. Strnad, *Die Register Innozenz' III.: 2. Pontifikatsjahr 1199–1200* (Rome/Vienna, 1979), 88–89.

13. As an example, K. Pennington, ZRG Kan. Abt. 72 (1986), 419 n.7, cited an Innocentian letter to Martin, bishop of Zamora: "Preter debitum officii pastoralis quod nos omnibus constituit debitores personam tuam tanto amplius diligimus et sin-

Fortunately, there is another possible explanation of the meaning of Innocent's two letters. Like many papal decretals dealing with doctrinal points subject to dispute, they both treated arguments to which Huguccio's *Summa* included pertinent "sedes materiae." This calls for comparison. Did Innocent refer perhaps to the *Summa* in his allusion to the bishop's "writings"? To begin with the rescript of 1209, IN QUADAM, the pope, as we have seen, attacked those who "falsely claim that no water but a watery substance had flowed from the wound Christ had suffered in his side." He continued by personally charging the bishop Huguccio, since he had "previously accepted" their opinion "in teachings and writings."[15] And indeed, the *Summa* correspondingly noted:[16]

Wine, namely, changes into blood . . . , water into other watery fluids, and stands for them. But did not real water flow from Christ's side? The Gospel says so, and so did others, too, asserting that it was real. . . . I do believe that

---

cerius amplexamur, quanto amplius es preditus scientia litterarum et tam in canonico quam civili iure peritus," Reg. 1.58 (6 March 1198), ed. O. Hageneder and A. Haidacher, *Die Register Innozenz' III.: 1. Pontifikatsjahr 1198–1199* (Rome/Vienna, 1964), 87. These lines seem to suggest the bishop's identity with Martin of Zamora, a contemporary canonist of some renown, whose teachings on the *Decretum*, 1 Comp, and 4 Comp are occasionally reported in the commentaries of the decretalists; cf. F. Gillmann, *Des Johannes Galensis Apparat zur Compilatio III in der UB Erlangen (Cod.349). Mit einem Anhang: Zur Inventarisierung der kanonistischen Handschriften aus der Zeit von Gratian bis Gregor IX.* (Mainz, 1938), 81–82 n.; but since this would imply that Martinus wrote glosses until the end of his pontificate, most scholars now reject this hypothesis: see R. Weigand, "Frühe Kanonisten und ihre Karriere in der Kirche," ZRG Kan. Abt. 76 (1990), 148–49; contra: A. Garcia y Garcia, "La canonística Ibérica (1150–1250) en la investigación reciente," BMCL 11 (1981), 54.

14. Identical names constitute very indeterminate evidence. Twelfth-century published charters from Pisa, for example, refer to, or are signed by, no less than 93 different persons called "Uguccio"; plus another 133 who appear as "Ugo"; see N. Caturegli, *Regestum Pisanum* (Regesta chartarum Italiae 24; Rome, 1938), 644–48 (index, eleventh-century charters excluded).

15. Reg. 12.7 (above nn.10–11), passim; similar comparisons in F. Holböck, *Der eucharistische und der mystische Leib Christi* (Rome, 1941), 183.

16. *Summa*, De cons. D.2 c.1 s.v. *quia utrumque*: "Vinum enim convertitur in sanguinem . . . , aqua convertitur in alios humores aquaticos et illos significat. Sed nonne vera aqua fluxit de latere Christi? Evangelium hoc dicit et dicunt quidam quod vera fuit . . . ; nos credimus quod non fuerit vera aqua sed fuerunt alii aquatici humores qui cum sanguine exierunt" (Admont 7, fol. 422rb; Klosterneuburg 89, fol. 364ra).

it was no real water but that there were watery fluids that came out along with the blood.

In the light of this opinion, the request sent by the bishop to the pope in 1209 appears almost as a natural consequence, provided that he was the *Summa*'s author.

The same may apply with regard to Innocent's response of 1199, QUANTO. Obviously, it was the papal reaction to a legal inquiry that the bishop of Ferrara had submitted to the Apostolic See. Paraphrased by Innocent in his "narratio," the problem had probably been formulated by Huguccio this way: "If one partner in a marriage turns to heresy, and the remaining one wishes to marry for a second time, can that happen legally?"[17] Such a question at first sight may have seemed pointless, since two pontiffs had very recently said that such a marriage could take place.[18] Yet the wording in which Huguccio had posed his question echoed one of the papal decisions, so that on his part, certainly, astonishment rather than ignorance was responsible for it.[19] In fact, the bishop's curiosity betrayed a controversial spirit. The Innocentian arenga ascribed his initiative to an opinion "once held in these matters," when he still "taught others the doctrine of canon law." Huguccio must have disagreed with the current state of papal legislation, for otherwise the letter would have been superfluous. As a result, he must have been pleased with the way Innocent decided to handle the case. At the beginning of his de-

17. Cf. Reg. 2.48(50), 88: ". . . altero coniugum ad heresim transeunte qui relinquitur ad secunda vota transire desiderat et filios procreare quod utrum possit fieri de iure . . ."; this reflected the bishop's own words as Innocent subsequently made clear: ". . . per tuas easdem nos duxisti litteras consulendos."

18. Urban III: JL 15734 (ca. 1185–87) = 1 Comp 4.20.5 = X 4.19.6; Celestine III: JL 17649 (ca. 1191–97): see next note.

19. There are indeed parallels between Huguccio's (via Innocent's: above n.16) and Celestine's formulations (cf. last note), the latter stating the case in this way (2 Comp 3.20.2 = X 3.33.1): "Viro propter odium uxoris Christum negante et sibi copulante paganam et ex ea filios procreante, Christiana in opprobrium Iesu Christi relicta cum assensu archidiaconi sui ad secundas nuptias convolarit et filios susceptit ex ipsis." The letter, originally sent to the bishop of Ancona, was incorporated in many of the decretal collections appearing between 1191 and 1210; cf. W. Holtzmann, *Studies in the collections of twelfth-century decretals*, ed. C. Cheney and M. Cheney (MIC B-3; Vatican City, 1979), 330 (index to JL 17649); also F. Cantelar Rodríguez, *El matrimonio de herejes. Bifurcación del impedimentum disparis cultus y divorcio por herejía* (Salamanca, 1972), 179 n.99. Huguccio must have known it through one of them.

cretal the pope already signalled that he himself shared Huguccio's viewpoint when he remarked that some of his "predecessors appear to have held a different opinion."[20] Innocent, in other words, chose the standpoint opposing Urban III and Celestine III, a standpoint previously adopted by Gratian and by Huguccio in his *Summa*. The pope could even have used the canonist's work along with the *Decretum* in order to reach his subsequent conclusions.[21] The first part of the decretal reproduced, if in a somewhat condensed form, almost all the ideas incorporated in Huguccio's gloss:[22]

HUGUCCIO	INNOCENT
Demum ostendit [Gratianus] quid iuris sit si alter de duobus coniugibus infidelibus convertatur ad fidem altero remanente in infidelitate,	Distinguimus . . . an ex duobus infidelibus alter ad fidem catholicam convertatur,
vel si alter de duobus coniugibus fidelibus discedat a fide altero remanente in fide.	vel duobus fidelibus alter labatur in heresim vel in gentilitatis errorem.

Innocent's central distinction between Christian and non-Christian couples thus exactly repeated the earlier one made by the *Summa* on the basis of Gratian's *Decretum*. In dealing then with the first case envisaged, the decretal's text again showed some resemblance to Huguccio's comment:[23]

20. "Licet quidam predecessorum nostrorum sensisse aliter videantur . . . ," Reg. 2.48(50), 89; the doctrinal implications of Innocent's response have been treated by O. F. Rink, "Die Lehre von der Interpellation beim Paulinischen Privileg in der Kirchenrechtsschule von Bologna, 1140 bis 1234," *Traditio* 8 (1952), 306–65; overlooked by D. Sguicciarini, *Il privilegio paolino in un testo inedito di Uguccione da Pisa* (Rome, 1973).

21. These affinities were previously pointed out by O. F. Rink, "Interpellation," 320–21, 330–32. Other extensive treatments of *Quanto* and its legal background are those by M. Maccarone, "Sacramentalità e indissolubilità del matrimonio nella dottrina di Innocenzo III," *Lateranum* 44 (1978), 501–4; and F. Cantelar Rodríguez, *El matrimonio*, 167–89.

22. C.28 q.1 a.c.1 s.v. *quidam* (MSS Lons-le-Saunier, 12.F.16, fols. 339vb–340ra; Klosterneuburg 89, fol. 285rb): also O. F. Rink, "Interpellation," 334–35; D. Sguicciarini, *Privilegio paolino*, app. iii-iv; F. Cantelar Rodríguez, *El matrimonio*, 97.

23. *Summa*, loc. cit. s.v. *quod autem*: The Roman numerals given in the text in-

HUGUCCIO	INNOCENT
Cum ergo alter coniugum infidelium convertitur ad fidem et alter non, refert an infidelis velit cohabitare cum fideli vel non.	Si enim alter infidelium coniugum ad fidem catholicam convertatur altero
[II] Si vero vult cohabitare, refert an abhorreat et blasphemet nomen Christi sive velit fidelem ad infidelitatem vel aliud peccatum mortale cogere vel non. Si abhorret et blasphemat vel velit cogere, licite dimittitur . . . [I] Si non vult cohabitare, contumelia Creatoris frangit vinculum matrimonii et licet fideli alii se copulare.	vel nullo modo vel saltem non absque blasphemia divini nominis vel ut eum pertrahat ad mortale peccatum ei cohabitare volente, qui relinquitur ad secunda si voluerit vota transibit. Et in hoc casu intelligimus . . . canonem [cf. C.28 q.2 c.2] . . . in quo dicitur quod contumelia Creatoris solvit ius matrimonii.

In this section Innocent came closest to the *Summa* in listing the impediments to a legal divorce between unbelievers. If one party converts to Catholicism, both texts argued, the nuptial bonds remain intact unless the infidel betrays a strong unwillingness to tolerate the other's new faith. Although the whole aspect did not directly bear upon the bishop's question, its treatment was quite conventional in such a context, as is testified by the *Summa*. Turning next to the Christian couple of which one partner has fallen into heresy, the pope, it is true, based his reasoning more on Gratian than on Huguccio. Perhaps he did so because the *Summa* paid no special attention to this problem in the context of Causa 28. All the same, the final decision against any resulting claim for a legal remarriage was unanimous:[24]

---

dicate that the original order of the paragraphs [I] and [II] has been inverted; in this way, they correspond directly to the line of thought adopted by Innocent.

24. *Summa* C.28 q.1 c.4 s.v. *imputabitur*; the text is printed in O. F. Rink, "Interpellation," 337; D. Sguicciarini, *Privilegio paolino*, ix.

HUGUCCIO	INNOCENT
Item propter talem fornicationem [sc. blasphemiam nominis Christi] vir fidelis licite dimittit uxorem fidelem et e contrario . . . , nec ob hoc frangitur matrimonium.	Si vero alter fidelium coniugum labatur in heresim . . . non credimus quod in hoc is qui relinquitur vivente altero possit ad secundas nuptias convolare licet in hoc casu maior appareat contumelia Creatoris. Nam etsi matrimonium verum inter fideles existat, non tamen est ratum. Inter fideles autem verum quidem et ratum existit quia sacramentum fidei quod semel admissum numquam amittitur ratum efficit coniugii sacramentum [cf. C.28 q.1 p.c.17].

Admittedly, neither the letter itself nor these comparisons explicitly reveal whether the bishop's opinion was "corrected or approved by the Apostolic See." They do suggest, however, that the bishop was somehow at odds with the pronouncements of Innocent's predecessors. Mutual agreement between the pope and the bishop on the legal point discussed in 1199 can be inferred, moreover, from the former's sympathetic tone, which stood in full contrast to that he later adopted in 1209.[25] Our evidence thus amounts to a coherent impression: Huguccio of Ferrara reacted exactly as the canonist would have done, in accordance with the doctrine set out in the *Summa*. In addition to that, a proper understanding of what caused both decretals almost requires recourse to the work itself. Huguccio obviously still kept an eye on canon law, his former scholarly domain, long after he had become the ordinary of Ferrara.

The identification of bishop and canonist faces, however, another objection. No contemporary author of a legal work ever asserted that bishop and canonist were one and the same. Only in the 1240s did

25. Innocent's flattering words therefore have to be understood in terms of business rather than personal friendship, as M. Sarti, *De professoribus*, 1.297 (1.372), and many students after him believed; cf. below n.38.

biographical hints of this sort begin to turn up in the glosses on Innocent's two decretals and elsewhere.[26] They soon multiplied and were handed down by medieval jurists like Johannes Andreae, who incorporated them into a coherent version of Huguccio's life. Thomas Diplovatatius ultimately summarized the biography in his work *De claris iurisconsultis* of 1511.[27]

In order to determine the reliability of these later testimonies, we must focus on the earliest phase of transmission. Indeed, the initial absence of all comment upon Huguccio's double identity raises suspicion. Such an argument from silence allows at least two different interpretations: Was an identification of bishop and canonist simply inconceivable among early thirteenth-century teachers at Bologna? Or did the teachers simply suppose that everybody knew about it?[28]

Our search for a possible answer must take into account the fact that originally our two Innocentian letters were known to the canonists as part of *Compilatio III* (1210). It was from there that the papal references to Huguccio of Ferrara and his "teachings and writings," or to his expertise in "matters of canon law" entered the minds of all students attending lectures of the Bolognese decretalists. In this respect, however, a sudden change was brought about when Pope Gregory IX in 1234 promulgated his decretal collection, the *Liber extra*.[29] Older compilations were now declared obsolete, although the

26. This statement is based on an examination of glosses to the above mentioned decretals (n.9), as they appear in the following commentaries to *Compilatio tertia* (i.e. before 1234): Vincentius Hispanus (MS Karlsruhe, Aug. XL); Johannes Teutonicus (MS Munich, Staatsbibl. lat. 3879); Laurentius Hispanus (MSS Karlsruhe, Aug. XL; Admont, Stiftsbibl. 55); the apparatus *Servus appellatur* (MS Paris, B.N. lat. 3967); Tancredus's *Glossa ordinaria* (MS Vatican, Bibl. Ap. Lat. 2509).

27. T. Diplovatatius, *De claris iurisconsultis* 2, ed. H. Kantorowicz, F. Schulz, and G. Rabotti, SG 10 (1968), 60–62.

28. One wonders in particular about the case of Johannes Teutonicus. His *Glossa ordinaria* to Gratian's *Decretum* (1215) borrowed much from Huguccio's *Summa*; for example, in discussing the nature of the fluid "flowing from Christ's side" (above n.10), Johannes wrote at De cons. D.2 c.4 s.v. *hec tria* (Admont, Stiftsbibl. 35, fol. 303va-b, Vienna, N.B. lat. 2082, fol. 226rb): "Alii tamen dicunt sed pessime quod aqua convertebatur in aquaticos humores, ut hec traduntur in extra iii de celebr. miss. CUM MARTHE (3 Comp 3.33.6)"; but he neglected to mention Huguccio's adherence to the rejected doctrine as well as Innocent's second letter on the same subject sent to the bishop of Ferrara in 1209.

29. For how this compilation took shape, see the illustrative examples of S. Kuttner, "Raymond of Peñafort as editor: The Decretales and Constitutiones of Gregory IX," BMCL 12 (1982), 65–80.

one designed to replace them drew heavily from their materials. When canonists now consulted our two Innocentian letters, they discovered that the *Liber extra* incorporated them in a dramatically shortened version. The entire biographically important passage was cut from the rescript of 1209, while that of 1199 retained only a trace of Innocent's original introduction, reduced as it was to the words "Since we know you as an expert of canon law."[30]

In view of these changes, it seems unlikely to be mere coincidence that the canonists, cut off as they were from any other biographical source, should begin to feel a need for dealing in more detail with Huguccio's identity. It was Johannes de Deo, professor of canon law at Bologna since 1229, who probably became the first to attest that the canonist and the bishop named Huguccio had been one and the same person. Composing his *Summa super iv causis decretorum* in 1243, about thirty years after the Ferrarese prelate's death, Johannes included a brief explanation of his purpose. As already mentioned, Huguccio's *Summa* had remained fragmentary, leaving a break from Causa 23 q.4 c.33 down to the end of Causa 26. Johannes de Deo intended to fill this gap. In an introductory letter he thus ventured to say something regarding the author of the *Summa* he hoped to complete: "Master Huguccio, most expert in the *Decretum,* was once bishop of Ferrara and wrote a commentary on [Gratian's] corpus of *decreta*. However," he went on, introducing a possibly erroneous assumption later to be repeated by Johannes Andreae and others, "prevented by death he was unable to finish it up entirely; for it ends at C.23 q.4 'Est iniusta' (c.33)."[31]

If we consider the subsequent statements by his fellow teachers, the prior part of Johannes's account most likely was based on an inference from Innocent's two decretals. To the biographical details he seems to have added a good guess. According to him, only death could have

30. "Quanto te magis novimus canonici iuris peritum . . ." = X 4.19.7 (cf. above n.12). E. Friedberg (ed.), *Decretales Gregorii IX* (Corpus iuris canonici 2; Leipzig, 1881), gives the excised sections in italics.

31. "Magister Huguccio summus in peritia decretorum olim Ferrariarum episcopus . . . composuit quandam summam super corpore decretorum, sed . . . morte preventus non potuit omnino perficere—deficit enim in xxiii Ca. q. iiii c. Est iniusta . . ." (Vat. lat. 2280, fol. 371ra); for further details about Johannes's supplement, see chap. II n.109 below.

been responsible for the sudden interruption of the *Summa*'s text at C.23 q.4 c.33.[32] While this assumption reduces the credibility of Johannes's remarks, in any case the biographical tradition as handed down by medieval canonists followed a different path. It rather departed from the gloss material growing around the two, now significantly shortened, Innocentian decretals. In one of the earliest complete commentaries on the *Liber extra*, Goffredus Tranensis (ca. 1241–43) supplied Innocent's incipit of 1209: "In a certain letter of mine . . . ," with the explanation, "Master Huguccio, bishop of Ferrara, had in mind the above-mentioned decretal, CUM MARTHE [X 3.41.6]."[33] About the same time, Bernardus of Parma likewise noted in his *Glossa ordinaria* (ca. 1234–66) to the *Liber extra*: "[Innocent answers] to the question of Master Huguccio, bishop of Ferrara, who shared the aforementioned opinion."[34] Bolognese teachers calling someone "master" were normally referring to their colleagues and predecessors, such as the school's founder, "magister Gratianus."[35] In giving Bishop Huguccio the title "master," both Goffredus and Bernardus very probably implied identity between him and the famous author of the *Summa*. At any rate, they offered a starting point for what later became a virtually uniform biographical tradition in the canon law school. Hostiensis (d. 1271) in his glosses to the *Liber extra* expanded the use of "master." Besides Goffredus's text, from which he borrowed literally, he applied the title to many other passages dealing either with an opinion of the canonist or with a state-

---

32. Modern scholars prefer another explanation for the *Summa*'s remaining incomplete: Huguccio did not cite decretals after *Compilatio prima* because a little earlier, in May 1190, his episcopal duties had turned him away from canonistic activities; see M. Sarti, *De professoribus*, 1.296 (1.371); F. Gillmann, "Abfassungszeit," 238–42; also F. Heyer, "Namen und Titel des gratianischen Dekrets," AKKR 94 (1914), 513 n.57; the problem is discussed below, chap. II.1–2.

33. Goffredus Tranensis, to X 3.41.8 s.v. *epistola decretali* (cf. n.10 above): "Magister Huguccio episcopus Ferrariensis respexit decretalem illam CUM MARTHE"; the gloss is cited in full by K. Pennington, ZRG Kan. Abt. 72 (1986), 420 n.13 (from MS Paris, B.N. lat. 15402, fol. 126rb).

34. Bernardus Parmensis, to X 3.41.8 s.v. *Respondemus* (Syracuse, N.Y., Univ. Lib., Arents Coll. 1, fol. 186rb): "Ad questionem magistri Huguccionis episcopi Ferrariensis, qui opinionem predictam secutus (est)."

35. On the meaning of "master" in late twelfth-century Bologna, in particular as used to designate canon law teachers, see J. Fried, *Über die Entstehung des Juristenstandes im 12. Jahrhundert* (Cologne/Vienna, 1974), 9–24.

ment of the prelate.[36] Hostiensis thereby became the great propagator
of the idea that canonist and bishop were identical. Two generations
later, Johannes Andreae gave a precise summation.

In publishing his *Additiones* to the Ordinary Gloss on the *Liber
extra* (before 1317), Johannes attached short remarks to Hostiensis's
biographical notes indicating whose "master" Huguccio had been.
"Our teacher," he said several times, now pointing beyond any doubt
to the author of the *Summa*.[37] He also wrote of "his teacher," thus
offering the first support for the belief that Innocent III had studied
canon law at Bologna, in close contact with Huguccio. This was certainly an inference to be drawn from the signs of reverence Hostiensis
had already discerned in Innocent's words.[38] Again relying on such
indirect evidence, Johannes Andreae later composed the first comprehensive account of Huguccio's life.[39]

36. Hostiensis, to X 3.41.8 (ed. Strasbourg, 1512), vol. 2, fol. 176vb, repeating
Goffredus (n.33 above); the statement had already appeared in an earlier draft of his
apparatus (before 1265), discovered by K. Pennington, "An earlier recension of the
'Lectura super X' of Cardinal Hostiensis," BMCL 17 (1987), 77–90, in MS Oxford,
New Coll. 205, fol. 163rb. To the other instances given by K. Pennington, "Legal
education," 72 n.10, a conspicuous one may be added: Hostiensis, to X 4.19.7 s.v.
per tuas (cf. n.17 above): "O magister Huguccio episcope Ferrariensis qui hanc movisti
questionem! Unde et dicit [sc. Innocentius]: 'Quanto te novimus,' quasi dicens: 'Tu
forsan melius scires solvere quam nos nisi quia quicquid diceremus ius est . . . et ad
nos talia pertinent.'" (Vienna, N.B. lat. 2114, fol. 111rb; ed. Strasbourg, 1512, vol.
2, fol. 239va). MS Oxford, New Coll. 205 (first recension) reads: "O magister Huguccio episcopo Ferrariensi facto . . ." (fol. 190rb).
37. *Additiones* to X 1.29.34 s.v. *Ferr. ep.* (cf. n.9h above): "magistro Huguicioni
antiquo doctori nostro" (Munich, Staatsbibl. lat. 15703, fol. 78ra); to X 3.43.3 s.v.
Veniens (cf. n.9c above): "Forte [sic!] loquitur magistro Hugutioni antiquo doctori
nostro Innocentius" (ibid., fol. 240rb). All these supplements (including those in the
next note) were still missing from Johannes's first recension of the *Additiones* in MS
Munich, Staatsbibl. lat. 6351, identified as such by K. Pennington, "Johannes Andreae's 'Additiones' to the Decretals of Gregory IX," ZRG Kan. Abt. 74 (1988),
328–47.
38. Cf. above n.36. On such grounds rejected as legend by K. Pennington, "Legal
education," 70–73; to his evidence, ibid., 72 n.11, add: "Ergo commendat doctorem
suum [sc. Huguccionem] de multa scientia," Johannes Andreae, *Additiones* to X 4.19.7
(n.9a above) s.v. *peritum* (MS Munich, lat. 15703, fol. 264va). The contrary view,
that a teacher-pupil relationship existed between canonist and pope, nevertheless still
finds support, e.g., W. Imkamp, *Das Kirchenbild Innozenz' III.* (Stuttgart, 1983), 38–
45; in a review, K. Pennington, ZRG Kan. Abt. 72 (1986), 417–21, has responded
to Imkamp's objections; cf. most recently J. More, "Lotario dei Conti di Segni (Pope
Innocent III) in the 1180s," AHP 29 (1991), 255–58. At any rate, Pennington has

2. BISHOP AND GRAMMARIAN?

a. The Chroniclers

Thus far, we have treated the question whether Master Huguccio, the canonist, ended his career as bishop of Ferrara. Incidentally, this has confined our investigation to the evidence that circulated in the schools of canon law. Not surprisingly, canonists completely ignored information available from other texts. They linked their former colleague and the bishop, but went no further.

The nonlegal sources, however, offer a very different version of Huguccio's life. Friar Salimbene of Parma, the earliest chronicler to mention the bishop (in 1283), summarized all pertinent biographical features when he included this passage in his work:[40]

> Huguccio was a Tuscan, citizen of Pisa, and bishop of Ferrara; he composed the *Liber derivationum*; ruled his diocese bravely and honestly and died after a praiseworthy life. He also wrote certain other little works [*opuscula*], which are useful and in the hands of many; which I have also seen and read more than once. A.D. 1210, on the last day of April, he went to Christ. He held the episcopate for twenty years minus one day.

Salimbene's knowledge is traceable to his residence at the Franciscan convent in Ferrara where he had spent seven years, from 1249 to 1256.[41] It is very likely that he took advantage of this sojourn to col-

---

correctly identified the point of departure for all later assumptions of a personal bond linking Innocent and Huguccio: Johannes Andreae.

39. Cf. the text quoted above, n.8: after mentioning the two Innocentian decretals, Johannes added the words "ut ibi dixi," thus pointing to the direct source of his biographical knowledge: the *Additiones*.

40. "Ugutio natione Tuscus, civis Pisanus, episcopus Ferrariensis fuit; librum derivationum composuit; viriliter et digne episcopatum rexit et laudabiliter vitam suam finivit. Et alia quedam opuscula composuit que sunt utilia et habentur a pluribus: que etiam vidi et legi non semel neque bis. Anno Domini mccx ultimo die Aprilis migravit ad Christum. Et stetit in episcopatu xx annis minus uno die," *Chronica*, ed. O. Holder-Egger, MGH SS 32 (Hanover, 1905/13), 27 n.5; ed. F. Bernini (Scrittori d'Italia 187; Bari, 1942), 36; ed. G. Scalia (Scrittori d'Italia 232; Bari, 1966), 38.

41. Biographical information in O. Holder-Egger (ed.), vii–xx; G. Scalia (ed.), 233.955–62; with special focus on the Ferrarese episode, F. Bernini, "Che cosa vide e raccontò di Ferrara il cronista Salimbene da Parma," *Rivista di Ferrara* 4 (1934), 28–35 (not seen).

lect historiographical material, which may well have included some information about the late bishop. At least in part, Salimbene had access to very good sources, as is suggested by the extraordinary precision of his dates. The assertion that Huguccio held the episcopate from 1 May 1190 to 30 April 1210 is corroborated by several other documents and makes specific the rough chronological boundaries established in those documents.[42] Yet two other hints are crucial for our purpose. Salimbene modelled his brief biographical note on a pattern usually applied to bishop lists, in which after items such as "name" and "origin" he included certain written works under Huguccio's "memorable achievements."[43] What is most striking in this context is the absence of any reference to the canonist's *Summa*. But Salimbene did refer to Huguccio's supposed other major text, the *Liber derivationum*. According to Salimbene, Huguccio of Ferrara therefore was a lexicographer and grammarian rather than a canonist, a conclusion that has little similarity with anything stated by Bolognese canon law teachers.

How did Salimbene know that Huguccio, bishop of Ferrara, wrote the *Derivationes*? His enumeration of Huguccio's works ends with an explicit assurance that he has personally consulted the *Derivationes* and other, minor writings "which I have seen and read more than once." Even if we presuppose only superficial acquaintance, Salimbene should still have noted the short preface right at the beginning of the dictionary, where he would have found the author identifying himself: "If someone asks who is the author of this work, it must be said: God. If someone asks who has been [His]

---

42. In effect, the previous bishop died before 4 April 1190 according to a letter mentioned in P. F. Kehr, *Italia pontificia* 5 (Berlin, 1910), 219; Huguccio himself first appeared as bishop in a document written on 24 August 1191: L. Barotti, *Serie dei vescovi ed Arcivescovi di Ferrara* (Ferrara, 1781), 31; Innocent III attested his still being alive in March 1209 (cf. n.9b above); and so probably did Emperor Otto IV a year later in a charter that put all heretics "secundum mandatum Ferrariensis episcopi" under ban, ed. L. A. Muratori, *Antiquitates Italicae medii aevi* 5 (Milan, 1741), n.89 (25 March 1210) = BF 352; whereas a decretal issued on 13 October 1210 (Po. 4103) added "pie memorie" (late) to Huguccio's name. Generally, it has been noted that "Salimbene clearly reveals . . . a fastidiousness for getting numbers right": A. Murray, *Reason and society* (Oxford, 1978), 182.

43. For the characteristics of this type of source, cf. M. Sot, *Gesta Episcoporum. Gesta Abbatum* (Typologie des sources du moyen âge occidental 37; Turnhout, 1981), 32–33.

instrument, the response must be: by origin a Pisan, by name Hu-guccio."[44]

As in Salimbene's account, the passage mentions Pisa as Huguc-cio's birthplace. Contemporary canonists did not associate Huguccio with Pisa, so that the appearance of Pisa so closely connected with the *Derivationes* supports the hypothesis that we are actually con-fronted with the piece of evidence on which Salimbene based his statement. A more careful reading of the *Derivationes* might have led Salimbene to the two "opuscula," which are cited there as Huguc-cionian products.[45] It is also possible that his reference stemmed from the various inscriptions to these little grammatical treatises, or from their peculiar transmission in the form of an appendix to the dictio-nary.[46] In any case, Salimbene most probably took only the dates of

44. "Si quis querat huius operis quis auctor, dicendum est quod Deus; si querat huius operis quis fuerit instrumentum, respondendum est quia patria Pisanus, nomine Ugutio" (MS Graz, UB 144, fol. 1ra). The entire prologue has been printed several times, e.g. by A. Marigo, "De Huguccionis Pisani Derivationum latinitate earumque prologo," *Archivum Romanicum* 11 (1927), 101–6, along with extensive notes; in a second edition, *I codici*, xiii–xiv, Marigo considered the quoted passage a later (au-thentic?) interpolation (cf. ibid. xi). In fact, it does not occur in two early copies of the *Derivationes*: MSS Florence, Laur. Plut. xxvii sin. 5; London, Brit. Mus. Addit. 18380. The Florentine exemplar, however, is so corrupt as to provide no adequate tool for textual reconstruction. Marigo referred to MS Paris, B.N. lat. 15462, as another MS that omits the final portion of the prologue (fol. 3ra), but a contemporary hand was quick to supply it in the lower margin. The author of the dictionary also reveals his origin in a well-known entry under the lemma: "[PIS]: Pise, -arum . . . De hac civitate oriundus extitit qui hoc opus multis laboribus et anxietatibus quadam tamen delectatione toleratis composuit" (MS Graz, UB 144, fol. 112va).

45. First, the *Liber de dubio accentu*, ed. G. Cremascoli, *Uguccione da Pisa. Liber de dubio accentu. Agiographia. Expositio de symbolo apostolorum* (Biblioteca degli Studi Medievali 10; Spoleto, 1978), 65–87. The *Derivationes* mention it twice: "[CERa]: opusculum quod de eorum accentu conscripsimus"; and again: "[QUIS]: in libello qui intitulatur de dubio accentu diligenter distinximus" (MS Graz, UB 144, fols. 33ra, 168va). Second, the *Rosarium*, preserved in four MSS, see G. L. Bursill-Hall, *A census*, 349: "[RODa]: unde et librum quem composuimus . . . rosarium in-titulavimus"; a similar remark occurs under: "[EDo]: libellum a nobis compositum sc. rosarium" (MS Graz, UB 144, fols. 55vb, 171rb). Moreover, the dictionary refers to another as yet unidentified work at: "[QUIS] Similiter componitur 'aliquando' acuto accentu posito super antepenultimam causa differentie ad istum ablativum 'aliquanto.' Licet enim 'd' et 't' sint diverse littere, habent tamen adeo affinem sonum quod ex sono non posset perpendi differentia. Quod patet lingua Teutonicorum sicut aperte dis-tinximus in alio nostro opere" (MS Graz, UB 427, fol. 122ra). For the lexicographer's possible authorship of the *Summa artis grammatice* (Munich, Staatsbibl. lat. 18908), see below n.120.

46. Six out of eleven MSS collated by G. Cremascoli (ed.), 18–23, have the *Liber*

Huguccio's episcopal consecration and death from a reliable local tradition, but obtained his other information from a copy of the *Derivationes*. The implications of such a procedure are obvious. Since his identification of Huguccio the bishop with the author of the etymological reference work is likely to have come from the latter's preface, the identification ultimately was founded on nothing except the similarity of names. Yet in order to find a definitive answer to the problem of Salimbene's reliability, we have to put his statement into a somewhat broader perspective.

Surviving only in a holographic manuscript, Salimbene's biographical account exerted, to be sure, no direct influence on later medieval writers.[47] His indications nevertheless happened to coincide in large part with those transmitted by a whole group of other testimonies. Among them, Riccobaldus of Ferrara stands out as principal source. Completing his *Pomerium* a little after Salimbene (about 1298–1300), he became the second chronicler to write about Huguccio of Ferrara and, as a matter of fact, the second also to identify the bishop with the lexicographer: "[A.D. 1190] Huguccio, bishop of Ferrara, composed the *Liber derivationum*."[48] The date (of composition?) he attached was new: 1190. Riccobaldus apparently deepened his acquaintance with Huguccio during the subsequent years, as is witnessed by a more elaborate *Compilatio chronologica*, finished in 1312. Turning once again to the subject of Huguccio's biography, he gave it a new twist: "[A.D. 1191?] Huguccio, born in Pisa, is accepted as bishop of Ferrara; appointed by the Apostolic See to be supervisor

---

de dubio accentu affixed to the *Derivationes*; they also carry inscriptions that regularly mention Huguccio as their author. Additional copies of the work can be found in P. Kristeller, *Iter Italicum* 4 (London/Leiden, 1989), 611 b (1 MS); and (4 MSS) in O. Limone, "Il 'Liber de dubio accentu' (cod. Ambr. E 12 inf.) falsamente attribuito ad Uguccione da Pisa," *Studi Medievali* 25 (1984), 320 n.18. Limone has also treated a number of MSS carrying inscriptions falsely claiming Huguccio's authorship; further examples of wrong attributions are given by G. L. Bursill-Hall, *A census*, 69, 237.

47. MS Vatican, Bibl. Apost. lat. 7260: O. Holder-Egger (ed.), xxvi–xxxi; G. Scalia (ed.), 987–1003; of course, a number of copies have been drawn from it since the sixteenth century, ibid., 1004–6.

48. "[A.D. 1190] Huguccio episcopus Ferrariensis librum Derivationum composuit," *Pomerium*, ed. L. A. Muratori, RIS 9 (Milan, 1726), 125; Riccobaldus repeated himself, ibid., 178, in his *Historia Pontificum Romanorum* (ca. 1300); and, again, in the *Compendium Romanae Historiae* (ca. 1318), ed. A. T. Hankey (Fonti per la storia d'Italia 108.2; Rome, 1984), 720.

of the abbot of Nonantola, a monstrous and unworthy man, he composed the *Liber derivationum*; in so doing, he drew from Papias's
book which is there."[49] In this restatement of Huguccio's biography,
Riccobaldus added the indication of origin: Pisa. As I have argued
above, he could have taken this information conveniently from the
Derivationes. His mention of "Papias's book" as a source demonstrates that he, like Salimbene, was familiar with the *Derivationes*.[50]
Also, Riccobaldus introduced a new question into the discussion:
When did Huguccio compose the *Liber derivationum*? He traced its
genesis to the monastery of Nonantola, at a time when the bishop of
Ferrara acted as a papal commissioner to correct the local abbot's
wrongdoings. Riccobaldus had probably plunged into the archival
records "there," which documented Huguccio's intervention, for we
know him as the only medieval writer ever to refer to it. Since then,
modern historians have confirmed that Huguccio's mission actually
took place, although they furnished the story with a date (1197–
1201) not corresponding to either one offered by Riccobaldus
(1190/1191).[51]

In sum, Salimbene, Riccobaldus, and some lesser, perhaps derivative witnesses show considerable agreement.[52] They all made their

49. "[A.D. 1191?] Hugutio natione Pisanus episcopus Ferrariensis agnoscitur,
qui datus adiutor a Sede Apostolica abbati Nonantulano homini prodigo et indigno
ex libro Papiae qui illic est librum derivationum composuit," ed. L. A. Muratori, RIS
9.245–46.
50. Papias, an Italian lexicographer, composed an etymological dictionary called
Elementarium doctrine rudimentum (ca. 1045); for his preface (with English translation), see L. W. Daly, B. A. Daly, "Some techniques in medieval Latin lexicography,"
Speculum 39 (1964), 229–35; further details in V. De Angelis, *Papiae Elementarium.
Litera A* 1 (Milan, 1977).
51. The first treatment on the basis of Nonantolan charters was that by the
eighteenth-century scholar G. Tiraboschi, *Storia dell'augusta badia di S. Silvestro di
Nonantola, aggiuntovi il codice diplomatico della medesima* (Modena, 1784/85),
1.126–27, 2.326–35. A more recent and well-documented account of the event is that
of G. Catalano, "Contributo," 15–36.
52. The other sources are: Francesco Pipini, *Chronicon* (1314), ed. L. Muratori,
RIS 9.635, who copied from Riccobaldus's *Pomerium* (see ibid., 101); the *Historia
Pontificum Romanorum* (n.48 above) was probably the source for the mention of Huguccio in an Italian *Chronica delle vite de' pontefici et imperatori Romani* (ca. 1371),
ed. Venice, 1507, 1534, also published in Florence in 1478 (Hain 12809) under the
title *Libro degli Inperadori et Pontefici*. Under either title, this work has been attributed
to Francesco Petrarca. Finally, a marginal note in the *Chronicon Estense* reads:
"Mcxci: Ugutio episcopus Ferrariae Librum Derivationum composuit," ed. L. Mura-

statements in the form of chronicles and treated Huguccio from a predominantly local viewpoint as a prominent figure of Ferrarese history.[53] The relation of the bishop to the *Derivationes* was their most distinct deviation from the biographical tradition handed down by medieval canonistic literature. Again, in what we may therefore call the local chronicler's version of Huguccio's life, the reference to Pisa as birthplace appears almost unmistakably bound to the grammatical work. Down to Riccobaldus's time, evidence asserting Huguccio's Pisan origin without any simultaneous link to the *Derivationes* does not exist.[54]

Ptolemy of Lucca is no exception to that generalization. His *Historia ecclesiastica* (ca. 1313–17) requires, nevertheless, special consideration, owing to its original way of presenting Huguccio to medieval readers. His approach was entirely unaffected by the earlier traditions we have treated so far. Ptolemy belonged to a small but growing number of chroniclers who occasionally consulted canon law texts for historiographical purposes and often used them to enrich their narratives.[55] This practice also induced Ptolemy to include some biographical sections on canonists in his work. Thus he treated, for example, the most famous among them:[56]

---

tori, RIS 15 (Milan, 1729), 535; a date for this entry cannot be established, cf. ibid., 297–98. But again, it strongly recalls Riccobaldus.

53. For Salimbene's links to Ferrara, see n.41 above; Riccobaldus had been born there. On his life (and works), A. T. Hankey (ed.), ix–xxii.

54. No canonist seems to have associated Pisa with the *Summa*'s author before Egidius Spiritalis de Perusio in his *Libellus contra infideles et inobedientes et rebelles Sancte Romane Ecclesie ac summo pontifici* (ca. 1323–28), ed. R. Scholz, *Unbekannte kirchenpolitische Streitschriften* (Rome, 1914), which includes an erratic reference to "Huguccio Pysanus" (111). In effect, this indication of the decretist's birthplace did not enter the biographical tradition at canon law school until T. Diplovatatius, *De claris iurisconsultis*, 62, who borrowed it from: "Dominus Rosellus in suo tractatu de sententia definitiva et interlocutoria, in prima columna: 'Huguccionem Pisanum egregium decretorum doctorem'"; this treatise of Rosellus de Aretio (fl. 1388), cf. T. Diplovatatius, *De claris*, 313–14, however, appears to be lost.

55. Surveyed by L. Schmugge, "Kanonistik und Geschichtsschreibung: Das Kirchenrecht als historische Quelle bei Tholomaeus von Lucca und anderen Chronisten des 13. und 14. Jahrhunderts," ZRG Kan. Abt. 68 (1982), 219–76.

56. Historia ecclesiastica 21.18: "[A. Mcli]: Isto eodem tempore scribit Martinus quod fuit Gratianus monachus de Tuscia civitate Clusina natus qui composuit Decretum apud Bononiam in monasterio sui ordinis ut Huguccio Pisanus de ipso scribit in

[A.D. 1151] During the same time, Martinus writes, lived Gratian, a Tuscan monk born in Chiusi, who composed the *Decretum* at Bologna, in the monastery of his order, as Huguccio of Pisa writes about him in his apparatus to the aforesaid *Decretum*.

The text, digressive in style, then continues to mix observations on Gratian with those concerning Huguccio. The basic question about Huguccio is identical to that of canon law tradition: Who was the author of the *Summa*?[57]

And note that Martinus says here, "i.e., during the times of Innocent." The Gloss of Johannes to C.2 q.6 c.5, however, asserts that he [Gratian] was a contemporary of Alexander III [1159–81], according to Huguccio's testimony; for he [Huguccio] said that . . . the *Decretum* was composed when Jacobus of Bologna taught in civil law and Alexander in theology. Whence it appears rather more correct that Gratian was a contemporary of Alexander III, and Huguccio of Innocent III [1198–1216] . . .

Thanks to Ptolemy's precise references to "Martinus" and the "Gloss of Johannes [Teutonicus]," the line along which he developed his argument is fairly clear. Interested in historical information about Gratian, he first followed Martinus and his chronicle. Then, comparing Johannes's gloss to the passage cited by Martinus, Ptolemy came to his conclusions. They betray in fact not only an attentive reading of the sources but also the critical efforts of someone who had no share in current opinions about Huguccio's life. Ptolemy, in other words, lacked all familiarity with the Innocentian letters to Bishop Huguccio and the canonists' speculation growing from them. Instead, he looked for textual evidence left by Huguccio himself. The same reason probably also accounted for a new element that Ptolemy

---

suo apparatu super dictum Decretum," ed. L. A. Muratori, RIS 11 (Milan, 1727), 1128; to this and the next passage, cf. L. Schmugge, "Kanonistik und Geschichtsschreibung," 246–48, who also discusses the hints to Martinus and Johannes Teutonicus.

57. "Et attende hic quia Martinus in isto loco ponit 'hoc est tempore Innocentii.' Glossa autem Iohannis, ii q.vi c. Forma, dicit ipsum fuisse tempore Alexandri III secundum relationem Hugonis. Dicit enim quod . . . tempore quo Iacobus Bononiensis docebat in legibus et Alexander in theologia fuit Decretum compositum. Unde verius videtur quod Gratianus fuit tempore Alexandri et Huguccio tempore Innocentii . . . ," *Historia ecclesiastica,* loc. cit.

introduced in the final half-sentence of his biographical passage on Huguccio: ". . . who wrote rich glosses to the aforesaid *Decretum* and in grammar rendered the etymological rules [*regulas derivationum*] into written form."[58]

Ptolemy thus became the first writer who explicitly attributed the *Derivationes* and the *Summa* to one author. Not inspired by canon law tradition, he obviously did not draw from his fellow chroniclers either. Otherwise, he would hardly have passed over a reference to the bishop of Ferrara, whom they never failed to mention. Therefore, what may have induced Ptolemy to formulate his statement remains unclear, unless we suppose that the attribution of both works to authors bearing identical names was the reason. No doubt, Ptolemy chose a textual approach when he dealt with the canonist. Why should we not assume that he treated the *Derivationes* in the same way? If he had read at least the preface, that would explain why he came to identify Huguccio as "Pisanus." At any rate, it is worthwhile to notice that here again the *Derivationes* and the indication of Huguccio's place of origin appear as inseparable biographical elements.

Ptolemy's unique combination never established a third medieval version of Huguccio's life. Nobody paid attention to it before the antiquarian Mauro Sarti (1769) combined it with the other two biographical traditions that circulated. Apparently none of them reached an audience broader than that originally addressed. Hence during the Middle Ages Huguccio remained a person at the same time famous and obscure.

Up to this point, what have we learnt about Huguccio, author of the *Summa decretorum*? Our survey of material bearing upon that question has thrown into focus three types of answers. To begin with, the canonists commonly identified Huguccio as the bishop of Ferrara. Influenced by local interests, chroniclers rather ascribed to the same bishop a widely read etymological dictionary called *Derivationes,* and repeatedly asserted his Pisan origin. Ptolemy of Lucca stood a little apart. Maintaining that *Summa* and *Derivationes* were written by a single author, he did not know that Huguccio had been a bishop.

Without hesitation, modern authors have conflated these noncon-

---

58. Ibid.: ". . . qui copiose glossavit dictum Decretum et in Grammatica regulas tradidit derivationum."

tradictory but oddly unrelated pieces of evidence. And indeed, their opinion about the alleged identity of bishop and canonist has been further corroborated here. Yet there seems to be a less solid foundation for seeing in Huguccio the great twelfth-century lexicographer as well. Instead, the medieval texts witnessing such an identification were confined to some local chronicles that appeared relatively late. Moreover, legal literature was absolutely silent on this connection. Very likely, the chroniclers therefore were led to their conclusion by the sheer coincidence of names. An initial passage of the *Derivationes,* "known to everybody" in the Middle Ages, ultimately may have offered the point of departure for combining their author, "by origin a Pisan, by name Huguccio," with the Ferrarese prelate.

b. The Derivationes

It remains an unsolved problem whether the canonist who was bishop of Ferrara wrote the *Derivationes.* Perhaps we can find an answer through a closer study of the dictionary itself. To begin with, doubt about attributing the work to the author of the *Summa* arises from an attempt to date Huguccio's lexicon. Riccobaldus's claim that the bishop wrote the *Derivationes* at Nonantola must be wrong. In the midst of episcopal duties, there was certainly little opportunity to complete such an enormous enterprise, especially when, at the same time, the *Summa* remained unfinished.[59] But there are more than such general reasons for doubt. The internal evidence of the *Derivationes* also contradicts Riccobaldus's chronology.

That the work was not composed after the bishop's consecration in 1190 is suggested, first of all, by manuscript evidence. Though roughly 200 copies of the *Derivationes* have survived, only four identify the author Huguccio as a bishop—in one case, bishop of Verona; in two cases, bishop of Ferrara.[60] The fourth text comes closer to

59. S. G. Mercati, "Sul luogo e sulla data della composizione delle Derivationes di Uguccione da Pisa," *Aevum* 33 (1959), 490–94, has summarized the possible objections to Riccobaldus's testimony.

60. According to A. Marigo, *I codici,* those are: Munich, Staatsbibl. lat. 14168 (15th c.): "Explicit liber derivationum Uguccionis Verronensis episcopi"; Venice, Bibl. Marc. lat. xiii. 16 (14th c.): "Uguitionis episcopi Ferrariensis liber incipit"; also in an abbreviated version at Oxford, Bodl. Lib. Can. misc. 201 (written in 1423). Remarkably enough, only nineteen copies of the *Derivationes,* often late, bear an inscription that refers to the author.

what, as we will see, the *Derivationes* itself reveals about its author. At the end of a thirteenth-century codex we read: "Here ends the Bolognese *Derivationes* of Master Huguccio, who due to his knowledge has been made bishop."[61] Apart from the hint at an eventual career as bishop, the setting for the *Derivationes* indeed happens to be reflected in the work itself. Above all, a careful reading shows that the lexicographer devoted not a single line to any question concerning Ferrara, whereas he was more communicative about his actual professional activity. It associated him with the liberal arts:[62]

[ARCeo, -ces]: whence art, because art corrects [*artat*] us by rules; and our art is the liberal one.

In more specific terms, the lexicographer was a grammarian:[63]

[DOCeo, -es]: as, for example, "I teach you grammar."

As such, he held the position of a master:[64]

[CERa, -e]: Therefore, no one should say without excuse "sinceris" and pronounce the penultimate syllable as short. So that if a verse of another master, or shall I rather say, of an uncultivated person, be found [to be wrong] due to defective learning, . . . it must be erased from the book of life, along with its author . . . and not be included among the just ones.

At Bologna:[65]

---

61. MS Berlin, Deutsche Staatsbibliothek Hamilton 335 (13/14th c.), fol. 231vb: "Expliciunt dirivationes Bolonienses secundum magistrum Hugutionem qui scientia sua factus fuit episcopus."

62. "[ARCeo, -ces]: unde ars, artis, quia regulis nos artat; et est ars nostra liberalis" MS Berlin, Staatsbibliothek Lat. fol. 621, fol. 13vb.

63. "[DOCeo, -es]: ut 'doceo te grammaticam,'" MS Graz 427, fol. 39va; the fact that Huguccio literally borrowed this line from Papias (cf. n.50 above) does not deprive it of all meaning.

64. "[CERa, -e]: Male igitur et sine omni excusatione dicitur 'sinceris' penultima correpta et accentu posito super antepenultimam. Si ergo versus factus fuerit ab aliquo magistro vel potius discolo et ex defectu scientie inveniatur, . . . abradatur cum suo auctore de libro vite et cum iustis non scribatur" (MS Vienna, N.B. lat. 1454, fol. 31va).

65. "[DUCo, -cis]: Conducere . . . est contrarium ad locare et dicitur in eius respectu. Ille hospicium locat qui pretium accipit de eo. Ille conducit qui precium pro eo dat; ut scholares conducunt hospitia, Bononienses locant ea" (MS Graz, UB 427, fol. 40rb).

[DUCO, -cis]: to rent [*conducere*] . . . is opposite to letting [*locare*], yet used in the same context. He who accepts money for a room lets it; he who pays for it, rents; just as scholars rent rooms, and the Bolognese let them.

We can safely rule out the drafting of these lines at Ferrara, because similar references to the city occur several times.[66] If anything, those four copies of the *Derivationes* imply that the work was finished before the author had "been made bishop." Whoever wrote it was neither a canonist nor particularly interested in legal terminology. In fact, there is hardly any entry in the whole dictionary that would prove the canonistic skills of the grammarian. In one passage, though, Huguccio does refer to canon law:[67]

[CERno, -nis]: whence decree, statute of the senators; whence decretal, as the so-called decretals which occur in a decretal collection [*in decretis*]; and decretist, who studies the decretal collection; in plural form *decreta*, the book is meant which contains decrees.

Did Huguccio here specifically have Gratian's *Decretum* in mind? Or did he think of canon law collections in general? His mention of "decretists" may favor the former conclusion. In last analysis, however, eight canon law references in the *Derivationes* to a source called "in decretis" rather point toward the latter possibility.[68] They must have

66. Such as those under "scoLaris, -ris" and "urbs, -bis" (MS Graz, UB 427, fols. 139vb, 160vb).
67. "[CERno, -nis]: Unde decretus, -a, -um; et hoc decretum, -ti, statutum patrum; unde hic et hec decretalis, et hoc -le; ut dicta decretalia que in decretis continentur; et hic et hec decretista, qui studet in decretis; pluraliter decreta, -torum, pro libro in quo decreta continentur" (MS Vienna, N.B. lat. 1454, fol. 32rb).
68. These are: (1) "[APologia]: Excusatio vel responsio, ab apo quod est re- et logos quod est sermo; quasi sermonis relatio i.e. responsio. In decretis Alexandri: 'Clerici qui alios accusant iustam accipiant apologiam,'" MS Vienna, N.B. 1454, fol. 10rb. (2) "[CAPio]: Capulo, -as. Unde in decretis pontificum: 'Lingua delatoris capuletur,'" ibid., fol. 24va. (3) "[CAPio]: Cauponor, -aris. . . . Unde in decretis Romani concilii: 'Sint ergo nobis anathema eo quod verbo veritatis audent cauponari,'" ibid., fols. 24vb–25ra. (4) "[CIo]: Concionabulum i.e. locus conciliorum vel concilium. Unde in decretis Innocentii pape: 'Si statim cedens de eius pessimo concionabulo,'" ibid., fol. 34ra. (5) "[LOGos]: Eulogia. Et sunt eulogie benedictiones, salutationes bone, bone donationes. Unde in decretis: 'De eulogiis ad sacra concilia deferendis,'" MS Graz, UB 144, fol. 113va. (6) "[PENdo]: Pense, -ius, -issime. Unde in decretis pape Felicis: 'In episcopio positi sunt in celesti militia que pensius ponderanda est,'" MS Graz, UB 427, fol. 190va. (7) "[SESqui]: Sescupla i.e. totum et dimidium sc. summa capitalis et dimidium. Unde in decretis: . . . ," ibid., fol. 132rb. (8) "[TERo]: Terrulenter. Et in decretis: 'Rem spiritualem terrulenter querere,'" ibid., fol. 148vb.

been taken from a book that cannot be identified with Gratian's.[69] They do not even seem to be the outcome of any direct consultation "in decretis," but formed part of the etymological material gathered by earlier grammarians. Five references can be traced literally to another Latin dictionary, the *Panormia* (ca. 1148–60).[70] Composed by Osbern of Gloucester, it was also responsible for most of the other illustrative quotations in the *Derivationes,* in what very likely establishes Osbern as Huguccio's immediate forerunner.[71] The grammarian, in other words, did not consult directly the sources of canon law.[72] The final interpretation of this disregard depends on whether we assume the identity of the lexicographer with the canonist or not. What can be said beforehand, though, is that the author of the *Derivationes* was not trained in law when he composed the work.

But when was it written? The *Derivationes* includes a chronological hint overlooked so far, which suggests a date earlier than that proposed by Riccobaldus and others:[73]

[DIA]: just as it is found in public charters: A.D. 1161.

69. Because three citations (see preceding note, under 3, 6, and 8) do not occur in the *Decretum.* The remaining ones (ibid.) correspond: (1) to C.2 q.7 c.16; (2) to C.5 q.6 c.5; (4) to C.1 q.1 c.111; (5) to D.18 c.8; (7) to D.46 c.9 or to D.47 c.2: T. Reuter and G. Silagi, *Wortkonkordanz zum Decretum Gratiani* (MGH—Hilfsmittel 10.1–5; Munich, 1990).

70. Compare, for example, the reference given above, n.68 under (1), to the *Panormia,* ed. A. Mai, *Classicorum auctorum e Vaticanis codicibus editorum* 8 (Rome, 1836), 56. Further parallels are: (3) = 128; (4) = 143; (6) = 445; (8) = 578. A. Mai's Vatican MS of Osbern is defective, though. Perhaps, a more complete copy might include the rest of Huguccio's quotations; cf. R. W. Hunt, "The 'lost' preface to the Liber Derivationum of Osbern of Gloucester," *Medieval and Renaissance studies* 4 (1952), 267–82 (= *The history of grammar in the Middle Ages,* ed. G. L. Bursill-Hall [Amsterdam, 1980], 151–56).

71. H. D. Austin, "The sources of Uguccione's illustrative quotations," *Medievalia et Humanistica* 4 (1946), 104–6, doubts this view, yet his statistics rather favor it, cf. R. W. Hunt, "Lost preface," 267 n.1 (151 n.1). It appears unlikely that Osbern's work found such a reception in Italy as early as in the 1160s (the date suggested below n.73). Did the grammarian Huguccio therefore use the *Panormia* during a possible stay at Paris around the same time? For further details, see n.120 below.

72. His interest in Roman law may have been stronger. The lexicographer incorporated a collection of Roman legal terms largely independent of other twelfth-century glossaries; printed in part by M. Conrat, *Die Epitome "Exactis regibus"* (Berlin, 1884; repr. Aalen, 1965), 204–9. For a comprehensive account of further contemporary Roman law dictionaries see H. Coing (ed.), 258–60.

73. "[DIA]: sicut in cartis publicis invenitur: Anno Domini Mclxi" (MSS Vienna, N.B. 1454, fol. 46ra; Graz, UB 427, fol. 36vb; Graz, UB 144, fol. 49rb; Lisbon,

It would be rash to conclude from this that in composing the *Derivationes* Huguccio in 1161 had reached the letter D (= DIA). A date included by a twelfth-century author in a charter formula need not reflect the moment of composition. Such ambiguity already arises from the fictitious character of the formula itself. Gratian, for example, on a similar occasion attached the year 1105 to a sample document that for merely illustrative purposes he had drawn up and incorporated into his compilation. He did so around 1140, so that his dating lagged behind the actual time by some thirty-five years.[74] To compare this case to that of the *Derivationes* requires cautious interpretation. Yet, in terms of probability, it should be remembered that in the overwhelming majority of such instances contemporaries inserted the date on which they actually wrote. For instance, Huguccio in his *Summa* reacted to Gratian's "1105" with skepticism: "I think," he said, "that the figure is corrupted and I do not think that so much time has elapsed since this book was composed."[75] He thus clearly expressed what he expected to find wherever a date appeared in a similar context: the present one. Contemporary sources such as the *Glossa Palatina* (1210–15) confirm this view. One of its early recensions can be dated through the same device the canonist Huguccio had tried to employ in commenting on Gratian.[76] If we assume that a similar principle was at work regarding the *Derivationes*, there is substantial reason to place Huguccio's dictionary in the decade around 1161.

Alcob. CCCXC/277, fol. 85vb). The date is consistent in all copies that offer a good text.

74. This date of composition for the *Decretum* is now generally accepted; cf. J. Noonan, "Gratian slept here," 158–61; the passage in question forms part of C.2 q.6 p.c.31.

75. "*MCV*: Hinc potest colligi quantum temporis effluxit ex quo liber iste conditus est. Sed credo hanc esse falsam litteram, nec credo quod tantum temporis effluxerit ex quo liber iste compositus est," *Summa* C.2 q.6 p.c.31, quoted after L. Schmugge, "Kanonistik und Geschichtsschreibung," 246.

76. See MS Arras, B.M. 500, containing the first recension (?) of the *Glossa Palatina*, in which a date (25 March 1207) appears s.v. *Libellorum*, C.2 q.8 p.c.5: according to A. M. Stickler, "Il decretista Laurentius Hispanus," SG 9 (1966), 511–13, this coincides with the indirect chronological evidence suggesting 1208–10 as the time of composition. On the same grounds, S. Kuttner and E. Rathbone once attributed the drafting of the Summa *Quoniam omissis* (MS Verdun, B.M. 35) to the year 1167: "Anglo-Norman canonists of the twelfth century," *Traditio* 7 (1949/51), 299 n.20, repr., with "Retractationes viii," in S. Kuttner, *Gratian and the schools*.

True, scholarly opinion has already come to similar conclusions. The *Derivationes* was attributed to Huguccio's youth, more specifically, to the 1160s.[77] But whereas research until now has been based upon the unquestioned identification of canonist and lexicographer and has consequently placed the *Derivationes* within a relative chronology of Huguccio's other works, the present chapter has reversed this approach. I have attempted to collect absolute textual criteria in order to date the dictionary and, in doing so, have questioned its possible link to the *Summa*. I have also shown that the traditional arguments advanced to identify the author of the *Derivationes* and the author of the *Summa* are inadequate. The insights gathered from Salimbene, Riccobaldus, and Ptolemy do not provide substantial or conclusive proof that Huguccio composed both works. As a result, all appears to come down to another crucial piece of evidence, the *Agiographia* of the canonist Huguccio.[78]

3. CANONIST AND GRAMMARIAN?

a. The Agiographia

Scholars have just begun to realize the *Agiographia*'s importance for the understanding of Huguccio's life. The little treatise was brought to their attention in 1943.[79] Since then it has been considered as a confirmation of those texts that previously had served biographical purposes and was cited merely to reinforce former conclusions. As we will see, however, the work deserves a more central place in any assessment of the exact circumstances of Huguccio's professional activities.

With marvelous precision, in his *Summa* the canonist Huguccio claims the authorship of another minor work:[80]

77. "The whole work, therefore, seems to be a product of his [i.e. Huguccio's] activities as a young student": A. M. Stickler, NCE 7 (1967), 200; "negli anni sessanta": G. Cremascoli (ed.), 96.

78. Its editor, G. Cremascoli, deliberately eliminated the initial "H" from the title; details below, n.84.

79. By S. Kuttner, "Bernardus Compostellanus antiquus. A study in the glossators of the canon law," *Traditio* 1 (1943), 283 n.1 (repr. in idem, *Gratian and the schools*, n.vii), who identified it in the Paris manuscript (below n.87); cf. also G. Cremascoli (ed.), 93–94.

80. Ibid., 93, quoted from MS Vatican, Bibl. Ap. lat. 2280, fol. 352rb: "Et di-

"Kalende" is derived from "kalo, -as" which means: "I call, you call." Because on that day people were called to the market; or they were called in order to listen to the announcement of a new month; or to learn which moon it was. If someone wants to get further instruction in this, he should read the small volume I have composed on such matters. Its name is *Agiographia,* and it starts like this: "Laboris assiduitas" etc.

The *Agiographia* has meanwhile been published in a carefully edited text, which facilitates our tracking of Huguccio's reference.[81] There is no doubt which passage he had in mind. In the *Agiographia*'s opening section there is a lengthy explanation of "kalende," also defined as "derived from 'kalo, -as' which means 'I call, you call.'"[82] The treatment of the term is quite elaborate and continues for twenty lines in its printed form.

Having established the link between the *Agiographia* and the *Summa,* scholars took a further step. In 1960, Alfons Stickler published a brief note and cited two pieces of evidence from the canonist's little treatise that apparently offered final proof that its author had written the *Summa* as well as the *Derivationes.* In one of them, the author of the *Agiographia* made the following remark on the word "scenofegia": "It is possible to pronounce this word stressed as well as unstressed, according to the wishes of the reader; and we have diligently noted the reason for this in the *Liber derivationum.*"[83] Stickler concluded that Huguccio thereby had created a complete chain of cross-references linking his grammatical and legal works.[84]

---

cuntur kalende a kalo, kalas, quod est voco, vocas, quia ea die vocabantur ad nundinas vel ad audiendum principium mensis vel ad audiendum quota esset luna. Si quis vult in his instrui legat modicum libellum quem de hac materia composuimus. Nomen eius est 'Agiographia' et sic incipit: 'Laboris assiduitas' etc." (*Summa,* De cons. D.3 c.19 s.v. *in predicto die kalendarum*).

81. G. Cremascoli (ed.), 137–74; later criticism includes a few emendations suggested by G. Orlandi, *Aevum* 53 (1978), 397–98; but all in all, the printing error in line two of Cremascoli's edition: "Laboris assiduitatis [!]," does not reflect the quality of the whole.

82. G. Cremascoli (ed.), 140, line 79: "Kalende a calo, -as, quod est voco, -cas. . . ."

83. "Licet in hoc nomine producere et corripere penultimam pro voluntate legentis. Et quare in Libro Derivationum diligenter assignavimus," G. Cremascoli (ed.), 156, lines 494–96; first cited by A. Stickler, LThK 5 (1960), 521–22.

84. The assumption that all these writings were interrelated later induced G. Cremascoli (ed.), 93 n.1, to eliminate the initial "H" from the *Agiographia*'s title. He

Since the identity of their authors was already taken for granted, however, Stickler rather placed his emphasis upon the following text. In a list of saints included in the *Agiographia*, he found a suggestive hint, which in his opinion narrowed the chronological limits of its composition. Forming part of a digression within the etymological treatment of "Alexander," it stated:[85]

[Alexander] is derived from "a" which is "without," and "lexis," that is, "language"; and "andros" which means "man": hence "A-lex-ander," i.e. "without man-like" or "human language," because his language did not seem to be human but divine. And if it is permissible to say so, for the same reason our Apostolic [Father] is called Alexander, since his words are not those of a human being but of God; whence he is no longer rightly [*iure*] said to be man, but God.

Since the *Agiographia* must have preceded the *Summa* (ca. 1187–90), there was sufficient reason for Stickler to suppose that the pope mentioned here as the present holder of the Apostolic See had to be Alexander III, whose pontificate lasted from 1159 to 1181.

Did all this in fact ultimately confirm that the grammarian and the canonist were identical? A closer look at the apparatus of sources attached to the edition of the *Agiographia* reveals something surprising: the extract on "kalende" just quoted had originally been copied almost word for word from the *Derivationes*![86] This raises the

---

based this editorial decision on the fact that the *Derivationes* included the entry of "hagios" under the letter "A." K. Miethaner-Vent, "Das Alphabet in der mittelalterlichen Lexikographie," in *La lexicographie au moyen âge*, ed. C. Buridant (Lille, 1986), 83–112, has provided the first adequate description of the arrangement of entries in the *Derivationes*.

85. "Alexander dictus est ab a quod est sine et lexis quod est sermo et andros quod est vir. Inde A-lex-ander quasi sine virili id est humano sermone. Non enim sermo eius videbatur hominis sed Dei. Et si fari licet, eadem ratione etymologie Apostolicus noster dictus est Alexander, quia eius verba non hominis sed Dei sunt. Unde iam non iure homo dicitur sed Deus" (ibid., 158–59, lines 537–43).

86. "[CALon]: Item *a calo quod est voco* he kalende, *quia eo die solebat pontifex ascendere turrim de consuetudine Romana et volens nuntiare quota esset luna eo die vel principium mensis, dicebat pluries calo calo calo quasi voco vos, venite et audite etatem lune vel principium mensis. Et ideo dies ille dictus est kalende quasi vocationes; vel aliter de consuetudine Romanorum erat quod in principio cuiuslibet mensis celebrabant nundinas et eas incipiebant in nonis. Quia ergo venturi nesciebant principium mensis, ideo semper in prima die mensis preco turrim ascendebat et totiens vocabat*

question why the author of the *Summa* cited an obscure little work in order to help the reader's understanding, instead of referring to a widely circulating and well-known dictionary. Probably, only one answer can account for Huguccio's preference, otherwise so odd: the canonist was able to introduce the *Agiographia,* but not the *Derivationes,* as a work of his own. This, of course, is an argument from silence. Yet the *Agiographia*'s text reveals additional evidence that renders questionable any connection between the author of the *Summa* and that of the *Derivationes.*

The *Agiographia* has appeared in a critical edition, but the editorial principles adopted in it are flawed and make one crucial argument about Huguccio's biography very problematic. To begin with, the treatise has survived in two copies, one from Paris (P), the other in Venice (V).[87] Each manuscript presents a significantly different version. P has a number of additions that are not in V, whereas V does not contain any text not in P, save the final portion of the work, missing from P altogether. Most importantly in this context and for the question of Huguccio's identity, the manuscript evidence also affects the two biographical passages just cited. Both appear in only one of

---

calo quasi voco vos ad nundinas quot dies restabant usque ad diem in quo volebant incipere forum, ut si in quarto [*Ag.*: quinto] *die* quater [*Ag.*: quinquies] *dicebat calo, si in sexto sexies* [*Ag.*: septimo septies]. *Unde et ille mensis habet quarto nonas, iste vero sexto nonas* [*Ag.*: quia semper in principio cuiuslibet mensis faciebant principium fori vel in quinto vel in septimo]; *quod ideo ita diviserunt ut latrones nescirent quando deberet esse forum, qui abscondebantur in silvis et venientes ad forum occidebant et predabantur. Et ideo dicte sunt kalende quasi vocationes. Et quia pluries dicebat calo, ideo ab illa pluralitate dictum est tantum pluraliter kalende, -arum;* Et nota quod pro hac figura c Greci scribunt k. Unde potest scribi kalende tantum per c secundum Latinos quantum per k secundum Grecos. Competentius tamen per k quia Grecum est sive notum nomen; *vel kalende dicuntur quasi colende quia* coli solebant apud veteres [*Ag.*: antiqui principium mensis semper solebant colere]" (MSS Graz, UB 144, fols. 21vb–22ra; Graz, UB 427, fol. 16vb). The italicized passages recur in the *Agiographia,* cf. above n.82.

87. Cf. G. Cremascoli (ed.), 115–18: (a) MS Paris, B.N. lat. 14877 (13th c.), fols. 124r–129v; formerly in St. Victor (Paris), shelf-mark KK 19 in the abbey's catalogue of 1514, ed. G. Ouy and V. Gerz-Van Buren, *Le catalogue de la bibliothèque de l'abbaye de Saint-Victor de Paris de Claude de Grandrue* (Paris, 1983), 197; as to the date (1250–1300), see also L. Delisle, *Le cabinet des manuscrits de la Bibliothèque Nationale* 2 (Paris, 1874), 219; (b) MS Venice, Bibl. Marc., lat. xiii. 16 [4521] (14th c.), fols. 197v–199r: interestingly, the treatise here is appended to the text of the *Derivationes* (see above n.60).

the extant transcripts (P), while the other (V) shows no trace of either
the reference to the *"Liber derivationum,"* or to a pope "Alexander."[88] These differences challenge the identification of the canonist
with the lexicographer. I will therefore attempt to establish the relationship of one manuscript to the other. In order to provide the
necessary background information for the ensuing philological discussion, let us first consider the main features of the text we are dealing with.

The Structure of the Agiographia

PROLOGUE (lines 1–15):[89] In the clear-cut manner also typical of
the canonist's writings, Huguccio initially set out his motives for
composing this little treatise. He wanted to explain by interpretation
or etymology the names of saints found in (his) calendar.[90] But in
order to introduce this argument, he first treated those terms which
usually provided the chronological framework, in an exposition of
days, months, and their meaning.

MONTH-NAMES (lines 16–77): From January through December.

ROMAN NAMES OF DAYS (lines 78–167): This section starts
with the passage on "kalende" referred to by Huguccio in his *Summa*.

NAMES OF WEEKDAYS (lines 168–274): Huguccio here included those names that were adopted by Christians (170–92), Jews
(193–214), and pagans (215–50), respectively. Then he pointed out
that the Church applied the names indiscriminately, regardless of
their Hebrew or Gentile origins (254–61). The Paris manuscript further summarizes the discourse with some practical advice to priests,
telling them how to announce correctly the dates of important events
in their churches (262–74).

NAMES OF SAINTS (lines 275 to end): Having provided the chronological frame, Huguccio added another short prologue (275–79)
in which he indicated his method for the main part of the work. Following the order of his calendar, he promised to begin with the saints

88. For an exhaustive treatment of the divergences between both exemplars see G.
Cremascoli (ed.), 97–108, 118–25.

89. The line numbers refer to Cremascoli's critical edition of 1978.

90. "Expositiones nominum sanctorum in kalendario conscriptorum interpre-
tando vel etymologizando explicare decrevimus" (ibid., 137, lines 6–8).

listed for January. If some names were missing, Huguccio noted, he could not find them in his hagiographical source.[91]

In outline, these are the major individual sections of the *Agiographia*, as they occur in the critical edition of Giuseppe Cremascoli. However, Cremascoli's text is seriously misleading. He did present a very faithful collation of what he found in the two manuscripts, but he did not thoroughly discuss his editorial principles. The key question he failed to ask was whether the Paris or the Venetian version came closer to Huguccio's original. Although P and V transmitted very different readings, Cremascoli decided in favor of the Paris rather than the Venetian exemplar simply because P contained additional material. He thought that V was an abbreviated copy. Also, P had been written slightly earlier (thirteenth century) than V (fourteenth century), which in his view further argued for its greater reliability.[92] Cremascoli did not, however, attempt to rule out the possibility that V rather than P was the original. He even admitted he had not been able to discern any mutual link between V and P.[93] In other words, he finally abandoned the task of determining their relationship.

For the rest of this section, I shall argue that Cremascoli's preference for P, based largely on intuition, was misguided. On the contrary, there is positive proof that V is closer to Huguccio's authentic version. As I will show, of the two recensions of the *Agiographia,* V represents the prior one. Then it can further be demonstrated that P's addenda did not stem from Huguccio's hand at all. To begin with,

91. Due to its importance, the text is given here in full: "His ergo premissis sequitur ut quod proposuimus de nominibus sanctorum exsequamur secundum ordinem incipientes a januario. Si tamen aliqua nomina sanctorum pretermiserimus, non erit hoc ex invidia sed ideo quia non omnia in nostro kalendario conscripta reperiuntur."

92. "Il codice veneziano trasmette un testo assai ridotto rispetto a quello del codice di Parigi, abbreviando assai l'elenco agiografico . . ."(ibid., 98); furthermore, concerning the principles of emendation: "In un caso perplesso [ibid., 168, lines 793–95] ho dato invece il testo di P quasi solo perché si tratta del codice più antico" (ibid., 124).

93. Ibid., 120: "Il testo nei due mss. . . . ebbe una propria ed indipendente vicenda." Therefore, the criticism has been voiced that the editor "non si domanda . . . se i due codici possano testimoniare l'esistenza di due diverse redazioni": M. de Marco, *Rivista di cultura classica e medioevale* 21/22 (1979/80), 210; whereas K. Pennington, "Huguccio of Pisa," DMA 6 (1985), 327, plainly speaks of "two manuscripts, each of which is a different recension."

TABLE I

	V	P
Major Features:	Version is complete	Version is fragmentary at the end
Textual Correspondence:	Rarely varies from P	Adds one-third of text not in V
Introductory Part (1–274):	Contains two-thirds of P's text	Includes supplements from the *Derivationes*
Names of Saints (275–902):	Lists 111 names	Adds 69 names to those in V

major discrepancies emerge from a juxtaposition of P and V (see Table 1). P is more comprehensive than V, but unlike V, fragmentary at the end.[94] This statement provides no basis from which to deduce which is Huguccio's authentic text. Proceeding to another set of differences, however, we discover that P includes sixty-nine names of saints in addition to those found in V.[95] Huguccio's assurance that he would treat the names of the saints "in the order" of his calendar provides a tool for ascertaining the nature of these differences in P and V. The key question is whether or not both texts kept the promise and followed his planned "orderly" path. If either manuscript failed to do so, it would suggest a later interpolation not based on Huguccio's scheme of "beginning in January."[96]

Cremascoli has endeavored to identify each saint according to his placement within the *Agiographia*'s chronological order, but concluded that Huguccio (despite his assertion) had sometimes neglected to follow the annual liturgical pattern.[97] The editor never considered

94. P breaks off at fol. 129v: "Britius [13 Nov.] dictus est quasi brateus a bravium . . .": G. Cremascoli (ed.), 172, line 902; the Venetian exemplar carries on down to Sylvester (31 Dec.), ibid., 174, line 936, offering another thirteen names.

95. G. Cremascoli (ed.), 119, counts seventy-three; of which, however, four were incorporated as mere derivatives of other entries, i.e., (a) Nathanael (lines 519–21), due to a preceding reference, cf. ibid., 101; (b) Marcellinus (line 345) from Marcellus; (c) Anastasia (lines 372–73) from Anastasius; (d) Juliana (line 427) from Julianus, see also ibid., 102.

96. As quoted above, n.91: "secundum ordinem incipientes a januario" and "in nostro kalendario" are the crucial passages.

97. "Uguccione . . . non si propone in primo luogo di illustrare uno schema di anno liturgico" (ibid., 99); Cremascoli was more successful in defining the "zona cultica" to which Huguccio's original calendar belonged, to Tuscany or the Emilia Romagna, ibid., 106–8.

TABLE 2

	P/V	Instead of
Christina(578–79)	May 10	May 12

the possibility of attributing incorrectly positioned saints to interpolations. By using dates drawn from the major hagiographical reference works, we shall determine which manuscript conformed more
closely to Huguccio's intention.[98] The results show that one saint
found in both V and P does not fit into the underlying annual circle
(Table 2). The transposition is minor. Perhaps, while writing the
Agiographia, Huguccio had skipped the name in his original and,
realizing his error a little later, supplied it immediately. But let us look
at the deviations occurring in P alone (Table 3). These 7 entries in P,
out of a total of 69 added to V, demonstrate that the author took
pains to put each of them into the right place. But he obviously made
significant mistakes. Compared to P/V, in which 1 of 111 names is,
though only slightly, out of order, in P the quota is 7 out of 69. In
the attempt to arrange the hagiographical material, the error rate for
P's supplements appears much higher (7/69) than that for entries P
and V have in common (1/111). Such a discrepancy suggests that the
additional portions did not come from Huguccio. One may conjec-
ture that in the course of revising the *Agiographia,* P's author tried
to fit a large number of saints from a second calendar into the original
pattern preserved in V. This conclusion seems even more likely if we
examine one particular example of P's mistakes.

At the top of our list of P's misplaced saints, "Barbatianus" raises
some perplexing problems. Although he occurs in all hagiographical
literature under December 31, P associated him with January 1. At
first sight, this represents just another minor transposition of the kind
from which V is not free either. Yet Huguccio's own words argue

98. Those are: H. Thurston and D. Attwater (eds.), *Butler's lives of the saints* 4
(New York, 1956), 681–707 (General Index); *Bibliotheca Sanctorum,* Suppl. (Rome,
1970), 231–92; *Lexikon der christlichen Ikonographie 5–8: Ikonographie der Heiligen,* ed. W. Braunfels (Freiburg/B., 1973–76); and the results obtained by G. Cremascoli (ed.), 97–108.

TABLE 3

	P	Instead of
Barbatianus (286)	Jan. 1	Dec. 31
Firmina (323)	Jan. 6–13	Oct. 9?/Nov. 24?
Tecla (430)	Feb. 10–13	Feb. 20
Quiricus/Julitta (684)	July 17	June 16
Euphrosynus (821)	Sept. 29–30	Nov. 3?
Leulinus (825)	Sept. 29–30	Nov. 24?
Heraclius (846)	Oct. 9–14	Oct. 3

against such an explanation. Only a few lines earlier in his treatise, we remember, he had been very explicit in stating that the *Agiographia* was designed to "begin in right order from January," just as the author had found it "written down in his calendar." Taken together with Barbatianus's odd position, these assertions help us to recognize the enormous error P had committed. If P's author actually had composed the work with a list of saints "beginning from January" in front of him, it meant that the entry of "Barbatianus" would have been moved from the very end of the list to the top of P. Such an operation seems unlikely. There remains only one plausible scenario to explain how the name of "Barbatianus" entered P on January 1 instead of December 31: A second redactor, who did not have Huguccio's plan firmly in mind, violated the first principle of the jurist's arrangement. This anonymous writer had a second calendar at hand that started not in January but at another date, most likely at Advent or Christmas. Hence, the transposition of "Barbatianus" became possible. Originally listed among other saints on December 31, this entry could easily have been transferred to the following day, January 1. Circumstantial evidence points to the same conclusion. As a matter of fact, Huguccio's calendar, with its beginning from January, formed an exception to the rule in medieval northern Italy. A survey of contemporary hagiographical texts has established that those which start somewhere in December clearly outnumber all others by at least ten to one.[99] Any list of saints that might have been used to supplement

99. G. Philippart, *Les légendiers latins et autres manuscrits hagiographiques* (Ty-

Huguccio's therefore was likely to include "Barbatianus" immediately before the date assigned to this name in P.

With a disproportionate number of names either misplaced or at least difficult to trace, P most probably represents a later, interpolated version of the *Agiographia,* while V, contrary to the view of Giuseppe Cremascoli, is closer to Huguccio's original. But this conclusion raises yet another question. Is P, after all, a second recension ventured by Huguccio himself? Since he had expressed regrets about the incompleteness of his name list, this suggestion seems possible.[100] However, there is proof that Huguccio was not the author of P, to be found in the *Agiographia*'s introductory part (1–274). Briefly mentioned above, P's interpolations in this section reveal a consistent feature. They fill in those texts from the *Derivationes* that Huguccio in V had deliberately cut out as superfluous or too long. To illustrate the procedure adopted in P, one major example will suffice.

P shared with V and the *Derivationes* the following account of names pagans usually applied to their weekdays:[101]

According to the Gentiles, however, the names of days correspond to those of the planets, and each day must receive its name from the planet that governs the first hour of that day. For example, Sun-day (or the day of the Lord), Moon-day, Mars-day, Mercury-day, Jupiter-day, Venus-day, Saturn-day. There are, namely, twenty-four hours per natural day. Natural day we call the extent of day and night distinguished into twenty-four hours. There are seven planets and they govern each of these twenty-four hours. In the following order, each of them governs three hours: the first has the first hour, the second the second, and so forth down to the seventh [hour]. Then, the first [planet] again has the eighth hour, the second the ninth, etc., down to the fourteenth. Then, the first [planet] has again the fifteenth [hour], the second the sixteenth, and so forth down to the twenty-first. Hence, the three hours which

---

pologie des sources du moyen âge occidental, 24–25; Turnhout, 1977), 79: thirty-three calendars from Italy begin on Advent, four on Christmas or New Year, one on Easter. Outside Italy, the situation is reversed: nineteen start on Christmas or New Year, eleven start on Advent, one on Peter and Paul. The sources surveyed by Philippart are listed in ibid., 13–16. Historical background to the "caput anni liturgici" provides W. Evenepoel, "La délimitation de l'année liturgique dans les premiers siècles de la Chrétienté occidentale," *Revue d'histoire ecclésiastique* 83 (1988), 601–16.

100. "Si tamen aliqua nomina sanctorum pretermiserimus, non erit hoc ex invidia sed ideo quia non omnia in nostro kalendario conscripta reperiuntur" (cf. above n.91).

101. Translated from G. Cremascoli (ed.), 145–46, lines 215–32; the *Derivationes,* s.v. "SABet" (MS Graz, UB 427, fol. 126rb) offers no major variants.

remain will be distributed like this: The planet having the first hour in that day will have the first hour of those three, the second the second, the third the third. And thus the day has finished, and the fourth planet which follows will have the first hour of the next day. And so that day will receive its name . . .

Having given an etymological basis for each term in a comprehensive and theoretical fashion, V then dismisses the subject with the lapidary statement "and so forth." Not so P. It continues by adding a lengthy paragraph that explains how to apply the pagan rules of calculating days. The original achievement of critically selecting appropriate material from the *Derivationes* was thus largely undone, because what V had left out, the author of P supplied line by line:[102]

. . . And to give an example, suppose that today be Saturday (as it is indeed!)[103] and that the order of planets be kept carefully. It begins according to the end of the preceding day: Saturn, Jupiter, Mars, Sun, Venus, Mercury, Moon; then again: Saturn, Jupiter etc. Saturn hence today has the first hour, Jupiter the second, Mars the third, Sun the fourth, Venus the fifth, Mercury the sixth, Moon the seventh, Saturn the eighth, . . . Mercury the twentieth, Moon the twenty-first; again Saturn the twenty-second, Jupiter the twenty-third, Mars the twenty-fourth, that is, the last hour. Sun which follows will accordingly have the first hour of the subsequent day, whence this day is also called Sun-day.

The contrast leaps to the eye. V had managed to condense that somewhat loquacious style of the *Derivationes* into a clear statement. The canonist Huguccio obviously used the work with discrimination. It is unthinkable that the same author could have departed from such an approach and relapsed into simply copying the whole text of the *Derivationes* when preparing a new recension (P).

As a result, we can reasonably conclude that another author, who possessed merely the qualities of a compiler, interpolated several sections from a second hagiographical source into Huguccio's original (V). Perhaps he felt entitled to do so by Huguccio's own excuse for the incompleteness of his list of saints. Likewise, he added what he

102. Ibid., 146, lines 232–46; *Derivationes,* loc. cit.
103. "Ut revera est": this brief remark of the *Derivationes,* another sign that the lexicographer took dates very seriously (see also above nn.73, 75), does not recur in P, cf. G. Cremascoli (ed.), 146, line 233.

conceived to be the missing portions of the *Derivationes*, so that all of the additions in P are probably inauthentic.[104] The *Summa*'s mention of the *Agiographia* instead of the much more famous *Derivationes*, the significantly increased rate of misplaced saints in P, and the example of "Barbatianus" favor this conclusion. Granted that, the *Agiographia*'s references to the *Derivationes* and a present pope "Alexander" lose their value as biographical evidence. With regard to the latter, it is perhaps possible to push our argument even further and to suggest another date of composition for P's recension of Huguccio's original work.

Those familiar with the twelfth-century doctrine of papal authority may consider as somewhat precocious the *Agiographia*'s praise of Pope Alexander's God-like qualities, who "is no longer rightly [*iure*] said to be man, but God [*non hominis sed Dei*]." Such an exalted formulation seems more consistent with a date not prior to Innocent III (1198–1216), who first put forward similarly extravagant claims.[105] At any rate, they do not coincide with the moderate position held by the canonist Huguccio in these matters.[106] Therefore, may we not better suggest that P's recension rather belongs to the time of Pope Alexander IV (1254–61)?

On the basis of this discussion, it has become evident that the *Agiographia* can serve our biographical argument only in a very restricted

104. It is likely that the same happened with one manuscript of the lexicographer's *De dubio accentu*: Oxford, Bodl. Lib., Laud. misc. 523 (14th c.), cf. G. Cremascoli (ed.), 21–22, 46–50. There, the copyist inserted a long gloss from the *Derivationes* into the original (ibid., 84, line 237). The assumed common authorship obviously made this text susceptible to such manipulations, too.

105. As, for example, in a letter of 1198 (Reg. 1.326 = 3 Comp 1.5.3 = X 1.7.3): "Non enim homo sed Deus separat, quos Romanus pontifex qui non puri hominis sed veri Dei vicem gerit in terris . . . non humana sed divina potius auctoritate dissolvit"; cited after K. Pennington, *Pope and bishops*, 16. By the middle of the thirteenth century, this formula had spilled over into many legal commentaries in order to describe the fullness of papal power; cf. Hostiensis in his gloss to X 3.41.1 s.v. *et Deo*: "Dispensationes summi pontificis ex causa facti non sunt hominis sed Dei" (ibid., 71 n.89). This is echoed by the *Agiographia* (n.85 above).

106. Huguccio showed restraint in his use of formulas extolling the papal position. He objected, for example, to expressions such as "pontifex universalis" and denied that the title of "vicarius Christi" was reserved to the papacy; see *Summa* D.99 c.3–5, C.33 q.5 c.19: S. Kuttner, "Universal pope or servant of God's servants," RDC 31 (1981), 109–50, at 118–20, 138–39 (reprinted, with "Retractationes viii," in idem, *Studies*).

sense. Lacking a consistent manuscript tradition, the treatise offers, to say the least, inadequate grounds for any conclusion about the supposed common authorship of the *Summa* and the *Derivationes*.

b. The Summa

With the identity of the canonist and grammarian still in doubt, we must turn, finally, to the canonistic *Summa*. Previous scholarship has scrutinized the commentary for biographical clues, yet, aside from a fairly accurate date of composition (1188–90) and brief references of the canonist to minor works of his own, the outcome was poor.[107] There are, to be sure, occasional remarks on particular customs of the Pisan church, which have sometimes been interpreted as manifestations of Huguccio's patriotic pride. As soon as the presumed link between the author of the *Summa* and the *Derivationes* is called into question, however, the same passages appear too casual to prove definitively that Pisa was the canonist's hometown. The testimony of Egidius Spiritalis de Perusio (ca. 1323–28) therefore remains the oldest explicit reference to associate the decretist Huguccio with Pisa.[108]

An evaluation of the biographical evidence of the *Summa* does little more than reinforce the ambiguities surrounding Huguccio's person. On the one hand, the text contains nothing that would suggest the canonist's authorship of the dictionary, in what indeed contrasts strikingly with his normal attitude betraying an eagerness not to leave any of his publications unmentioned.[109] We have seen that the can-

107. Concerning references from the *Summa* to other treatises of the canonist, see n.80 above, n.109 below. The date of composition will be fully discussed below, chap. II.1.

108. Cf. n.54 above. In the *Summa*, evidence pointing toward Pisa as the canonist's birthplace amounts to only one comment: C.16 q.7 c.32 s.v. *clericorum*: "quod fit in multis locis et maxime Pisis," cited after C. Leonardi, *La vita*, 52 n.35; not compelling as an isolated case in view of other formulations such as D.25 c.1 s.v. *ad primicerium* (MSS Klosterneuburg 89, fol. 35va; Admont 7, fol. 35ra): "Hunc dicunt quidam esse cantorem, sed in multis ecclesiis per se est primicerius et per se est cantor, sicut Luce"; or D.89 c.2 s.v. *vicedominium* (Admont 7, fol. 114ra-b): "Vel forte loquitur de quadam alia singulari dignitate que vocatur maioritas et est in quibusdam locis, ut Vercellis." P. Erdö, *L'ufficio*, 178–90 (71–84), notes several occasions, *Summa* D.21 c.1, D.99 c.1–2, where Huguccio mentioned the archbishop of Pisa among other "primates" of the Church. This was unprecedented in older decretist literature and could be interpreted as a sign of local patriotism.

109. Besides the *Agiographia* (n.80 above), the *Summa* thus cited a separately pub-

onist decided to attribute the definition of "kalende" to the *Agiographia* rather than the *Derivationes,* its ultimate source. This may well imply that he simply could not speak of the *Derivationes* as a product of his own.[110]

On the other hand, the *Summa* consistently used the *Derivationes* in order to formulate its etymological definitions.[111] Only a few among the more than one hundred cases cannot be traced to this source.[112] That reminds us of the manner in which the canonist had exploited the dictionary in drawing up the *Agiographia.* In both instances, however, the simple use of it offers no compelling proof of authorship, since Huguccio's having recourse to an up-to-date and

---

lished *Questio* treating marriage impediments at C.35 q.5 c.8 s.v. *in altero*: "Hec tamen questio solet esse scholastica et quandoque eam diligentius tractavimus et in scriptum redegimus"; cf. A. M. Landgraf, "Diritto canonico," 381 n.35; MSS Klosterneuburg, Stiftsbibl. 89, fol. 329rb; Admont, Stiftsbibl. 7, fol. 401va. Moreover, in a reference unnoticed so far, Huguccio confirmed his authorship of the *Expositio de symbolo apostolorum* (G. Cremascoli, [ed.], 227–55; N. M. Häring, ed., "Zwei Kommentare von Huguccio, Bischof von Ferrara," SG 19 [1976], 365–98; cf. also F. Gastaldelli, "Le 'Sententiae' di Pietro Lombardo e l'"Expositio de symbolo Apostolorum' di Uguccione da Pisa," *Salesianum* 39 [1977], 318–21): *Summa, De cons.* D.4 c.73 s.v. *sic credatur in ecclesiam catholicam*: "Sed dicit [Augustinus] sic debere intelligi: 'Credo in sanctam ecclesiam catholicam' i.e. in ecclesia sancta et catholica conversans. 'Credo in Deum,' sed melius 'in' prepositio pretermittitur et non repetitur et 'credo' et 'catholicam' i.e. fidem catholicam tenentem. 'Esse sanctam' i.e. bonam et iustam vel 'esse sanctam' i.e. sancitam et firmatam et semper perseverantem [ed. perseveraturam]; ita quod numquam deficiet. Vel credo sanctam ecclesiam catholicam esse unam et in unitatem totam consistere. Sed hoc melius aliter determinatur sc. in expositione quam fecimus super 'Credo in Deum'" (MS Admont, Stiftsbibl. 7, fol. 470ra). There is a literal correspondence to the *Expositio,* G. Cremascoli (ed.), 249, lines 669–72, 677–78; 250, lines 701–3, 704–5. Consequently, this theological treatise predates the *Summa.* Meanwhile, it remains an open question whether the *Expositio dominice orationis* (N. M. Häring [ed.], 398–416) likewise came from the canonist's pen. A comparison of their respective exegetical passages to "dimitte nobis," i.e. between the *Summa, De pen.* D.3 c.20 s.v. *delet et illa,* and the *Expositio* (ed. 406–7), shows no similarities.

110. Another instance of Huguccio's preference for his own treatises over the *Derivationes* is his definition of "symbolum," at *Summa* D.15 c.1, which, although based on that of the dictionary, s.v. "BONUS," follows exactly the wording adopted in the *Expositio* (cf. last note), G. Cremascoli (ed.), 228.34–42.

111. As observed by C. Leonardi, *La vita,* 101–2. The canonist, however, did not copy his word explanations "ex integro dalle Derivationes alla Summa Decretorum," but was again (cf. nn.102–3 above) rather selective.

112. The three Isidorian etymologies of "concilium" (D.15 c.1), "metropolitanus" (D.21 c.1), and "raptus" (C.36 q.1 c.1) thus owed their inclusion in the *Summa* to the fact that Gratian had partly included them in his *Decretum.*

locally published, all-encompassing etymological lexicon represented the most plausible choice anyway. Despite a complete lack of research on that question, we can point to at least one other Bolognese canonist who, in dealing with difficult terminology, seems to have consulted the *Derivationes* in the same fashion.[113] Therefore, no convincing clue as to the possible link between the two texts derives from considerations like these.

To explain how the *Summa* actually adopted the etymological definitions, let us finally illustrate their use by a brief discussion of those few cases in which the canonist indicated a source. All in all, this happened on no more than four occasions, out of a total of approximately 125 etymologies (including doubles). We have already noted that Huguccio had preferred to mention his *Agiographia* instead of tracing a terminological digression on "kalende" to the *Derivationes*. As for the remaining three instances, the canonist once referred to St. Augustine for an interpretation of "Pascha" which had been absent from his standard etymological source.[114] Concerning "tremissis," the first definition explicitly associated with Isidore, the *Derivationes* again failed to provide any such entry.[115] When we turn to the second term purportedly drawn from Isidore, however, things appear to be slightly more complicated. The *Summa* had incorporated the Isidorian reference into a set of definitions of the word "territorium." To

---

113. The *Summa Casinensis* (*Continuatio prima*), written during the early pontificate (1185/86) of Pope Urban III (cf. chap. II.4 below) is possibly dependent on the *Derivationes*, given the appearance of the etymological definition of "dipticis," C.24 q.2 c.6: "i.e. cartis, a dico, dicis, iuxta illud: 'Clerice dypticam lateri ne dempseris umquam,'" MS Montecassino, Bibl. Abbaz. 396, p. 164a. This hexameter (= H. Walther, *Carmina medii aevi posterioris Latina* II.1 [Göttingen, 1963] no. 2826) comes either from our lexicon (s.v. "DICO," MS Graz, UB 144, fol. 50vb), or from its direct source, Osbern's *Panormia*, ed. A. Mai, *Auctorum*, 158. Considering the Bolognese environment of the anonymous author of the *Continuatio*, the latter option seems unlikely.

114. *Summa*, De cons. D.3 c.21 (MS Admont, Stiftsbibl. 7, fol. 446rb): "Pascha . . . nominatur phase Ebraice, pasca Grece, transitus Latine"; this is well in line with the *Derivationes*, s.v. "FASE" (MS Graz, UB 144, fol. 65ra). Not so, however, the following Augustinian etymology: "Augustinus dicit divina inspiratione hoc nomen pascha compositum esse a Greco 'paschi,' quod 'passio' sonat, et Ebreo 'phase,' quod transitus interpretatur."

115. "Tremissis, ut dicit Ysidorus est tertia pars solidi; et dicitur 'tremissis' quasi 'ter missus,' quia ex tribus tremissibus missis i.e. computatis solidus completur," *Summa* C.1 q.1 c.102 (Admont, Stiftsbibl. 7, fol. 140va-b). Cf. Isidore, *Etymologiae*, ed. W. M. Lindsay (Oxford, 1911), 16.25.14.

show its unusual independence from the *Derivationes,* it is worth-while presenting parallel texts:[116]

Derivationes	*Summa*
[TERO] . . . Item a tero, terra, -re, quia assidue teratur; vel a torreo, quia siccitate torreat . . . Quod autem dicitur terra quasi "rastris trita" ethimologia est . . . Item a terra . . . territorium, modicus locus vel districtus alicuius. Vel *territorium* dicitur *quasi tauritorium* i.e. *tritum bobus et aratro. Antiqui enim sulco ducto et possessionum et territoriorum limites designabant.*	Dicitur territorium secundum Ysidorum quasi "tauritorium" quia tauris aratrum trahentibus solebant antiqui fines suarum positionum sulco abinvicem dividere; vel, ut Pomp. ait in Digesto [Dig. 50.16.239.8]: "Territorium dicitur universitas agrorum inter fines cuiuslibet civitatis." Et tunc dicitur a terreo, terres, quia inter fines sue civitatis terretur i.e. iurisdictionem suam exercent iudices loci.

To be sure, this is not a representative example of how the canonist used to handle his principal etymological source. Nevertheless, it demonstrates a selective attitude that prevails throughout the *Summa.* Regularly, Huguccio avoided copying longer sections word for word, despite the fact that he followed other texts literally. What accounted for this inclination to pass over the important contribution of the dictionary? No straightforward response is possible. But there is still another curious illustration of Huguccio's disregard. He once commented on the Isidorian etymology of "raptus," which had entered the *Decretum* as chapter 1 of C.36 q.1 ('a corrumpendo dictus'): "Raptus, namely, derives from 'corumpere.' And why not from 'rapere?'"[117] In fact, if the canonist had looked at the corresponding

116. Left column: *Derivationes,* s.v. "TERO" (MS Graz, UB 144, fol. 202rb). The italicized section exactly reproduces Isidore, *Etymologiae* (ed.) 14.5.22; right column: *Summa* C.16 q.5 c.1 (MS Admont, Stiftsbibl. 7, fol. 280va). Dig. 50.16.239.8 reads: "Territorium est universitas agrorum intra fines cuiusque civitatis."

117. "A corrumpendo quasi raptus. Et quare non a rapiendo?" *Summa* C.36 q.1 c.1 (MS Admont, Stiftsbibl. 7, fol. 404va). Gratian's Isidorian fragment traces to Etymologiae 5.26.14. Other examples of the canonist's critical use of the *Derivationes* have been treated above, nn.86, 110.

passage in the *Derivationes,* he might well have found an answer to his open question:[118]

[RUMPO] From "rumpere" also "rapere" . . . ; whence "rapto" . . . ; and from "raptare" (derives) "raptus."

4. CONCLUSION

Our reevaluation of the evidence regarding Huguccio's life has rendered very likely the canonist's identity with the bishop of Ferrara. The earliest statements to that effect made at the Bolognese canon law school seem to derive from the two Innocentian letters, QUANTO (X 4.19.7) and IN QUADAM (X 3.43.8). Although they contain only indirect references to the former "teachings and writings" of the bishop, the doctrinal concerns expressed in the letters and the canonistic *Summa* coincide to such a degree as to suggest the involvement of one and the same Huguccio.

Steven Wight has kindly pointed out to me a hitherto unnoticed piece of biographical evidence, which corroborates this conclusion. In the *Quinque tabule salutationum,* written by a contemporary of Huguccio, the Bolognese rhetorician Boncompagno da Signa (ca. 1195), he has discovered a passage proposing the rule that the writer of a formal letter should never address a bishop in his former capacity of master, because this is against the principles observed by the papal chancery. Boncompagno's text then gives as an example the bishop of Ferrara: "If someone writes the bishop of Ferrara," it reads, "he ought not to call him 'master.'" It is obvious that in order for this reference to be striking to Boncompagno's Bolognese audience, the holder of the Ferrarese See in about 1195 would have to be an important *magister;* most appropriately Huguccio, the famous author of the *Summa decretorum.*[119]

---

118. "[RUMPO]: Item a rumpo, rapio, -pis, rapui, raptum. Qui enim rapit quasi rumpit. . . . Rapto, -tas, frequentivum. . . . Item a rapto . . . hic raptus, -tus, actus vel passio rapiendi," *Derivationes* (MS Graz, UB 144, fol. 172ra). The text continues with the Isidorian etymology.

119. Boncompagno de Signa, *Quinque tabule salutationum*: "Si aliquis modo eligatur in patriarcham, archiepiscopum, episcopum, aut cardinalem vel abbatem, et vocabatur primo 'magister,' extinguitur propter dignitates istas nomen magistrale et

At the same time, the hitherto unquestioned link to the author of the *Derivationes* has been challenged. Doubts arose from the fact that the medieval testimonies combining the bishop and the canonist can be grouped strictly separately from those associating the Ferrarese prelate with the lexicographer. Hence, the argument moved on to the twofold textual tradition of the *Agiographia,* to examine if the work could serve as the decisive proof for an identification. In the final analysis, though, the little treatise could not present a reliable basis for such an argument either. Its original version did not contain the cross-references of the later one, which modern historians thought would tie together the *Summa* and the *Derivationes.* The *Summa,* finally, only added to the ambiguities by combining constant recourse to the *Derivationes* in etymological matters with an obvious restraint in quoting it at the expense of the canonist's own, minor treatises. Moreover, the *Summa* nowhere identifies Pisa as Huguccio's birthplace, as the author of the *Derivationes* did. Any conclusion favoring the ascription of both works to the same person thus remains founded merely on the identity of names.[120]

It is perhaps appropriate to end with yet another ambiguous piece of biographical evidence, which was already intriguing Mauro Sarti more than two hundred years ago. In the fourteenth-century copy of

---

postea non appellatur 'magister' nec debet appellari. Unde . . . et dominus papa tacet nomina magistralia in dignitatibus." To give an example, he further referred to the bishop of Ferrara: "Unde si aliquis scribat episcopo Ferrariensi non debet eum appellare 'magistrum,' nec ipse se vocat 'magistrum'" (MSS Munich, Staatsbibl. lat. 23499, fol. 63vb; Rome, Bibl. Vallicelliana, C.40, fol. 5vb). My thanks to Steven M. Wight (University of California, Los Angeles) for sharing with me these acute observations.

120. A very tenuous connection indeed; see the remarks above, nn.13–14, 44. The most intriguing contemporary namesake, however, is a master of grammar by name "Oguicio," who wrote the *Summa artis grammatice,* uniquely preserved in MS Munich, Staatsbibl. lat. 18908 (early 13th c.). A careful analysis of the work has appeared in C. H. Kneepkens, *Het Iudicium Constructionis. Het leerstuck van de constructio in de 2de helft van de 12de eeuw* (Nijmegen, 1987), 1.139–43. It depends on the treatise *Breve sit* by the Parisian master Robert (ed. Kneepkens, *Het Iudicium,* 2.1–326), whom "Oguicio" identifies as "magister noster" (fols. 1ra, 25rb). This Huguccio, in other words, had studied the liberal arts in France (cf. n.71 above), although the *Summa artis grammatice* itself was probably composed at Bologna (mentioned twice, fols. 6rb, 29va) during the 1160s or 1170s. On the possible identity with the lexicographer and the canonist Huguccio, Kneepkens did not go beyond asserting the existence of an "identiteitsproblematiek" (1.142).

a Bolognese document originally drafted in 1199, he had discovered
the subscription of a "Magister Ugicio Pisanus," who also might be
considered identical with the grammarian. Unaware that he was
creating a circular argument, however, Sarti declared this appearance
of Huguccio's name an interpolation, given that at the same time he
was bishop of Ferrara.[121]

Obviously, we have reached a dead end in our attempts to shed
further light on Huguccio's biography. Because similar case studies
offer support to either side of the dispute, it would require new testimonies to proceed beyond this point and to weigh definitively the
contradictory evidence for and against a personal union of the grammarian and the canonist.

121. "Sed quis credat duos circa idem tempus Hugucciones Pisanos Bononiae
fuisse doctrina claros et magistri titulo insignes?" M. Sarti, *De professoribus*, 1.299
(1.371). The document has been edited ibid., 2.iii.A (2.165–66), from a copy of 1395,
now at Bologna, Arch. Comm., Demaniale 1/829. The original reportedly carried the
date of 1 January 1199; cf. G. Catalano, "Contributo," 9 n.15b.

The *Summa Decretorum*

H UGUCCIO'S *Summa* not only presents an exhaustive commentary on Gratian's *Decretum* but also figures among the longest works of canonistic literature ever written. While during his lifetime it may have recommended his candidature for the bishopric of Ferrara, for posterity the work remained a monument to his exceptional legal learning. To be sure, a substantial amount of Huguccio's teaching has also been preserved in the contemporary gloss apparatus *Ordinaturus magister* (1180/90). As the research of Rudolf Weigand has shown, both of its recensions were produced under Huguccio's strong influence. The generation of canonists succeeding him acknowledged that by attributing the opinions expressed in *Ordinaturus* altogether to "H⟨uguccio⟩." And yet, for them, as for scholars today, it was the *Summa* that secured Huguccio a central place in the history of medieval jurisprudence.[1]

As is attested by the surviving manuscript evidence, scholarly interest in the work kept medieval copyists busy down to the fifteenth century. There was, however, no early printed edition made, and Huguccio's text fell into total disregard during the early modern period. Only with the general rise of historiographical activity after the early 1800s did Huguccio again become the subject of serious scrutiny. In due course, publications by Friedrich Maassen (1857) and Johann

---

1. For introductory bibliographical information about the *Summa* and the apparatus *Ordinaturus magister,* see Introduction, nn.10, 13, 18 above.

Friedrich von Schulte (1875) helped to reestablish his place in the history of canon law.[2] Based on their efforts, later generations of scholars devoted themselves to the task of examining the *Summa*'s teachings and made additional portions of its text available in print. The pioneering studies of Franz Gillmann (d. 1941) certainly deserve a particular mention in that respect. But the endeavors toward a fuller acquaintance with the work became continuous only after the appearance of Stephan Kuttner's *Repertorium* (1937).[3] They reached their peak during the two decades following the Second World War, when an international project undertook the task of preparing a critical edition. Since the mid-1960s, these initiatives have been at a virtual standstill, despite the promising beginnings that led to the collation of some thirty manuscripts.[4] It may therefore be useful to devote a comprehensive chapter to the textual shape and tradition of the *Summa,* which has not received significant treatment in recent years. Along with an updated list of manuscripts and some additional remarks on the date and stages of the *Summa*'s composition, the ensuing discussion will also include a thorough analysis of *Continuatio prima,* the most common supplement to Huguccio's great but fragmentary achievement.

I. DATE OF COMPOSITION

In 1914, Franz Gillmann wrote a magisterial article in which he placed the composition of the *Summa* in the years 1188–90.[5] Among

2. F. Maassen, "Beiträge zur Geschichte der juristischen Literatur des Mittelalters: Die Summa des Huguccio," *Sitzungsberichte der philosophisch-historischen Classe der Kaiserlichen Akademie der Wissenschaften* 24 (Vienna, 1857), 35–46; J. F. v. Schulte, *Geschichte,* 1.156–70; cf. also the bibliographical survey by G. Cremascoli, "Uguccione," 132–37, 140. Point of departure for modern scholarly interest in Huguccio was Mauro Sarti, *De professoribus,* published in 1769.

3. S. Kuttner, *Repertorium,* 155–60; cf. the review of Kuttner by F. Gillmann, appended to idem, *Johannes Galensis,* 54–94 (repr. in R. Weigand [ed.], *Schriften Franz Gillmann,* 1, n.16); N. del Re, *I codici Vaticani della "Summa Decretorum" di Uguccione da Pisa* (Rome, 1938).

4. Most of the information published on the manuscripts (see below, section 3) goes back to that period. For a contemporary report, A. M. Stickler, "Problemi di ricerca e di edizione per Uguccione da Pisa e nella decretistica classica," *Bibliothèque de la Revue d'histoire ecclésiastique* 33 (1959), 111–28. On current editorial efforts, cf. S. Kuttner, "Annual report," BMCL 18 (1988), xvi.

5. F. Gillmann, "Die Abfassungszeit," 233–51; reprinted in R. Weigand (ed.), *Schriften Franz Gillmann,* 1, n.8.

the pieces of evidence he culled from the work in support of his conclusion, there was hardly anything that spoke of a date outright. Instead, he relied on circumstantial proofs, which in effect narrowed the chronological margin down to this triennium. Various quotations made it clear that Huguccio wrote after the fall of Jerusalem (July 1187) and the short pontificate of Gregory VIII (October to December 1187), i.e., during that of his successor, Clement III (December 1187–1191).[6] Regarding the latter chronological boundary, moreover, Huguccio's habit of citing new papal decretals merely as "extra" betrayed a lack of familiarity with *Compilatio prima,* published in 1191.[7] The indirect clues thus substantiate the sole actual date (1188) to be drawn from the *Summa,* which Huguccio had included in his commentary as part of a sample intended to help his students in drawing up a charter.[8]

Later scholarship has found little reason to challenge Gillmann's findings. Only minor modifications have been proposed. Gillmann himself was aware, for instance, that in all the manuscripts available to him the *Summa* contained a mention of the decretal LITTERAS TUAS, which Pope Innocent III had issued as late as 1201![9] While

6. Ibid., 238–42. Convincing evidence for a date after Gregory's pontificate comes from a passage at C.11 q.3 c.24 s.v. *more penitentium*; Huguccio mentioned Pope Clement III s.v. *inter eos et ecclesie rusticos,* D.89 c.5: "Ar. quod papa potest delegare iudici ecclesiastico causam que vertitur inter laicos vel inter clericum actorem et laicum reum; quod his diebus fecit dominus papa Clemens de causa que vertebatur inter quandam conversam Sancti Salvatoris et Hugolinum de Mozone reum. Quam dominus papa delegavit archipresbitero Sancti Petri et mihi. Sed utrum hoc potuerit dubitatur" (Klagenfurt xxix.a.3, fol. 78va; Admont 7, fol. 114va; Munich, Staatsbibl. lat. 10247, fol. 90ra; published by F. Gillmann, "Abfassungzeit," 240 n.3; cf. also S. Kuttner, *Repertorium,* 158 n.1). It is rather perplexing that most of the MSS read "inter clericum actorem et clericum reum"; only Paris, B.N. lat. 15396, fol. 90rb, has "inter clericum actorem et laicum reum," which alone coincides with the facts of the case to which Huguccio refers.
7. Following F. Gillmann, "Abfassungzeit," 241–42, most scholars today favor Huguccio's election to the see of Ferrara on 1 May 1190 as the event that made the canonist abandon his task as a commentator; cf. above, chap. I, n.32.
8. Ibid., 241 n.2: "Sic ergo formetur inscriptio accusationis: A. D. mclxxxviii, indictione tali, imperii Frederici sacratissimi principis anno tali." Mauro Sarti, *De professoribus,* 1.296 (1.370), had misread the same date as "mclxxviii," so that some modern accounts still claim that Huguccio had given lectures in canon law as early as 1178: details above, Introduction, n.10.
9. *Summa,* to C.23 q.1 c.4 s.v. *quod sibi iubetur:* "Ar. quod pendente causa matrimonii propter dubium licite videtur posse reddi utrumque debitum. . . . Quod ta-

Gillmann for chronological reasons declared it an interpolation, others have been more hesitant to do away with it. For them, the awkward passage can be interpreted either by insisting, along with Gillmann, on a date prior to *Compilatio prima* (1191), never quoted by Huguccio, or by pushing the *terminus ante quem* far into Huguccio's reign as bishop of Ferrara (1190–1210). To be sure, the latter option would require that the canonist had deliberately avoided citing other decretals after the new collection of 1191. This would not only be without any parallel in contemporary canonistic literature but also highly impractical for a nonliterary text. It is therefore a less-than-likely explanation.

In addition, Gillmann's continuing search for relevant evidence led him to two other passages, previously overlooked. Since he published them in rather inconspicuous places, they will be discussed here in greater detail.

First of all, Huguccio included a clear chronological indication in the following gloss: "This year the archbishop of Pisa set himself the task of helping the Christians against the persecutions of Saladin. He once tried to go on the journey, but could not yet fulfill his vow due to the rough sea, which forced him to return."[10] Huguccio told this little episode to illustrate a moral maxim in the pertinent canon, stating that "circumstances adverse to good intentions and vows are to

---

men non est usquequaque observandum, ut in extra Innocentii III 'Litteras tuas' [= Po.1560 from 1201]"; cf. S. Kuttner, "Retractationes vii," *Gratian* (London, 1983), 12. The reference is transmitted in at least six MSS (Vatican, Bibl. Apost. lat. 2280, fol. 244ra–b; Florence, Laur. S. Croce Plut.i sin. 4, fol. 278va; Florence, Laur. Fesul. 126, fol. 101ra; Admont, Stiftsbibl. 7, fol. 318ra; Lons-le-Saunier, Arch. dép. 12.F 16, fol. 306va; Paris, B.N. lat. 3892, fol. 267ra). The other four are: Madrid, B.N. lat. 11962, Rouen, B.M. 749, Tarazona, Cath. 151 (3), Verona, Chapter cxciv. Its exceptional character is evident, however, considering that out of the roughly two hundred decretals quoted by Huguccio (see Appendix I), LITTERAS TUAS represents the sole instance of a papal letter issued at any time after 1190.

10. "Sicut archiepiscopus Pisanus hoc anno propositum habuit succurrendi Christianis contra persecutionem Saladini. Et incepit iter, sed repulsus tempestate maris votum suum adhuc complere non potuit," C.7 q.1 c.48 s.v. *bonis votis*, ed. F. Gillmann, *Zur Lehre der Scholastik vom Spender der Firmung und des Weihesakraments* (Paderborn, 1920), 4 n.2 (from MS Vatican, Bibl. Apost. lat. 2280, fols. 154vb–155ra), also in MSS Florence, Laur. Fes. 125, fol. 310va; Lons-le-Saunier, Arch. dép. 12.F 16, fol. 193vb; Klagenfurt, Bischöfl. Bibl. xxix.a.3, fol. 139ra; Admont, Stiftsbibl. 7, fol. 205va; Paris, B.N. lat. 15396, fol. 149vb.

be considered as a test of virtuousness."[11] An event occurring "this year" offered him a case in point. But to which year and what kind of promise by the Pisan archbishop did the canonist refer in his example? Gillmann regretted that "presently" (1920) he was unable to investigate these questions any further. As a matter of fact, historians do have notice of a vow publicly taken by the prelate, but know nothing of a failed attempt to fulfill the obligation. Instead of reporting his departure and premature return due to bad weather, Pisan annalists speak only of an archbishop's success in gathering and joining a fleet of crusaders. The *Summa* thus contributes an unknown detail to the city's history, which nevertheless can safely be located in the year 1188. After the loss of Jerusalem to Saladin in July 1187, Pope Clement III had spent the early months of his pontificate mainly in Pisa, where sometime between January and February of 1188 he received a vow from Archbishop Ubaldus and the commune that obliged them to go on Crusade. Already by September a large number of ships had been brought together and duly departed for the Holy Land. However, the fleet, led by Ubaldus, did not reach Tyre until the beginning of April 1189, after a long wintering off the Sicilian coast. The *Summa* may allude either to this delay or to an earlier attempt to set sail that had ended in Ubaldus's temporary return.[12] When Huguccio insisted on the continuing obligation to fulfill the vow, his attitude reflected circumstances that occurred at some point between the spring and winter of 1188. This passage therefore again recommends Gillmann's date of composition.

On the other hand, Gillmann found two passages in the *Summa* that seem to defy a similarly straightforward chronology. One of the remarks in fact suggests that Huguccio had already begun the final draft of his work a year earlier. It occurs in the first part of the com-

11. The text of canon 48 begins: "Adversitas que bonis votis obicitur, probatio virtutis est."

12. For historical information regarding Pisa during the early years of the Third Crusade, W. Heywood, *A history of Pisa* (Cambridge, 1921), 217; H. Möhring, *Saladin und der dritte Kreuzzug* (Wiesbaden, 1980), 67–68, 164; and the fourteenth-century *Cronaca di Pisa da Ranieri Sardo,* ed. O. Banti (Fonti per la storia d'Italia 99; Rome, 1963), 36: "Negli anni Domini 1188 missere Ubaldo arciveschovo di Pisa andò al passagio chollo inperadore Barbarossa chon 52 navili pisani per chonquistare la Terra Sancta."

mentary, where Huguccio discusses a chapter (D.81 c.15) ascribed
by Gratian's *Decretum* to a certain Pope Gregory. Quoting this pope
as the author of the text, the *Summa*, among other things, glosses the
words "beato Gregorio": "[Gregory] here does not talk about himself but another Gregory. There were seven [popes called Gregory].
Thus it is clear that this chapter is not by Gregory I."[13] Speaking of
seven popes by the name of Gregory, Huguccio had not just committed an error in counting. Instances to be found in the later sections
of the *Summa* unanimously witness his familiarity with the correct
numbering in formulations such as "Gregorius papa octavus."[14] This
makes it unlikely that the canonist would have spoken of seven pontiffs called Gregory at any time after the election of Gregory VIII in
October 1187.

But instead of moving backward the beginnings of Huguccio's final
draft by at least one year, Gillmann presented another text from the
Summa as a counterargument. To the words of the *Decretum*, D.20
a.c.1: "the rules . . . of the younger [pope] Gregory," Huguccio remarked briefly: "I do not know which of the eight [Gregorys] he
was."[15] Following the legal order of the *Decretum*, this text (based
on D.20 a.c.1) precedes the reference to the seven popes by the name
of Gregory, which Huguccio included in his comment on D.81 c.15.
To reconcile it with the rest of the chronological evidence, we therefore must assume an oversight on Huguccio's part. While adding the
final touches to the *Summa*, he probably failed to revise the passage
on D.81 c.15, thereby leaving it in a stage of development reached
already before Gregory VIII became pope in October 1187. This re-

13. "*Beato Gregorio* Non loquitur de se sed de alio Gregorio. Septem namque
fuerunt. Unde patet quod hoc non est capitulum primi Gregorii," ed. F. Gillmann, *Die
Notwendigkeit der Intention auf Seiten des Spenders und des Empfängers der Sakramente nach der Anschauung der Frühscholastik* (Mainz, 1916), 33 n.1 (from MS Bamberg, Can. 40, fol. 64va). "Septem" is the reading in all of the MSS I consulted: Paris,
B.N. lat. 3891, fol. 84va; Paris, B.N. lat. 3892, fol. 89vb; Admont 7, fol. 106rb;
Florence, Fes. 125, fol. 161rb; Klagenfurt xxix.a.3, fol. 72vb; Vatican, Lat. 2280, fol.
75ra; Lons-le-Saunier 12.F 16, fol. 100rb; Klosterneuburg 89, fol. 95va; Paris, B.N.
lat. 15396, fol. 83va; Munich, Staatsbibl. lat. 10247, fol. 83ra.
14. Instances have been printed by J. F. v. Schulte, *Geschichte,* 1.130 n.4; F. Gillmann, "Abfassungszeit," 240 n.2.
15. "Quis de octo fuerit nescio," *Summa* D.20 c.1, s.v. *regule minoris Gregorii,*
ed. F. Gillmann, *Notwendigkeit,* 33 n.1 (from MSS Bamberg, Can. 40., fol. 14va;
Vatican, Bibl. Apost. lat. 2280, fol. 18rb).

minds the reader that the genesis of the voluminous work certainly required a considerable period of time. Impossible to imagine that Huguccio possessed the mental stamina to produce a four-hundred-folio text within the limits of, say, 1188. To be sure, Gillmann's principal purpose was to determine the date of completion rather than that of composition. But to achieve a fuller understanding of the chronology and its implications, we must go beyond this point and try to discern the successive stages in which Huguccio's commentary took shape.

2. STAGES OF COMPOSITION

Scholars have always known that, in composing the *Summa,* Huguccio occasionally departed from the order of Gratian's *Decretum.* The gap he left between C.23 q.4 c.33 and C.27 was an all-too-visible sign. Friedrich Maassen further called attention to a passage in which Huguccio himself attested to the piecemeal fashion he adopted. Instead of treating Gratian's treatise on penance (C.33 q.3) right after C.33 q.2, the canonist briefly indicated that he would move on to C.33 q.4 and reserve the intermediary questio for a later and more extensive treatment.[16] Manuscripts of the *Summa* also often omit well-defined sections of the text, another hint at a genesis involving an intermittent pattern.[17] Fortunately, the work includes many cross-references, which help to place each of these sections in a relative chronology. They show that the composition of the *Summa* went through five successive stages.

I. Initially, Huguccio seems to have followed closely the order of the *Decretum.* He first completed the major bulk of his work in a straightforward fashion, in the order Prologue; D.1–101; C.2–22; C.27–C.33 q.2; C.33 q.4–C.36. All of these textual portions are linked by a network of mutual citations. When referring to subsequent parts, Huguccio promised to treat them by applying future

16. C.33 q.3 pr.: "Hic intitulatur tertia questio in qua prolixius tractatus interseritur de penitentia, qui quia specialem exigit laborem ei ad presens supersedeo," MS Admont 7, fol. 385va; cf. F. Maassen, "Beiträge," 38.

17. After an examination of the textual tradition, Luigi Prosdocimi, "La Summa Decretorum," 359–60, came to the conclusion that "proprio la C.1 e il De cons. siano le ultime parti composte . . . , dopo di che non sarebbe rimasto ad Uguccione che accingersi al commento delle Causae Haereticorum."

tense ("ut dicemus"), whereas he used past tense to indicate preceding ones ("ut diximus"). Here and there, the former category is combined with the invocation of God, "Deo volente," which reveals that Huguccio put emphasis on something he had not yet written.[18]

II. Next, he turned to Causa 1.[19] The special treatment of Causa 1 was hardly exceptional, considering that later Bolognese curricula often reserved for it a lecture of its own. By way of references pointing from the rest of Huguccio's comment toward Causa 1, moreover, we can infer that it was finished prior to all of the other portions the author had passed over in the first place.[20]

III. After his treatment of Causa 1, he next took up *De consecratione*. Obviously, the canonist decided to focus on this theologically oriented treatise on sacraments in general before proceeding to deal with penance in particular. In *De penitentia*, he quoted the comment on consecration as a work already accomplished.[21]

18. The application of future tense in Huguccio's use does not always take on a meaning in terms of time, but also may have a spatial dimension; when, for example, the *Summa* calls the reader's attention to a distant passage by adopting forms like "invenies" or "sicut distinctum est," the temporal aspect often has to be reduced to the mere references "below" and "above." Not so, however, wherever Huguccio speaks of himself in the first person: "a nobis expositum" regularly points to something accomplished earlier, "faciemus" to a comment yet to be written. In this fashion, a remark at D.54 c.15 points to C.17 q.4 c.34 ("sicut ibi dicemus"); another one advises the reader to interpret C.7 q.1 c.3 in connection with C.11 q.1 c.25 ("ibidem melius assignabimus"); on the other hand, at C.12 q.2 c.15 the *Summa* refers backwards to D.23 c.6 ("ut dixi"), at C.32 q.4 c.11 to the prologue ("ut in principio huius operis diximus"). In addition, Huguccio employed the formula "Deo volente" in his commentary on C.2 q.2 a.c.1 (with regard to C.3 q.1), C.3 q.4 c.12 (to C.11 q.3), C.13 q.1 a.c.1 (to C.16 q.1 c.42), and C.22 q.4 c.20 (to C.32 q.2 p.c.10).

19. Cf. *Summa* C.1 q.1 c.17 s.v. *Qui perfectionem* (MS Admont 7, fol. 130ra): "Si quis tamen velit in his plenius instrui legat distinctionem quam de his fecimus infra, viiii q. i Quod ordinatio [a.c.1]."

20. For details on Causa 1, see L. Prosdocimi, "La Summa Decretorum," 356–61; indicative passages are De cons. D.2 c.73: "Nos vero idem dicimus de hoc sacramento quod de aliis sc. quod hoc sacramentum potest confici a quolibet heretico . . . dummodo forma ecclesie servetur et conferens habeat ordinem qui ad tale sacramentum exigitur. Sed hoc plenius distinximus i q.i Si fuerit [c.30]," Admont 7, fol. 436ra; also De cons. D.4 c.140; De cons. D.4 c.31 (ed. F. Gillmann, *Notwendigkeit*, 36 n.4); while writing these lines, Huguccio had not yet completed De pen. and the fragment on Causa 23: see next note.

21. De pen. D.3 c.21: "Hoc capitulum invenitur infra, de con. di.v Nichil [c.23], et ibi est diligenter a nobis expositum" (Vat. Lat. 2280, fol. 304vb); and already earlier, at De pen. D.3 c.7: "Assignavimus iam et alias causas quare huiusmodi pene . . . remaneant post baptismum . . . , ut infra de con. di.iiii Sine penitentia [c.99]" (Admont 7, fol. 491va).

IV, V. The fourth and fifth stages deal with *De penitentia* and *Cause hereticorum* (C.23–C.23 q.4 c.33). Although there exists no adequate proof that Huguccio's comment on penance was an earlier achievement of his, its priority can be taken for granted. After all, a different order would be less than likely in view of the fragmentary state of the explanations to the *Cause hereticorum* (C.23–26). Such evidence suggests that Huguccio started working on this section of the *Summa* only after the completion of *De penitentia*.[22]

This relative chronology of the *Summa* is largely based on intrinsic evidence. It will now be illustrative to correlate these findings with the extant manuscript material.

3. THE MANUSCRIPT TRADITION

a. A Survey

For more than two decades, the search for manuscripts of the *Summa* in European libraries has not resulted in any new discovery, so that their total of 42 has remained unchanged.[23] The two most recent lists of copies, published in the 1950s, contain 41 and 43 items respectively, of which two have been eliminated.[24] While the increase

---

22. Despite the questionable date (above n.9), Huguccio's authorship for the fragment on C.23 has been confirmed by F. Gillmann, "Abfassungszeit," 244n., who first quoted its gloss to C.23 q.4 c.24 §7 s.v. *sunt in illa clerici* etc. It referred to *Summa* D.12 c.8, which indeed included a text that corresponds well to the remark "sicut ibi exposuimus." That the same fragment belongs to the latest parts of Huguccio's work is proved by a passage to C.23 q.4 c.24 §6 s.v. *Est enim et tale*: "Hic ponit alium modum inferendi. Hoc multo melius intelliges si que diximus de istis duobus modis inferendi infra, de con. di.v Numquam [c.33], respexeris" (Admont 7, fol. 322va, Lons-le-Saunier 12.F 16, fol. 311rb). Accordingly, the question of priority concerns *De penitentia* only. If we accept the date of 1201 for Huguccio's fragment on C.23 (cf. n.9 above) as authentic, moreover, the precedence of his comment on *De penitentia* is confirmed through its references to a scholastic setting: *Summa*, de pen. D.2 c.44 s.v. *innocentes* (Lons-le-Saunier 12.F 16, fol. 393vb): "disputationibus relinquimus"; de pen. D.4 a.c.1 s.v. *Quia vero* (Lons-le-Saunier 12.F 16, fol. 399va–b): "Sed hec melius in disputationibus disquiruntur." These remarks (cf. also A. Landgraf, "Diritto canonico," 411–12) should reflect Huguccio's activity as a full-time teacher, before his elevation to the Ferrarese See in 1190.

23. MS Madrid, B.N. lat. 11962, represents the most recent discovery, cf. below, nn.48, 105. As Prof. Antonio Garcia y Garcia (Salamanca) has kindly pointed out to me, there is another copy (or abbreviation?) of the *Summa* in the libraries of Málaga (Spain).

24. A little older but more descriptive is the list by C. Leonardi, "La vita," 89–

in the number of testimonies was rather modest, scholars have added more accurate descriptions of already-known manuscripts in a series of scattered articles and notes.[25] The following survey of the surviving textual tradition will provide an update of earlier work and will also classify each copy according to the different phases of composition we have discerned. In order to do this, all known copies of the *Summa* will be treated in a systematic fashion, to show the enormous impact of Huguccio's stage-by-stage completion on the outward appearance of the surviving texts. Only one-fifth (9) of them offer the entire *Summa*. More than one-third (18) of the incomplete exemplars owe their imperfect state to the absence of one or more of the above-mentioned later additions (stages ii–v) from the bulk of text completed in the first place (stage i).[26]

I. MSS Containing None of Huguccio's Later Additions:

1.1 [Vatican, Arch. S. Pietro C.114] (s.xiii in.): i[27]

1.2 Calahorra, Cath. 8 (s.xiii): i[28]

98; whereas that published in *Traditio* 11 (1955), 441–44, rather presents an analysis of contents. Of the MSS mentioned therein, cancel MS Kassel, Landesbibl. Jur. 28: L. Prosdocimi, "I manoscritti della 'Summa Decretorum' di Uguccione da Pisa: Iter Germanicum," SG 7 (1959), 251–72; MS Milan, Bibl. Ambr. 238 inf.: *Traditio* 13 (1957), 469. Two Spanish MSS do not contain Huguccionian material in the proper sense, either, although they have been identified as such: MS Madrid, B.N. lat. 251, merely includes heavily abbreviated excerpts of the *Summa* in the third layer of its marginal glosses on Gratian's *Decretum:* R. Weigand, *Die Glossen*, 823–25; while MS Madrid, Fundación Lázaro Galdiano 440, contains in its fifth (sixth) layer of glosses a redaction of Huguccio's and Alanus's comments, not finished until after 3 Comp. (1210): ibid., 827–31; cf. also F. Cantelar-Rodríguez, *El matrimonio de herejes*, 123–25.

25. Besides the two lists just mentioned, see especially the contributions by L. Prosdocimi, "Summa Decretorum," and idem, "I manoscritti"; A. Vetulani, "Trois manuscrits canoniques de la Bibliothèque Publique de Leningrad," SG 12 (1967), 195–201; T. Lehnherr, "Der Einschub in die Huguccio-Handschrift der Kapitelsbibliothek von Verona," AKKR 153 (1984), 56–76; additional notes have appeared in *Traditio* 12 (1956), 563; 13 (1957), 469; 17 (1961), 534; 19 (1963), 534; BMCL 1 (1971), 71–72.

26. In the following manuscript survey, these symbols and abbreviations will be used: Roman numerals (i–v) indicate the stages within the relative chronology given above. An asterisk (*) marks appended or shifted texts. Square brackets ([. . .]) indicate that the classification of a MS is conjectural. For full information regarding the MSS, their locations, and signatures, see Bibliography, part I below.

27. Prologue: fol. 1r; D.1–101: 1r–116r; C.2–22: 117r–267v; C.27–C.33 q.2: 269r–323r; C.33 q.4–C.35 q.8 c.1: 323r–340v: C. Leonardi, "La vita," 95. That this incomplete copy originally belonged to the group of texts without any supplement is

1.3 Luxembourg, B.N. 144 (s.xiii ex.): i[29]
1.4 [Salamanca, Univ. 1930] (s.xiii–xiv): i[30]
1.5 Munich, Staatsbibl. lat. 10247 (s.xiv): i[31]

II. MSS Containing One Later Addition:

2.1 Fulda, Landesbibl. D. 22 (s.xiii): i and ii[32]
2.2 Paris, B.N. lat. 3891 (s.xiii): i and iii[33]
2.3 Klosterneuburg, Stiftsbibl. 295 (s.xiv): iii[34]

III. MSS Containing Two Later Additions:

3.1 Paris, B.N. lat. 15396–97 (s.xiii): i, iii, iv*[35]
3.2 Bamberg, Can. 41 (s.xiv): i, iii*, iv*[36]
3.3 Bamberg, Can. 40 (s.xiv in.): i, ii, iii[37]

---

suggested (a) by its age (perhaps the oldest copy still extant) and (b) by its mutilation right before the end of part ii (C.36), most likely to be attributed to the loss of a few final folios.

28. G. Fransen, "Manuscrits canoniques conservés en Espagne," *Revue d'histoire ecclésiastique* 49 (1954), 153.

29. Prologue: fol. 1ra–b; D.1–101: 1rb–147va; C.2–22: 160ra–329rb; C.27–C.33 q.2: 342ra–400va; C.33 q.4–C.36: 400va–423vb. Described from microfilm. For further details, below nn.75, 78, 86, 100.

30. Formerly MS Madrid, Palacio II(509): C.2–22; C.27–C.33 q.2; C.33 q.4–C.36. G. Fransen, "Manuscrits canoniques conservés en Espagne," *Revue d'histoire ecclésiastique* 48 (1953), 231–32; see also n.98 below.

31. Prologue: fol. 1ra–b; D.1–101: fols. 1rb–98vb; C.2–22: fols. 99ra–226vb; C.27–C.33 q.2: fols. 227ra–263va; C.33 q.4–C.36: fols. 263va–280ra. Described from microfilm.

32. Prologue: fol. 3r; D.1–101: 3r–98r; C.1: 98v–106r; C.2–19: 106r–218r; C.20–22: 219r–230v; C.27–C.33 q.2: 231r–276ra; C.33 q.4–C.36: 276ra–291r. L. Prosdocimi, "I manoscritti," 261; cf. also nn.80, 83 below.

33. Prologue: fol. 1r–v; D.1–101: 1v–100v; C.2–22: 101r–230r; C.27–C.33 q.2: 231r–267v; C.33 q.4–C.36: 267v–280v; De cons.: 280v–320v. C. Leonardi, "La vita," 94; see also below n.85.

34. De cons.: fols. 110r–238v. C. Leonardi, "La vita," 93.

35. MS 15396: Prologue: fol. 2ra–b; D.1–101: 2rb–99vb; C.2–13: 108ra–191vb. MS 15397: C.14–22, fols. 3ra–46vb; C.27–C.33 q.2: 59ra–95rb; C.33 q.4–C.36: 95vb–110rb; De cons.: 110va–151ra; De pen.: 151ra–171va. Described from microfilm; see also below, nn.74, 89.

36. Former signature: P.ii.28. Prologue: fol. 1r–v; D.1–101: 1v–125v; C.2–22: 135r–309r; C.27–C.33 q.2: 325r–375ra; C.33 q.4–C.36: 375ra–394v; De pen.: 395r(new quire)–418v; De cons.: 419r(new quire)–477v. L. Prosdocimi, "I manoscritti," 258. See also below nn.76, 87.

37. Former signature: P.ii.25. Prologue: fol. 1ra–b; D.1–101: 1rb–76vb; C.1: 77ra–91va; C.2–22: 91va–196vb; C.27–C.33 q.2: 196vb–229rb; C.33 q.4–C.36:

3.4 Klosterneuburg, Stiftsbibl. 89 (s.xiv): i, ii, iii[38]
3.5 Klagenfurt, xxix.a.3 (s.xiv): i, ii, iii[39]
3.6 Lincoln, Cath. 2 (s.xiv): i (Pars i only), iv, iii[40]

IV. MSS Containing Three Later Additions:

4.1 Leningrad (s.xiii ex.): i, ii, iii*, iv*[41]
4.2 Vatican, Borgh. 272 (s.xiv): i, ii, iii, iv*[42]
4.3 Rouen, B.M. 749 (s.xiv): i, ii, v, iv*[43]
4.4 Cambrai, B.M. 612 (s.xiii/xiv): i–iv[44]
4.5 Tarazona, Cath. 97(9): i, ii, iii, iv*[45]

V. MSS Containing All of the Later Additions:

5.1 Admont, Stiftsbibl. 7 (s.xiv): iv*[46]
5.2 Florence, Plut.I sin. 4 (s.xiii/xiv): iv*, iii*[47]

229rb–242vb; De cons.: 242vb–279vb; cf. L. Prosdocimi, "I manoscritti," 257, 268–72.

38. Prologue: fol. 1r; D.1–101: 1r–112vb; C.1: 113ra (new folio after blank space)–133vb (rest of folio blank); C.2–22: 134ra–273vb (with wrong headings occasionally); C.27–C.33 q.2: 274ra–316r; C.33 q.4–C.36: 316r–332vb (rest blank); De cons.: 333ra–386v. Described from microfilm. For the date, C. Leonardi, "La vita," 95, has suggested s.xiii.

39. From the Episcopal Library. Prologue: fol. 1ra–b; D.1–101: 1rb–86vb; C.1: 86vb–103ra; C.2–22: 103ra–221va; C.27–C.33 q.2: 222ra–259rb; C.33 q.4–C.36: 259rb–273va; De cons.: 273va–313vb. Description based on microfilm.

40. Prologue: fol. 2r–v; D.1–101: fols. 2v–176v; De pen.: 176v–214v; De cons.: 215r–307r. C. Leonardi, "La vita," 93.

41. Shelf-mark: Lat. fol. ii.vel.10. Prologue: fol. 1ra–b; D.1–101: 1rb–(?); C.2–C.2 q.1 c.7: (?)–83vb: C.1–C.1 q.1 c.74: 84r–91v; C.1 q.1 c.74–C.2 q.1 c.7 (later insertion): 92r–109v; C.2 q.1 c.7–22: 110r–239; C.27–C.33 q.2: 239v–(?); C.33 q.4–C.36: (?)–290va; De pen.: 300ra–323r; De cons.: 324ra–376r. *Traditio* 12 (1956), 563; A. Vetulani, "Trois manuscrits," 195–201; see further below nn.77, 88, 108.

42. Prologue: fol. 1r; D.1–101: 1r–57r; C.1: 57v–67r; C.2–22: 68r–143r; C.27–C.33 q.2: 154r–175r; C.33 q.4–C.36: 175r–184r; De cons.: 184r–218v; De pen.: 219r–232r. C. Leonardi, "La vita," 96; see also below n.103.

43. Fols. 1–332; C. Leonardi, "La vita," 95; also below n.91.

44. Fols. 1–385; C. Leonardi, "La vita," 95; cf. below n.84.

45. Prologue; D.1–101; C.1; C.2–22; C.27–33 q.2; C.33 q.4–C.36; De cons.; De pen.; G. Fransen, "Manuscrits canoniques," 232; *Traditio* 15 (1959), 499; below n.101.

46. Prologue: fol. 2ra–b; D.1–101: 2va–126vb; C.1: 127ra(after blank space)–151va; C.2–22: 152ra–316va; C.23–C.23 q.4 c.33: 316va–324ra; C.27–C.33 q.2: 335ra–385va; C.33 q.4–C.36: 385va–405va; De cons.: 406ra–473rb; De pen.: 473va–500rb (ends at D.5 c.1 s.v. *fructus*). Description based on microfilm; see also below n.92.

47. From the *Biblioteca Laurenziana*. Prologue: fol. 1r; D.1–101: 1r–108v; C.1:

5.3 Madrid, B.N. lat. 11962 (s.xiii): iv*, iii*[48]
5.4 Tarazona, Cath. 151(3) (s.xiv): iv*, v*, iii*[49]
5.5 Vatican, Bibl. Ap. lat. 2280 (s.xiv)[50]
5.6 Paris, B.N. lat. 3892 (s.xiv)[51]
5.7 Verona, Arch. Cap. cxciv (s.xiv)[52]
5.8 Lons-le-Saunier, Arch. Dép. 12 F.16 (s.xiv)[53]
5.9 Florence, Bibl. Laur. Fes. 125–26 (s.xv)[54]

This scheme shows the correlation between the external features of each copy and the relative chronology of the *Summa,* composed stage by stage in a nonlinear fashion. Twenty-eight out of forty-two surviving exemplars have been distributed into five categories, rendering evident the genesis of the work. Huguccio's final comment on

---

109r–128r; C.2–22: 128r–277r; C.23–C.23 q.4 c.33: 277r–284r; C.27–C.33 q.2: 295r–335r; C.33 q.4–C.36: 335r–350v; De pen.: 351r–370v; De cons.: 371r–417r. C. Leonardi, "La vita," 92. For the date, L. Prosdocimi, "La Summa Decretorum," 362; cf. also below n.94.

48. Prologue: fol. 2ra–b; D.1–101: 2rb–85vb; C.1: 86ra–(?); C.2–22: (?)–(?); C.23–C.23 q.4 c.33: 232ra–249vb; C.27–C.33 q.2: 250r–(?); C.33 q.4–C.36: (?)–304va; De pen.: 304va–324va; De cons.: 324va–369vb. A. Garcia y Garcia, "Canonistica Hispanica iv," BMCL 1 (1971), 71–72; see further n.105 below.

49. Prologue; D.1–101; C.1; C.2–22; C.27–C.33 q.2; C.33 q.4–C.36; De pen.; C.23–C.23 q.4 c.33; De cons.; *Traditio* 15 (1959), 498–99; see nn.79, 102 below.

50. Prologue: fol. D.1–101: 1va–89rb; C.1: 89rb–106vb; C.2–22: 109ra–243ra; C.23–C.23 q.4 c.33: 243ra–248rb; C.27–C.33 q.2: 256ra–292rb; De pen.: 292rb–311ra; C.33 q.4–C.36: 311ra–326va; De cons.: 326va–370vb. Description from microfilm. Cf. nn.95, 106 below.

51. Prologue: fol. 1ra–va; D.1–101: 1va–106vb; C.1: 106vb–126vb; C.2–22: 127ra–265vb; C.23–C.23 q.4 c.33: 265vb–272ra; C.27–C.33 q.2: 281va–322vb; De pen.: 322vb–341vb; C.33 q.4–C.36: 341vb–357ra; De cons.: 357ra–400vb. Seen on microfilm; cf. below nn.96, 107.

52. Prologue; D.1–101; De pen.; C.33 q.4–C.36; De cons.; C.1: 217ra–(?); C.2–22; C.23–C.23 q.4 c.33; C.27–C.33 q.2; L. Prosdocimi, "La Summa Decretorum," 358 nn.11, 364. Compare nn.81, 104 below.

53. Prologue: fol. 2ra–va; D.1–101: 2va–120ra; C.1: 120rb–142va; C.2–22: 142va–304vb; C.23–C.23 q.4 c.33: 305ra–313ra; C.27–C.33 q.2: 325rb–378vb; De pen.: 378vb–405rb; C.33 q.4–C.36: 405rb–426vb; De cons.: 427ra(begins at D.1 c.7)–483vb. Described from microfilm. Also, see n.97.

54. MS Fes. 125 contains the Prologue: fol. 1ra–vb; D.1–101: 1vb–191vb; C.1: 193ra–226vb; C.2–C.13 q.2 c.1: 227ra(after blank space)–388v; continued in Fes. 126: C.13 q.2 c.1–C.22: 1ra–98vb; C.23–C.23 q.4 c.33: 99ra(after blank space)–109rb; C.27–C.33 q.2: 127ra–210rb;; De pen.: 211ra–247vb; C.33 q.4–C.36: 248ra–277vb; De cons.: 278ra–369va. Described from microfilm; for the date, cf. K. Pennington, *Pope and bishops,* 81 n.21; see also C. Leonardi, "La vita," 92; and n.99 below.

Causa 23 (stage v), for example, appears in none of those MSS that contain only half or less of his (four) additions (groups ii and iii). Also, a striking coincidence emerges from a look at the texts that happened to comprise some, but not all, of the critical sections (ii to iv). These partial reconstructions inserted Causa 1 (ii) on nine occasions, De cons. (iii) on nine (appended twice), and De pen. (iv) on two (appended six times). Huguccio's fragmentary comment on Causa 23 (v) again stands out, in that it appears in only one such case. In other words, whenever medieval scribes supplied later portions of Huguccio's *Summa,* they were likely to copy the oldest and omit the latest section. The paleographical evidence, moreover, seems to attest to the same fact by pointing up a correspondence between age and completeness.

The remaining manuscripts are incomplete or defective to such a degree as to defy any attempt at classification. Nonetheless, some of them also contribute to the understanding of the genesis of the *Summa,* either by omitting certain additions or by transmitting them separately. They thus provide further witness of the presence of traces in the manuscript tradition of the author's original inconsistencies in drawing up his work.

VI. *Fragments:*

Worcester, Cath. Lib. F.12 (s.xiii): i, iv, iii[55]
Assisi, Bibl. Comm. 213 (s.xiii): i[56]
Leipzig, Univ. 985 (s.xiii): i[57]
Marburg, Univ. 83 (s.xiii/xiv): i[58]
Volterra, Bibl. Guarn. 6370 (s.xiv): i[59]

55. C.11 q.3 c.97–C.22; C.27–C.33 q.2; De pen.; C.33 q.4–C.36; De cons. The presence of De cons., along with that of De pen., suggests a later stage in the transmission of Huguccio's text. Perhaps the copy once also included the commentary on Causa 1, as do most texts containing these two additions.

56. Prologue twice: fol. 1r–v, 3r; D.1–101: 3r–88v; C.2–C.17 q.2 c.1: 89r–182v. C. Leonardi, "La vita," 91; *Traditio* 11 (1955), 441.

57. C.2–22: fol. 9r–233v. L.Prosdocimi, "I manoscritti," 262; cf. also below n.93.

58. Old class mark: C.2. Prologue twice: fols. 105r, 106r; D.1–101: 106v–186v, 195r–196r; C.2–C.11 q.3 c.62: 187r–194v, 197r–246v. L. Prosdocimi, "I manoscritti," 264.

59. Prologue: fol. 1r; D.1–D.21 c.2: 1r–20v; C.2 q.7 c.41–C.3 q.7 c.18: 21r–30v; C.27–C.33 q.2: 31r–80r; C.33 q.4–C.36: 80r–100r. C. Leonardi, "La vita," 96.

Parma, Bibl. Pal. 1222 (s.xiii): i[60]
Paris, B.N. lat. 3918 (s.xiii): i[61]
Barcelona, Univ. 504 (s.xiii): i[62]
Vienna, N.B. lat. 2061 (s.xiii): i[63]
Bamberg, Can. 42 (s.xiii): i[64]
Bernkastel-Kues, Hosp. 228 (s.xiv): iv, ii, i[65]
Vatican, Bibl. Ap. Lat. 2491 (s.xiv): i[66]
Cambridge, Pembr. Coll. 72 (s.xiv ex.): i[67]
Munich, lat. 28193 (s.xiv): i[68]

In analyzing the textual tradition of the *Summa*, the ultimate goal, short of a critical edition, must be the qualitative assessment of each copy. The enormous size of the work, however, has impeded the process of examination and comparison. For the transcription and systematic collation of the *Summa* begun during the 1950s, under the guidance of Alfons Stickler, MS Munich, lat. 10247, was selected as the basic text.[69]

By contrast, other scholars used copies in a random fashion, often led by considerations of availability and legibility. Their casual remarks on textual variants and superior readings were sometimes contradictory yet suggested the soundness of Stickler's principal editorial decision.[70]

60. Prologue; D.1–101; C.2–C.15 q.8. *Traditio* 11 (1955), 442.
61. Prologue: fol. 1r; D.1–D.50 c.17: 1r–26vb; C.2–C.6 q.1 c.22: 27ra–42vb; C.16 q.3 c.4–C.22 q.1 a.c.1: 43ra–54vb. F. Heyer, "Namen und Titel," 513 n.57.
62. D.1 c.4–D.101: fols. 1ra–170vb; C.2–C.16 q.1: 170vb–338vb. *Traditio* 17 (1961), 534.
63. Intercapitular gloss to the *Decretum*, C.2–C.11 q.1 c.39, fols. 1ra–172vb. Ends s.v. *deputentur*: "i.e. delegentur. Potest enim episcopus delegare causas suorum clericorum, ut ii q.vi Placuit/ . . .."
64. Former shelf-mark: P.ii.15. C.27–C.27 q.2 c.21: fols. 1ra–8vb. L.Prosdocimi, "I manoscritti," 258.
65. De pen. D.1 c.13–D.7 c.6: 45ra–74vb; C.1 q.1 c.1–C.1 in fine: 75ra–103v; C.2–C.2 q.3 p.c.8: 103v–110vb. L. Prosdocimi, "I manoscritti," 259.
66. In form of a marginal gloss. D.1–D.25 p.c.3 §4: fols. 1ra–36va. S. Kuttner and R. Elze, *A catalogue of canon and Roman law manuscripts in the Vatican Library* 2 (Studi e testi 328; Vatican City, 1987), 60–61.
67. Prologue: 116r–v; D.1–D.54 p.c.21: 116v–159v. C. Leonardi, "La vita," 91.
68. Contains a fragment of Huguccio's prologue, fol. 126v. L. Prosdocimi, "I manoscritti," 266.
69. Cf. n.4 above. According to my estimate, the text of the *Summa*, typed single-spaced (50 lines, 60 characters each), would cover ca. 3200 pages.
70. The use of the *Summa* has left recent authors with sometimes strikingly dif-

Compared to some of his colleagues, Huguccio took great care in editing his commentary. The argument is always presented with clarity, little variation in the vocabulary, and a uniform syntactic structure. Obscure or garbled passages are regularly signs of a corrupted text, which in most cases can be emended through the consultation of a second or, if necesssary, third manuscript. More extensive collations often prove to be monotonous exercises, and there is no sign of different recensions or authentic manipulations. As a result, striking distortions of Huguccio's opinions in the literature rarely find an excuse in distorted manuscript readings.[71]

The preceding survey may facilitate access to the best manuscripts of the *Summa*. It is based on the assumption that the texts closest to Huguccio's original are those that still reflect the seams of the editorial process. Stickler's MS Munich, for example, represents the most primitive stage of completion, omitting all of the later additions. MSS Vatican, Arch. S. Pietro, Calahorra, Salamanca, and Luxembourg, very likely belong to the same category, provided none were written by scribes who performed the task poorly. Also of interest are those copies that include the later additions in an appended position. The same copies should be consulted, too, when dealing with Causa 1, De cons., De pen., or the *Cause hereticorum*. Although it is by no means a foregone conclusion that the external shape of a copy correlates with its intrinsic qualities, scholarly work operating on the basis of this premise has yielded the most reliable textual results.[72]

---

ferent impressions. For example, K. Pennington, *Pope and bishops*, xiii, has remarked that "it is especially difficult to establish a good text for Huguccio's *Summa*." For R. Benson, *Bishop elect*, 397, on the other hand, "the manuscripts of Huguccio's *Summa* show surprisingly little textual variation"; similarly, T. Lehnherr, "Der Begriff," 33, finds the textual variants "nicht sehr erheblich." The selection of manuscripts may well account for their disagreement. While Pennington worked with MSS Admont; Klosterneuburg; Florence, Fes.; and Vatican, lat. 2280, all representing later stages (iii and v) of composition, Benson and Lehnherr both chose MS Munich (stage i) as their basic text; cf. also n.72 below.

71. A notable exception to this rule, however, is discussed by G. Catalano, *Impero*, 21–24, who corrects the text of the *Summa* D.2 c.4, in MS Vatican, lat. 2280 (stage v). The corrupted version led S. Mochi Onory, *Fonti canonistiche*, 162–77, to serious misinterpretations regarding Huguccio's view of the relationship between the emperor and the kings (cf. Introduction, nn.21–22 above).

72. Accordingly, the MSS most often used in the literature, Vatican, lat. 2280, and Admont 7 (both stage v), are among the least recommendable. Besides MS Munich,

b. Non-authentic Additions

The consultation of the *Summa* is complicated by the intrusion of foreign material into many of the Huguccionian texts. For more than a century, these nonauthentic interpolations have prompted numerous misattributions, while even today it remains uncertain if all of them have actually been identified. In this respect, the more recent investigations into the manuscripts have proved particularly fruitful. They have shown that the gaps left in Huguccio's own comment on the *Decretum* were supplied from other decretist works in the following fashion:

II. *Causa 1:*

a. *Nihil quod dicitur*: in Paris, B.N. lat. 15397*[73]
b. *Continuatio prima*: in Paris, B.N. lat. 15396–97[74]
c. *Summa Lipsiensis*: in Luxembourg, B.N. 144[75]
d. *Ecce vicit leo*: in Bamberg, Can.41[76]; Leningrad*[77]

III. De consecratione:

a. *Summa Lipsiensis*: in Luxembourg, B.N. 144[78]
b. *Ius naturale* (?): in Tarazona 151(3)[79]

---

lat. 10247, which for most purposes is available on microfilm only (ink faded), I consider MS Paris, lat. 15396–97, a carefully written and very reliable text.

73. This decretist comment (inc. C.1 q.1 c.1 s.v. *Gratia* [fol. 172ra]: "Nichil quod dicitur gratia in veritate gratia est nisi gratis detur et accipiatur . . ."; expl. C.1 q.7 c.26 s.v. *sorciendis* [fol. 175vb]: "i.e. obtinendis per interpositam personam et fraude legis huius et sacramenti sui") forms a unit with another one on C.23–26, "Quod utrumque" (ibid., fols. 176ra–183va); details n.84 below.

74. Paris, B.N. lat. 15396, fols. 100ra–107rb (ends at C.1 q.7 c.27 s.v. *Pro nihilo computantur*: ". . . admitti poterit etiam socius criminis, ut di. lxviiii Si quis papa/ . . ."; fol. 107v is blank); oddly, an initial portion of the *Continuatio*, C.1–C.1 q.1 c.20 s.v. *Cum omnis*, expl.: ". . . numquam divinatio accipitur in bona significatione/ . . . ," appears again at the beginning of MS lat. 15397, fol. 2ra–2vb (first three lines of the final column only); see further above n.35, below n.89.

75. Fols. 148ra–159bis(rb); see also above n.29, below nn.78, 86, 100. The Anglo-Norman *Summa Lipsiensis* ("Omnis qui iuste iudicat") was the most comprehensive commentary on Gratian before Huguccio (ca. 1186): S. Kuttner, *Repertorium*, 196–98.

76. Fols. 126r–135r. The French apparatus *Ecce vicit leo* has survived in two recensions, one prior to 1200, the other after 1205: S. Kuttner, *Repertorium*, 59–66; H. Müller, *Der Anteil*, 157 n.8. Cf. also above n.36, below n.87.

77. Shelf-mark: Lat. fol. ii.vel.10. The fragment of *Ecce vicit leo* covers C.1–C.1 q.7 c.9 only and is inserted after C.36 of the *Summa*, fols. 292r–299vb: *Traditio* 12 (1956), 563. See also n.41 above, nn.88, 108 below.

78. Fols. 424ra–437ra; cf. above nn.29, 75, below nn.86, 100.

79. Inserted after Huguccio's C.36 and before his treatise on De pen., inc.: "Ex-

IV. De penitentia:

a. Alanus ab Insulis: in Fulda D. 22*[80]
b. *Transitum ponit*: in Verona cxciv*[81]

V. Cause hereticorum:[82]

a. *Quid culpatur*: in Fulda D. 22*[83]
b. *Quid utrumque*: in Paris, B.N. lat.15397*[84]
c. *Continuatio prima*: in Paris, B.N. lat. 3891(3)[85]; Luxembourg, B.N. 144(3)[86]; Bamberg, Can. 41(1)[87]; Leningrad(3)[88]; Paris, B.N.

---

pleto de matrimonio tractatu. . . ." That this text originally formed part of the apparatus *Ius naturale* (1191/1205) by the English canonist Alanus is called into question by MS Seo de Urgel, Cab. 2882, which ascribes it to "R. de parui passu": S. Kuttner, "Retractationes vii," *Gratian*, 13. Also n.49 above, n.102 below.

80. Fols. 291r–294r; the work by Alanus ab Insulis is printed in PL 210.111–98: L. Prosdocimi, "I manoscritti," 261. Cf. nn.38, 83.

81. Fragment of one column, appended after C.36 of the *Summa* (fol. 456v): *Traditio* 11 (1955), 443. See further n.52 above, n.104 below.

82. The bracketed numbers after the MSS indicate that the given text covers: (1) C.23–26; (2) C.23 q.4 c.34–C.26; (3) parts of C.23 pr.(–C.23 q.1 a.c.1) only.

83. Appended after C.36 of the *Summa*, fol. 294ra–vb, and covering C.23–C.24 q.1 c.8 only; cf. L. Prosdocimi, "I manoscritti," 261: "Trattasi di un testo derivato certamente dalla Summa di Rufino, e molto vicino alla cosidetta Summa Conditio." The fragment probably dates into the early 1170s. See nn.32, 80 above.

84. Inc. C.23 q.1 a.c.1 s.v. *Quod militare* etc. (fol. 176ra): "Quod utrumque sc. et iniuriam propulsare a se et iniuriam propulsare a sociis . . ."; expl. C.26 q.7 c.17 s.v. *Quis existi.* etc. (fol. 183va): ". . . Hec sunt verba Gratiani. *Demonium* [c.18]." This excerpt, together with the preceding comment on C.1 by the same author (n.73 above), forms part of a hitherto unknown decretist apparatus, written probably at Bologna. The text contains a reference, C.25 q.2 p.c.16 s.v. *si preces veritate* (fol. 182), to the decretal EX PARTE VENERABILIS (JL 14317), ca. 1174–81. The conciliar decrees of Lateran III (1179) are nowhere mentioned, so that the commentary can be dated between 1174 and 1179. The explanations follow the *Decretum* very closely, which may suggest the influence of Bazianus. R. Weigand, "Bazianus- und B-Glossen zum Dekret Gratians," SG 20 (1976), 453–96 at 475, has observed that Bazianus focused strictly on literal exegesis. Moreover, C.23 q.5 c.11 s.v. *absque eo ubi caritas pericli.* (fol. 178va): "i.e. preter illum casum cum castitas periclitatur, quasi dicens 'et in persecutionibus et etiam in hoc casu' cum sc. castitas periclitatur. Et ponitur hic 'absque eo' reclusive sicut in Canticis Canticorum: 'Pulchra sunt omnia mea absque eo quod interius latet,' " offers the oldest version of an opinion that the later tradition, from *Continuatio prima* (ca. 1185/86; printed n.150 below) to *Ordinaturus magister* (second rec., ca. 1190; Munich, Staatsbibl. lat. 10244, fol. 138va) and the *Glossa ordinaria* (cf. my article, "Lucretia and the medieval canonists," BMCL 19 [1989], 13–31 at 24–25), unanimously associated with Bazianus.

85. Covers C.23 pr.–a.c.1, fol. 230ra: L. Prosdocimi, "La Summa Decretorum," 370; cf. also n.33 above.

86. C.23 pr.–a.c.1, fol. 329rb; L. Prosdocimi, "La Summa Decretorum," 370; see further nn.29, 75, 78 above, n.100 below.

87. C.23–26, fols. 310r–324v; cf. nn.36, 76 above.

lat. 15397(1)[89]; Cambrai, B.M. 612(3)[90]; Rouen, B.M. 749(2)[91]; Admont 7[92]; Leipzig, Univ. 985[93]; Florence, Plut.[94]; Vatican, Lat. 2280(2)[95]; Paris, B.N. lat. 3892(2)[96]; Lons-le-Saunier, 12.F.16(2)[97]; Salamanca 1930(1)[98]; Florence, Fes. 126(2)[99]

   d. *Summa Lipsiensis*: in Luxembourg, B.N. 144[100]

   e. *Ius naturale*: in Tarazona 97(1)[101]; Tarazona 151(2)*[102]

   f. *Ecce vicit leo*: in Vatican, Borgh. lat. 272(1)[103]

   g. *Ostenditur hic*: in Verona cxciv[104]

   h. Johannes de Deo: in Madrid, B.N. lat. 11962[105]; Vatican, Lat. 2280*[106]; Paris, B.N. lat. 3892*[107]; Leningrad*[108]

---

88. C.23 pr., fol. 271vb; see nn.41, 77, 108.
89. C.23–26, fol. 46vb (immediately following C.22 of Huguccio's *Summa*)–58rb; see above nn.35, 74.
90. C.23 pr., fol. 271vb: L. Prosdocimi, "La Summa Decretorum," 369; see also n.44 above.
91. C.23 q.4 c.34–C.26, fols. 245rb–256va: L. Prosdocimi, "La Summa Decretorum," 371 n.47; see further n.43 above.
92. Begins at C.24, fols. 325ra–333vb. Cf. also n.46 above.
93. Fragmentary, C.23–C.24 q.3 c.29, fols. 234ra–254rb (leaving most of the column blank): seen on microfilm; cf. L. Prosdocimi, "I manoscritti," 262, and n.57 above.
94. C.23 q.4 c.34–C.26, fols. 284ra–294ra; see above n.47.
95. C.23 q.4 c.34–C.26, fols. 248rb–256ra; see above n.50, below n.106.
96. C.23 q.4 c.34–C.26, fols. 272ra–281va; cf. above n.51, below n.107.
97. C.23 q.4 c.34–C.26, fols. 313ra–325rb; see above n.53.
98. Beginning at C.23; cf. above n.30.
99. C.23 q.4 c.33–C.26, fols. 109rb–125rb; see n.54 above.
100. C.23–C.26 q.2, fols. 330ra–341vb (ends at C.26 q.6 c.3 §1 s.v. *benedictionem*); as indicated by a reference, "Residuum quere in fine voluminis," the rest of the text follows on fol. 437rb–va, though partly mutilated; cf. L. Prosdocimi, "La Summa Decretorum," 370. Also nn.29, 75, 78, 86 above.
101. C.23–26: *Traditio* 15 (1959), 499; cf. n.45 above.
102. From C.23 q.4 c.33(!) onward inserted, along with the Huguccionian fragment, between the *Summa*'s texts on De pen. and De cons.: *Traditio* 15 (1959), 498–99. Cf. nn.49, 79 above.
103. C.23–26, fols. 144r–153v; cf. above n.42.
104. Begins at C.23 q.4 c.33(!); analyzed by T. Lehnherr, "Der Einschub," 56–76, who dated the insertion in the years 1212–17; perhaps it is slightly earlier (1210–15), as R. Weigand, "Huguccio," 490, has suggested; cf. nn.52, 81 above.
105. Fols. 232ra–249vb, inserted into the text (n.48 above) of the *Summa*, right after C.22.
106. After the text of the *Summa*, fols. 371ra–388ra: F. Gillmann, "Abfassungszeit," 243–44n. See also nn.50, 95 above.
107. Appended to Huguccio's work (nn.51, 90 above), fols. 401ra–419v.
108. Contains on the last folio (376) an entry drawn from the prologue (cf. n.109 below): A. Vetulani, "Trois manuscrits," 200; and nn.47, 77, 88 above.

Thanks to the *horror vacui* of the medieval scribes, the textual tradition of the *Summa* came to contain other decretist writings. While most of them have also survived outside of it, there are five instances in which material is uniquely preserved in Huguccio's work. There are, to begin with, the half-page fragment replacing the treatise on *De penitentia* in MS Verona and a one-folio excerpt covering parts of the *Cause hereticorum* in MS Fulda. The commentary on the same section in MS Verona and the two appendices to Huguccio's *Summa* in MS Paris 15397 are certainly more significant. All of these additions owe their transmission to mere accident. The final one by Johannes de Deo was, on the other hand, designed specifically to fill the lacuna in Huguccio's work. To convey this purpose to his readers, Johannes emphasized it in a foreword and a versified epilogue.[109] He also took up the glossator's pen at the very point where Huguccio had abandoned it: at C.23 q.4 c.33.

The most conspicuous feature of the preceding list, however, is the presence of numerous excerpts from the so-called *Continuatio prima*. Their occurrence in Huguccio's unfinished *Cause hereticorum* (C.23–26) constitutes something like the usual pattern, which makes the reader think of particular ties between this comment and Huguccio's *Summa*. In fact, *Continuatio prima* has only once been preserved outside of the Huguccionian tradition.[110] In interpreting the work, moreover, scholars have come to very different conclusions. Therefore, the question of the *Continuatio* deserves a more detailed discussion.

---

109. Both printed by F. Gillmann, "Abfassungszeit," 243–44n; The motive of Johannes emerges from the prologue (printed chapter I, n.3 above) as well as from his concluding verses: "En ego quem genuit Yspania clara, sodales / Hoc opus explevi precibus magis, imperiales / Hugo quod presul perficere forte nequivit / . . . / Ceptum perfeci tutans pia virgo Maria / . . ."; In MS Cambrai 612, fol. 271v, the copyist was probably inspired by Johannes, when he noted at the beginning of Causa 23: "Hic nece defecit Huguccio Ferrariarum . . ." (quoted from L. Prosdocimi, "La Summa Decretorum," 361–62). For a short biographical sketch on Johannes and his works, A. de Sousa-Costa, "John de Deo," NCE 7 (1967), 996.

110. In MS Montecassino, Bibl. Abbaz. 396, pp. 136–75, between commentaries on C.1 and De cons. by the same author; identified by S. Kuttner, "Bernardus Compostellanus," 283 n.23 (repr. with "Retractationes vii" in idem, *Gratian*).

4. CONTINUATIO PRIMA

Previous scholarship dealing with the *Continuatio* has approached the text for the most part from a perspective similar to that adopted by Johann Friedrich von Schulte in his first description of 1875.[111] Schulte's greatest concern was to show that the author of this final supplement to the *Summa* was not Huguccio himself but another canonist, whom he mistook for Johannes de Deo. The latter error was soon corrected.[112] Still, Schulte's treatment established a model, in that it accorded to the commentary the status of a mere appendix of the *Summa*. This perspective has remained predominant until today, although the information furnished since then rather suggests that the *Continuatio* represents a decretist work in its own right.

Once again, a groundbreaking contribution to the question has come from Franz Gillmann. In 1912, he presented an analysis of those parts of the commentary that supplied the gap left by Huguccio (Causa 23 q.4 c.34—Causa 26). His conclusion stated that an anonymous author had completed it prior to the *Summa,* during the pontificate of Urban III (1185–87).[113] In other words, the little work originally had been designed for purposes other than that of serving as a complement to Huguccio's massive comment, which was begun only afterwards. About one generation later, two studies by Stephan Kuttner further confirmed the independent character of *Continuatio prima.*[114] The *Repertorium* (1937) listed several Huguccionian manuscripts in which the text not only extended to the unfinished section of the *Summa* but also comprised the initial parts of Causa 23. While this observation was still one step short of attributing to the *Continuatio* the status of a *Summa* of its own, a little later (1943), Kuttner published another discovery of consequence. In a manuscript from Montecassino, Bibl. Abbaz. 396, he had found the only known text of the *Continuatio* preserved outside of the Huguccionian tradition.

---

111. J. F. v. Schulte, *Geschichte,* 1.155 n.5, 1.157–61.

112. By L. Tanon, "Etude de litterature canonique: Rufin et Huguccio," *Nouvelle Revue historique de droit français et étranger* 13 (1889), 694.

113. F. Gillmann, "Paucapalea und Paleae bei Huguccio," AKKR 88 (1908), 471n. (repr. in R. Weigand [ed.], *Schriften Franz Gillmann,* 1, n.14); see also Gillmann's book review published in AKKR 92 (1912), 367; and his "Abfassungszeit," 246n.

114. S. Kuttner, *Repertorium,* 158; idem, "Bernardus Compostellanus," 283 n.23.

In addition to the gloss on the *Cause hereticorum,* the copy also contained comments on Causa 1 and *De consecratione,* apparently by the same author. In the *Repertorium,* Kuttner had not yet realized the identity of *Continuatio prima* and the pertinent text in Montecassino 396, so that he had called it *Summa Casinensis.* Once he had established the link, however, he decided to change the name of the whole comment to *Continuatio prima,* which, as he continued to believe, was written by a "pupil" of Huguccio.

By retaining the term *Continuatio* and by speaking of the doctrinal dependence of its author on Huguccio, Kuttner has helped to perpetuate the traditional view, which placed the work in close connection with the *Summa.* This tendency was further reinforced by Luigi Prosdocimi, who in 1955 combined his manuscript study of the *Summa* with the theory that the *Continuatio* "in sostanza" consisted of the notes someone had taken during Huguccio's lectures.[115] To be sure, his hypothesis lacked the support of any new evidence. Subsequent scholarship never fully accepted it, but it continued to play a role in strengthening the old interpretation of the *Continuatio* as a derivative of Huguccio's teaching. While at times this led to the straightforward attribution of the text to Huguccio, in other cases no effort was made to distinguish clearly between his opinions and those of the anonymous Continuator. A recent illustration of these uncertainties can be found in a study by Titus Lehnherr (1987), in which the author endeavored to reconcile Prosdocimi's claims with his own findings.[116] While editing a series of comments from the *Continuatio,* Lehnherr noted several references to the canonist Bazianus, as well as certain divergences from Huguccio's views. Still, he was content to correlate the evidence with the rather circumstantial proofs of Prosdocimi, and to describe the *Continuatio* as a collection of notes drawn from the lectures not only of Huguccio but also of Bazianus.

115. See L. Prosdocimi, "La Summa Decretorum," 366–73, on the question of the *Continuatio* (368): "non potrebbe essere, nella sua sostanza almeno, di Uguccione stesso?" In conclusion, he suggested (ibid., 371) that the *Continuatio* represents a "prima redazione scolastica del suo commentario . . . nata . . . dalla lectura."

116. T. Lehnherr, *Die Exkommunikationsgewalt,* 226–29, especially 226 n.46; the study includes the collation of a series of texts from the *Continuatio,* published in an appendix (288–96). Longer excerpts from the *Continuatio* are further printed in the appendix to A. Zeliauskas, *De excommunicatione vitiata,* 86*. Zeliauskas quoted the text as *Summa Cassinensis.*

Considering that *Continuatio prima* has been treated largely in its subsidiary relationship to the *Summa,* this chapter will adopt a different approach. To avoid earlier preconceptions, it will discuss the actual content of the text without reference to the peculiarities of textual transmission. There have been arguments in favor of such a procedure ever since the days of Franz Gillmann and the early work of Stephan Kuttner. And yet, most scholars have been content to reproduce previous findings. The misleading title, *Continuatio prima,* is a case in point. Apart from the fact that a work completed at least three years earlier (1185–87) than Huguccio's *Summa* (1188/90) was certainly never intended to serve as a continuation, it does not even represent the oldest addition in the manuscript tradition. Another fragment on Causa 23–24, inserted in MS Fulda, derives from a decretist treatise composed shortly after 1170.[117] As a result, mere convention accounts for the continuing use of the denomination of *Continuatio prima.*[118]

a. The Text

As mentioned earlier, *Continuatio prima* has survived mainly in the form of a supplement to those later portions of Huguccio's *Summa* for which medieval scribes did not have an original text at their disposal. A look at the list of Huguccionian manuscripts shows that in almost all cases *Continuatio prima* filled the gap of the so-called *Cause hereticorum* (C.23–26). The only exception occurs in MS Paris 15396–97, where it further supplied the comment on Causa 1. Elsewhere, the *Continuatio* covers the entire section of the *Cause hereticorum* four times (in MSS Bamberg, Can. 41; Paris 15397; Salamanca; Leipzig), whereas on seven occasions it completes the part Huguccio had never finished, from Causa 23 q.4 c.34 onward. Compared to this quite impressive array of testimonies transmitting the text alongside Huguccio's *Summa, Continuatio prima* has survived independently in but one copy, MS Montecassino 396 (pages 113–90), which in addition to the commentaries on C.1 and C.23–

---

117. Details above n.83; the first to describe this excerpt was A. Stickler, "Decretistica Germanica adaucta," *Traditio* 12 (1956), 601–2.

118. A. Stickler has asserted the independent character of the *Continuatio* ever since his article "Der Schwerterbegriff," 206–7. He thus became one of the earliest proponents of this criticism.

26 includes another, fragmentary, treatise by the Continuator on *De consecratione*.

Stephan Kuttner, who first found the crucial manuscript in the library of Montecassino, has ascribed the three treatises without hesitation to one author. In so doing, he relied on external features. They were all written by one hand, and the scribe left just a few lines of blank space to distinguish the three parts one from another.[119] One is therefore under the impression that the three texts not only form a unit but also go back to an original that did not contain any additional materials. An attentive reading of the three parts, however, does not confirm this observation. There is, after all, one cross-reference that seems to tie them to a larger commentary, going beyond the presently known scope of *Continuatio prima*. In the context of Causa 1, the Continuator thus relegates his reader to a doctrine he had expounded in a chapter belonging to Causa 9![120] *Continuatio prima,* in other words, may once have formed a much larger composition than the one that survives today.[121]

Regardless of its original size, the work doubtless flowed from the

119. Though less obvious, this is true not only of the transition between C.23–26 and De cons. (p. 175b), but also of that between Causa 1 and the following treatise on the *Cause hereticorum*. The three words at the top of page 136a in MS Montecassino 396: "Si quis neque," complete the explicit of Causa 1 (omitted in Paris, B.N. lat. 15396, fol. 107rb: cf. n.74 above) from the preceding page (135b), q.7 c.27 s.v. *exteris*: "Cum enim de aliis criminibus temporalis nuntiatur penitentia, de hoc perpetua imponitur, ut supra q.i Reperiuntur [c.7], Tales (p. c.111); [inc. p. 136] Si quis neque [c.115]." The commentary on Causa 23 follows immediately.

120. Cf. C.1 q.1 p.c.97 s.v. *quamvis* (MSS Montecassino 396, p. 123a; Paris, B.N. lat. 15396, fol. 103rb): "Hic ponit magister aliam solutionem quam approbamus. . . . Qualiter eam approbemus, per que capitula, alibi dictum est sc. viiii q.i Ordinationes [c.5]."

121. Another, fragmentary commentary on the *Decretum* in MS Aschaffenburg, Hof- und Stiftsbibl. Perg. 26, fols. 218ra–227rb, shares many characteristics with *Continuatio prima*. The text, covering C.12 q.1 a.c.1–c.23, and ibid., c.28–C.12 q.2 c.73, has been discussed by H. Van de Wouw, "Notes on the Aschaffenburg MS Perg. 26," BMCL 3 (1973), 100–101. It displays similarities of style: the same argumentative pattern ("Signatur contrarium—sed ibi—hic," in *Continuatio prima* [n.116 above] and MS Aschaffenburg, ed. H. Van de Wouw, "Notes," 100); parallel use of references (Huguccio and Bazianus cited far more often than Gandulph and Cardinalis, ibid., 101); same origin and similar dates of composition (Bologna, after 1179 and prior to Huguccio's *Summa*); as well as a particular preference for matters related to southern Italy (cf. the mention in MS Aschaffenburg of the "rex Apulie" prior to the kings of France, England, and the emperor, ibid., 101, and n.155 below). Are we therefore confronted with another fragment of *Continuatio prima*?

pen of a single canonist, as is evident from the inclusion of explicit cross-references. Twice in his commentary, such remarks involve passages to be found in more than one of the three extant parts of the *Continuatio*. As is to be expected, the author composed parallel comments to each of them. In this fashion, he provided a link between the treatises on Causa 1 and those on *De consecratione* when he expounded a phrase that qualifies simony as "prima heresis":[122]

Causa 1	De consecratione
Signatur contrarium de con. di.ii Prima inquit (c.44).	
Nam ibi dicitur quod prima heresis suborta est a duritia sermonis Domini.	i.e. precipua vel prima in novo testamento. Et hoc dico de symonia.
Sed dici potest quod hic dicitur "prima" quoad novum testamentum quod incipit in Christi morte. Finis enim veteris fuit cum dixit: "Consumatum est."	Nam hoc factum est in veteri testamento quod in morte Christi consumatum est. Et ita solvuntur contraria.

A second comment, included in De cons., substantiates the assumption of common authorship with regard to the *Cause hereticorum*:[123]

Causa 23	De consecratione
Loquitur ergo quando una civitas iniuste movet bellum contra aliam. Tunc illa auctoritate sui iudicis potest se defendendo pugnare. Nisi enim defenderet, videretur temptare Deum quod	Contra . . . xxiii q.viii Si nulla [c.17]. . . . Distingue ergo: Si aliquis puniatur corporaliter pro suo peccato primo debet recurrere ad Deum. . . . Si vero iniuste puniatur ab

122. Montecassino 396, p. 114b (left column, C.1 q.1 c.13 s.v. *ante omnia,* collated with Paris 15396, fol. 100va) and p. 190b (right column, De cons. D.2 c.44 s.v. *Prima*); Huguccio's *Summa,* it should be noted, rejected the opinion expressed by the Continuator, at C.1 q.1 c.13 s.v. *ante omnia:* "Non valet quod quidam dicunt 'ante omnes' in novo testamento, quia heresis de manducanda carne Christi prima fuit tempore quoad novum testamentum, ut de con. di.ii Prima [c.44]. Melius ergo dicitur ante omnes i.e. pre omnibus" (Klosterneuburg 89, fol. 114vb).

123. Left column: C.23 q.8 c.17 s.v. *tamquam* (Montecassino 396, p. 154a; Lons-le-Saunier 12.F 16, fol. 316vb); right column: De cons. D.1 c.69 s.v. *ad ipsum prius* (Montecassino, p. 183a).

non debet aliquis dum habeat
quod opus sit facere. Contra
de con. di.i Omnis [c.69].
Responsio: Ibi reprehenditur
qui statim exercet vires
suas et cum videt se nil
posse proficere postea ad
Deum revertitur.

alio non debet expectare
quod Deus liberet ipsum.
Quod hoc esset temptare
Deum. Hic
debet vires
suas experiri.

Of course, the obvious parallels that emerge from these comparisons represent merely one category of the intrinsic evidence. Other internal features also speak in favor of attributing all three of the comments in MS Montecassino 396 to a single author. However, they will be treated in different contexts.

b. Date and Place of Composition

Thanks to the lively interest shown by the author of *Continuatio prima* in contemporary events, there is sufficient material to date the work. On the basis of those textual portions that supplied the gap in Huguccio's *Summa*, Franz Gillmann has associated the commentary· with the pontificate of Urban III (1185–87): "Hoc hodie non facit Urbanus," he cited from C.23 q.8 c.8 s.v. *Scire*. Besides this direct mention of the pope, he produced another reference in which the *Continuatio* criticized the current attacks by the imperial legate Bertoldus on the town of Faenza, an event reported by the Bolognese annals under the year 1185.[124] Turning our attention to the parts of the work unknown to Gillmann, we discover other hints that argue for a composition during the first year of Urban's pontificate. For one thing, the date is recommended by the fact that Urban's name appears

---

124. *Continuatio prima* to C.23 q.4 c.40 3 s.v. *de sedibus,* ed. F. Gillmann, AKKR 92 (1912), 367: "Ar. quod Christiani sedes inimicorum ecclesie possunt occupare et tenere. Similiter aliorum hostium, unde sedium occupatio de iure gentium dicitur esse, ut di.i Ius [c.9]; infra e. q.v Dicat [c.25]. Et nota quod quedam sunt de iure gentium, que et sunt de iure divino. Hoc autem non habet locum in Faventinis que parati sunt obedire nec sunt hostes. Unde peccat Bertoldus nec etiam precepto imperatoris excusatur, cum etiam imperator eos iuste non possit persequi" (Vat., lat. 2280, fol. 248rb; Montecassino 396, p. 144b). Cf. L. Savioli, *Annales Bolognesi,* 2.1 (Bassano, 1789), 130; peace was to be restored in late 1185 (ibid., 132, 137; also K. Borchard, "Archbishop Gerard," 580–81), but obviously had not yet occurred by the time these lines were written.

only once, whereas that of his predecessor, Lucius III (1181–85), occurs in the same text no fewer than five times.[125] But that Lucius died prior to the drafting of the *Continuatio* can be inferred from the following note: "Alexander III approved [of this]. He did not think that those who were ordained by schismatics had to be reordained. He offered them dispensation, so that they could remain in their orders. However, Lucius, who did not enjoy great authority around here, thought they had to be reordained."[126] This formulation, applying past tense when discussing the degree of authority enjoyed by Pope Lucius, certainly implies that his pontificate had already come to an end. But that the memories regarding this pope were still fresh seems just as evident from casual remarks such as "while he was at Verona" (Fall 1184).[127] Similarly, the most recent datable entry from the treatise on *De consecratione* does not suggest a much earlier date for the drafting, either. There the anonymous author once observed, "And in the town Lucius consecrated the altar of St. Peter."[128] Lucius III consecrated the altar of Saint Peter at Bologna on 4 July 1184. Thus, the brief sentence combines a chronological clue with one regarding the place where the *Continuatio* was composed. No scholar, it is true, has ever expressed doubts about its Bolognese origins. The *Continuatio* in fact corroborates this common assumption in another interesting passage, which also sheds light on the electoral procedures during the early days of the Bolognese commune:[129]

They say that the bishop of this town once did this during the election of Antoninus. When, in the election of the podestà, the citizens could not come

125. (1) C.1 q.1 c.38 s.v. *quolibet horum* (cf. next note); (2) C.1 q.6 a.c.1 *electioni non refutatur*; (3) C.23 q.8 c.17 *Ut pridem* (see also below n.127); (4) C.24 q.1 c.2 *non sineret*; (5) De cons. D.1 c.19 *denuo* (below n.133).

126. C.1 q.1 c.38 s.v. *quolibet horum*: "Approbavit Alexander III qui non censuit reordinandos eos qui in scismate fuerint ordinati, dispensans cum eis ut in ordinibus suis permaneant. Lucius tamen, cuius non magna fuit auctoritas in hac parte, reordinandos eos censuit" (MSS Montecassino 396, p. 117a; Paris 15396, fol. 101rb).

127. C.23 q.8 c.17 s.v. *Ut pridem*: "Supple 'notificamus.' Et similis casus accidit Lucio pape dum esset Verone" (Lons-le-Saunier 12.F 16, fol. 316vb).

128. De cons. D.1 c.19: "Et in civitate Lucius consecravit altare Sancti Petri" (Montecassino 396, p. 178b). As to the date of the event, L. Savioli, *Annales*, 123.

129. C.26 q.2 c.11 s.v. *Licet pollutum*. The Latin text differs significantly in the manuscripts, see below, Appendix II). Once again, the *Continuatio* used the expression "in hac civitate" to refer to Bologna at De cons. D.2 c.22 *pars in altari*, printed below n.142.

to an agreement, the bishop wrote the name of Antoninus on a piece of parchment, and on another the name of another honorable man, and that of a third on a third piece. Then he told a simple boy that he should draw one of the lots and that the one whose name was picked by the boy would be the podestà. They say, however, that in order to rule a city properly, a ruler needs to be elected according to skill rather than luck.

Local historiography reports that Antonino de Andito di Piacenza served the commune of Bologna as podestà in 1183.[130] In agreement with Gillmann's findings we can therefore conclude that the *Continuatio,* in the form transmitted by MS Montecassino 396, originated from Bologna at the time of Pope Urban III, most likely from the first year of his pontificate (1185/86).

c. Relationship to Huguccio's Summa

Another important task of the present research is to determine the relationship between Huguccio's *Summa* and the *Continuatio.* As we have seen, scholars have been rather impressed with the suggestive force of the textual tradition. In their view, the *Continuatio* deserved attention mainly as a substitute for the *Summa,* a circumstance that was rarely considered purely accidental. Luigi Prosdocimi, for example, proposed Huguccio's indirect authorship of the *Continuatio,* while Stephan Kuttner more cautiously assumed doctrinal dependency on the Continuator's part. A closer look at the internal evidence, however, complicates the picture. It has been known since Schulte (1875) that the text contains explicit references to Huguccio. No study to date, however, has attempted to elaborate on these observations and to determine specifically the impact of Huguccio's teachings on the Continuator.

In the parts of the *Continuatio* known to him, Schulte found two mentions of Huguccio.[131] Three other instances can be added.[132] Hu-

---

130. L. Savioli, *Annales,* 108 ("Antonio dall'Andito piacentino"); A. Hessel, *Geschichte der Stadt Bologna von 1116 bis 1280* (Berlin, 1910), 130 n.100; ital. trans. ed. by G. Fasoli (Bologna, 1975), 69 n.100 ("Antonino de Andito di Piacenza").

131. (1) C.23 q.5 c.41 *invito telum* (MSS Paris, B.N. lat. 15397, fol. 50vb; Montecassino 396, p. 150b); (2) C.24 q.3 c.17 *episcopale iudicium*: ed. J. F. v. Schulte, *Geschichte,* 1.158 n.9, from MSS Bamberg, Can. 41, and Leipzig 985; it should be noted, however, that the second reference does not occur in Lons-le-Saunier 12.F 16, fol. 322ra; Admont 7, fols. 329vb–330ra: further details n.134 below.

guccio is not cited either in his gloss to Causa 1 or in his gloss to the section of the *Cause hereticorum* preceding C.23 q.4 c.34, yet occurs seven times in the treatise on *De consecratione*. This amounts to a total of twelve references.[133] If we compare that number to the frequency with which other canonists are quoted, Huguccio comes in third. His contemporary Bazianus is far ahead of him with more than thirty citations, while the name of Johannes Faventinus appears in the commentary of the Continuator fourteen times. The author obviously showed great eagerness to give the names of those canonists whose opinions he included. He pursued this tendency most consistently with regard to Bazianus, whereas the distribution of the references to Huguccio (twelve), Cardinalis (seven), and Gandulphus (six), is somewhat uneven. Huguccio and Gandulph are never mentioned in the context of Causa 1, while Cardinalis does not occur in *De consecratione*. In sum, the numerical considerations offer a first insight into the Continuator's intellectual formation, indicating that Bazianus rather than Huguccio played a decisive role.

The textual tradition of the *Continuatio* also shows considerable fluctuation in the number of references. Thus, Prosdocimi (1955) observed that certain quotes attributed to Huguccio were absent from several copies. Since these omissions can be explained by *homoteleuton*, however, they do not point up original readings.[134] The situation

132. (3) C.23 q.5 c.6 *Culpa levis*: "Nota quod hug. dixit Ieronimum disputare contra eos qui dicebant malos bis a domino iudicandos" (Leipzig, Univ. 985, fol. 241vb; Lons-le-Saunier 12.F 16, fol. 314va); (4) C.24 q.1 c.35 *removendum*, see n.134 below; (5) C.24 q.1 c.40 *Si quem*: "Sed queritur: Cum cordis contritio ad salutem adulto sufficiat, quare permittitur catholico ut baptismum recipiat de manu heretici in necessitate, et non eucharistiam que similiter est sacramentum necessitatis? Dicit Bar.: Quia per sacramentum baptismi corporaliter suscepti aliquid plus accipit Christianus quam si continetur et non accipit. . . . Dicunt Gan. et Hug. rationes Bar. non sufficere dicentes hoc prohibitum propter reverentiam corporis Domini, quod ab immundis tractandum non est, quia recipere corpus Domini non est preceptum sicut recipere baptismum" (Montecassino 396, p. 162a–b; Lons-le-Saunier 12.F 16, fol. 320ra; Bamberg, Can. 41, fol. 319va).

133. (6) De cons. D.1 c.19 *Si motum* (Montecassino 396, p. 178b); (7) De cons. D.1 c.19 §1 *denuo consecretur* (p. 179a); (8) De cons. D.2 c.2 *Nam si tantum* (p. 184b); (9) ibid., *non est aqua sola* (p. 184b); (10) ibid., *nisi utrumque* (p. 184b); (11) De cons. D.2 c.7 *Quod quam sit* (n.135 below); (12) De cons. D.2 c.11 *totiens* (p. 186a). In addition, most copies contain a reference to Huguccio at C.23 q.1 c.5 *Militare*, which, however, is interpolated; for details, see next note.

134. L. Prosdocimi, "La Summa Decretorum," 372–73. His claim that the pas-

is different for some of the inconsistencies that emerge from a systematic collation of the well-documented *Cause hereticorum* (covered by up to eleven manuscripts). Interestingly, it is the passages related to Bazianus that betray the greatest susceptibility to manipulation (see Appendix II below). In various cases they seem to have entered the *Continuatio* only after the completion of the original draft. As a result, we can speak of a connection between the *Continuatio* and Bazianus that permeates the whole work.

The following example sheds some light on the personality and intellectual background of the Continuator.[135]

---

sages citing Huguccio have to be considered as later additions to the original *reportatio* of the canonist's own lectures cannot be confirmed through a consultation of the MSS. Of the three references in the section on C.23 q.4 c.34–C.26 that do not figure in all of the texts (missing parts in square brackets), two are very likely original: (a) C.24 q.3 c.17 *episcopale iudicium* (n.131 above): "Dicitur quod presbiter excommunicare potest. Sed hoc capitulum non negat. [Secundum Hug. potest], secundum bar. non potest." Complete in MSS Montecassino 396, p. 167b; Paris 15397, fol. 55vb; Bamberg, Can. 41, fol. 321va; Leipzig 985, fol. 253va; *om.* Vat., lat. 2280; Admont 7; Paris 3892; Florence, Fes. 126; Lons-le-Saunier 12.F 16; (b) C.24 q.1 c.35 *removendum* (cf. n.132 above): "Tamen multi sunt quibus non placet hec solutio dicentes quod statim excommunicare non potest ex quo dampnatam heresim [sequitur licet non publice. Hug. dicit quod licet iam dampnatam] sequatur [heresim], antequam convincatur non incidit in canonem date sententie," ed. T. Lehnherr, *Exkommunikationsgewalt*, 293: full text in Montecassino 396, p. 161b; Paris 15397, fol. 54ra; Leipzig 985, fol. 249vb; *om.* Vat. lat. 2280; Admont 7; Paris 3892; Florence Fes. 126; Lons-le-Saunier 12.F 16; Bamberg, Can. 41. It is clear that both omissions were caused by *homoteleuton*. The case is different with another, obviously intruded gloss mentioning Huguccio at C.23 q.1 c.5 Militare (Montecassino 396, p. 137a–b): "Intentio enim substantiam negotii variat et perficit. Et est ar. quod dare elemosinam propter vanam gloriam est peccatum. Sed non est verum. [Hoc non concedit Ug. Immo dicit hoc esse verum et totum depravari propter adiunctum.] Intentio enim sola est peccatum." Huguccio's conflicting view (in square brackets) is justly omitted from MS Paris 15397, fol. 47rb, which offers one of the most reliable texts of *Continuatio prima* (cf. below, Appendix II).

135. De cons. D.2 c.7 *Quod quam sit*: "Hic est diversitas magistrorum. Nam dicunt quidam hoc non referre nisi ad tria membra tantum nec in capitulo fieri mentionem de reprobatione quarti membri. Nos dicimus quod istud quod refertur ad quatuor membra licet quartum expresse non reprobet hoc enim ipso quod simul eo copulavit similem formam dat intelligi, ut vii q.i Denique [c.9]; xxii q.vii Apostolus [c.3]; ff., de verborum oblig. Titius [Dig.45.1.126.1]; et preterea quia dominus hoc non fecit, ut in capitulo dicitur. Et est ar. quia quod non invenitur constitutum intelligitur esse prohibitum. Dicit Hug. reprobationem quarti in capitulo contineri ibi: 'Ergo quando' etc." (Montecassino 396, p. 185a–b). Huguccio's *Summa* argues along the same lines, ibid.: "Dicunt quidam quod hoc non refert nisi ad prima tria pre-

Here is a disagreement among the masters [*diversitas magistrorum*]. Some of them say that this refers only to the [first] three propositions and that the chapter never mentions the rejection of the fourth one. We say [*nos dicimus*] that this refers to [all of] the four propositions, despite the fact that [the author of the chapter] does not explicitly reject the fourth, because by simply linking it to the other ones he implies a similar form of interpretation, as in C.7 q.1 c.9; C.22 q.7 c.3; Dig. 45.1.126.1. . . . Huguccio says that the rejection of the fourth [proposition] is to be found in the chapter, at "Ergo quando" etc.

The passage deals with a chapter that enumerates four dogmatic propositions. Canonists wondered if the text condemned as heretical only the first three of them, or if it declared the last one unorthodox, too. Of course, the reason for citing these explanations does not concern matters of canonistic doctrine. It is rather to attest to attitudes that are typical of the author and epitomize certain characteristics of the commentary as a whole. A principal objection against any attempt to reduce the role of the Continuator to that of a mere "pupil" thus arises from the self-confident manner in which he interferes in an ongoing dispute between the masters of the discipline. The formula "We say" (*nos dicimus*) places him not only in the forefront of the *diversitas magistrorum* but also side by side with his purported teacher Huguccio, whom he briefly mentions in support of his own view. The authoritative expression "nos dicimus" echoes repeatedly through the *Continuatio*; it often invokes Huguccio or another teacher in order to add weight to an argument. To return to the above-cited text, however, "We say" (*nos dicimus*) still provides another clue. For as the author himself reveals a little later, he merely backed up a view originally proposed by another canonist, Bazianus:[136]

---

missa. . . . Ego autem credo ultimum . . . omnino sit illicitum. . . . Si enim non esset illicitum quare inter alia reprehensibilia notaretur? . . . Unde valuit in hoc sicut in predictis eandem formam prohibitionis intelligi; ar. vii q.i Denique [c.9]; et xxii q.vii Apostolus [c.3]. Similiter dicitur in lege . . . , ut ff., de vo. o. Ticia [Dig.45.1.126.1]. Preterea ultimum ultimo loco repetitur et improbatur" (Klosterneuburg 89, fol. 347ra). To *Ergo quando botrus* (fol. 347rb), Huguccio noted correspondingly: "Abhinc videtur repetere de quarto errore."

136. De cons. D.2 c.7 *Omnis talis error*: "Per hoc et per illud quod habetur ibi 'quod quam sit' etc., quia relatio ad proximum fit probat Bar. quod sicut cetera prohibet ita et ultimum, licet ad ultimum non exequatur executio. Ideo enim quod hoc dixit, de alio tacuit quia similem formam intelligi voluit" (Montecassino 396, p. 185b).

Bazianus proves that, just as [the author of the chapter] prohibits the other ones, so he prohibits the last one, despite the fact that the argument does not proceed to the last one. For the same reason that he said this [much], he remained silent about the other [final] one; because he wants a similar form of interpretation.

Regarding the question of the relationship between the Continuator and Huguccio, however, a great difference between them can be discerned from their treatment of Bazianus. As indicated by the statistics, the *Continuatio* admits its indebtedness to him on almost every page. By contrast, the huge *Summa* cites him on no more than three occasions.[137] Such an obvious disregard may well suggest the existence of professional rivalries among the Bolognese canonists, with Huguccio as the principal opponent of Bazianus.

Also, considering that both Huguccio and the Continuator worked in the same intellectual climate, it appears necessary to define doctrinal influences in terms other than those of a straightforward teacher-pupil relationship. More often than expected, the *Continu-*

---

137. *Summa* D.68 p.c.2 *sola unctione* (ed. R. Weigand, "Huguccio," 506); C.1 q.3 c.4 *sub cuius redemptione* (cf. n.143 below); C.11 q.3 c.42. At the same time, Johannes Bazianus is the most cited civilian. MS Admont 7 refers to him eleven times as "Iob." (see chap. III n.39). These disproportions, as well as the consistent use of the siglum "bar." for the canonist argue against the identification of both, proposed recently by A. Belloni, "Baziano, cioè Giovanni Bassiano, legista e canonista del secolo xii," TRG 57 (1989), 69–85; and D. Maffei, "Fra Cremona, Montpellier e Palencia: Ricerche su Ugolino de Sesso," RIDC 1 (1990), 13 n.16 (also in REDC 47 [1990], 34–51, at 38 n.16). Maffei cites Ugolinus de Sesso (fl. 1195), who in one of his procedural treatises, *De recusatione iudicum,* (printed by G. Martínez, "Tres lecciones del siglo xii del estudio general de Palencia," AHDE 61 [1991], 391–449, at 412–17) refers to a legal opinion apparently attributed to his teacher Bazianus (MS Barcelona, ACA Cugat 55, fol. 139va ed. 413): "Probari non debet causa recusationis sed sufficit dicere: 'Recuso te iudicem quia es meus inimicus.' Et ita de omni alia causa recusationis . . . secundum bar. et Ug. [wrongly identified in ed. 398 as Hugo de Porta Ravennate instead of Huggucio]." The same opinion is cited as that of Johannes Bazianus by the *Dissensiones Dominorum* attributed to Ugolinus de Presbyteris (ca. 1217), ed. G. Haenel (Leipzig, 1834; repr. Aalen, 1961), 346, and in the *Glossa ordinaria* to Cod. 3.1.14(16) s.v. *recusare*. However, regarding the reliability of the sigla in MS Barcelona one might find another reference to Bazianus, ibid., fol. 140va, ed. 421–22 (quoted after Maffei), rather dubious: "Super hoc magister Ugo et bar. dixerunt quod excommunicati iuste non possunt acusare vel testificari etiam post absolutionem. Remanent infames. . . . Sed magister bas. et alii dicunt quod excommunicatus post absolutionem non est infamis et potest acusare vel testificari." For different reasons, the identification of "bar." and "Iob." has now been refuted by A. Gouron, "A la convergence des deux droits: Jean Bassien, Bazianus et maître Jean," TRE 59 (1991), 319–32.

atio is an accurate testimony to second-hand information from the *Summa,* which is indicated by simple references to "quidam" and the like. A few incidental passages have already been quoted.[138] Since the Continuator had formulated his remarks several years prior to the writing of the *Summa,* they may well have served as Huguccio's model. The same is illustrated by the following example, in which the *Continuatio* has a strong case as Huguccio's direct forerunner:[139]

Continuatio prima	*Summa*
There is in the Lateran Church a wooden altar in the form of the Ark of the Testament. But even though the cover is made of wood, the relics themselves are kept in stone.	In the Lateran Church, they say [*dicitur*], there is a wooden altar resembling an Ark, upon which sacrifice is made. But they say that there is an altar of stone underneath.

The information about the altar of the Lateran Church in Rome was handed on by the *Summa* along with the explicit assurance (*dicitur*) that its author had not seen the wooden altar himself. The *Continuatio* was most likely Huguccio's informant. Besides the absence of any similar argument in earlier decretist literature, the work repeatedly attests to the great familiarity of the author with Rome and the adjacent regions.[140] This in fact suggests the originality of his reference.

138. Cf. above n.122, where Huguccio rejects the opinion held by "quidam" who might be identical with the Continuator; also, the *Summa* and the *Continuatio* once phrased their corresponding views very similarly, see above n.135.

139. *Continuatio,* De cons. D.1 c.31 s.v. *altaria lapidea*: "In ecclesia Lateranensi est ligneum altare in modum arche testamenti. Sed quamvis superior tabula sit lignea, lapis est tamen ubi condite sunt reliquie" (Montecassino 396, p. 180a); *Summa,* ibid., s.v. *lapidea*: "In Lateranensi ecclesia dicitur esse altare ligneum quod est quasi quedam archa super qua sacrificatur. Sed dicitur subesse altare lapideum" (Klosterneuburg 89, fol. 338ra).

140. Details below, nn.155–57. To establish the origin of the hint at the Lateran's wooden altar, I have consulted the following decretist commentaries on De cons. D.1 c.31: (a) Bolognese: Rufinus, ed. H. Singer (Paderborn, 1902), 545; Johannes Faventinus, MS Munich, Staatsbibl. lat. 14403, fol. 2v; Simon of Bisignano (c. 1177–79), Bamberg, Can. 38, p. 100a; Sicardus, MS Munich, Staatsbibl. lat. 8013, fol. 96r; (b) French: Summa *Fecit Moyses tabernaculum,* ed. J. F. v. Schulte (Giessen, 1891), 267; Summa *Tractaturus magister* (ca. 1182/85), Paris, B.N. lat. 15994, fol. 87vb; (c) Anglo-Norman: *Summa Lipsiensis* (ca. 1186), Rouen, B.M. 743, fol. 134vb; Summa *De iure canonico tractaturus* by Honorius (ca. 1188–90), Laòn, B.M. 371bis, fol. 164va. Among the noncanonical sources, the almost contemporary *Descriptio ecclesie Lateranensis* (ca. 1159–81), revised by Johannes Diaconus under the title *Liber de*

Although the *Continuatio* predates Huguccio's work, scholars have ascribed all the teachings they have in common to the author of the *Summa*. They explain the chronological difficulty by assuming a teacher-pupil relationship and by stressing that the impressive learning and all-encompassing range of Huguccio's literary achievement presuppose a long phase of preparation in the classroom. The qualities of the *Summa*, it is true, immediately eclipsed the obscure and less elaborate work of the Continuator. Yet this does not allow us to consider the latter as Huguccio's mouthpiece. Even if we admit that he was not a thinker of Huguccio's own status, he continues to deserve credit as the representative of a wider spectrum of learned opinions, as they circulated on the eve of Huguccio's great accomplishment. Most importantly, his work preserves a large part of what we know about the teachings of Bazianus.

d. The Contribution of Bazianus

For all we know, Bazianus played a prominent role among the Bolognese glossators by the time the *Continuatio* was written (1185/86). He enjoyed a reputation rivalled only by that of Huguccio and that of Johannes Faventinus, their common predecessor, who had left Bologna around 1175.[141] It is consequently rather logical that the Continuator shared many views with these famous colleagues. But the omnipresence of the siglum "bar." suggests that there was a particularly close relationship. Some of these references to him in fact require the Continuator's personal attendance at the lectures of Bazianus, which may also have prompted several unrelated or even appended accounts of opinions held by "bar."[142] Does that indicate that

---

sanctis sanctorum, was the first to state that the wooden altar symbolized the Ark of the Covenant: ed. R. Valentini and G. Zucchetti, *Codice topografico della città di Roma* 3 (Rome, 1946), 325–73, at 335; cf. also J. M. Powell, "Honorius III's 'Sermo in Dedicatione Ecclesie Lateranensis' and the historical-liturgical traditions of the Lateran," AHP 21 (1983), 199–209, at 199–204.

141. R. Weigand, "Bazianus und B-Glossen zum Dekret Gratians," SG 19 (1976), 453–96, has edited and discussed many decretist glosses signed by "bar."; he has also emphasized his impact as a teacher of canon law at Bologna during the 1180s, ibid., 455–56, and idem, *Die Glossen,* 617–18; on the recent debate concerning the possible identity of Bazianus with the civilian Johannes Bazianus, see n.137 above. For bibliography concerning the career of Johannes Faventinus, see Introduction, nn.8–9.

142. A gloss that seems to reflect the liveliness of Bazianus's lectures is *Continu-*

the Continuator lacked personal judgment and can be considered a mere mouthpiece, if not of Huguccio, then of Bazianus?

Indeed, it looks at times as if the personalities of Bazianus and our Continuator would merge. A striking instance to that effect has kindly been pointed out to me by Professor Rudolf Weigand (Würzburg). In an article of 1985, he published a comment from Huguccio's *Summa* that contains this interesting mention of "bar.":[143]

Here one usually finds a note [*notula*] of Master Bazianus in which he says that both parties committed simony. That the bishops had the right to institute already seems clear, considering that the monks bought [the right]. Also, how would there be simony on the account of one party and not the other? But I say, as I have said, that the monks rightfully possessed it and owned it and that they gave [money], not in order to acquire the right, but in order to retain peacefully what they had acquired.

There is no need in the present context to explore the doctrinal issue with which the passage deals, except to say that it rejects a view held by Bazianus. Obviously, he and Huguccio disagreed on whether, in a case offered in the relevant chapter of Gratian's *Decretum*, simony had been committed by both parties or just by one. The "note" (*notula*) of Bazianus favored the former interpretation. With regard to the same "notula," Rudolf Weigand's article then makes the crucial observation that despite Huguccio's assertion of its frequent occurrence in the manuscripts (*haberi solet*) he could not find it in any of the almost 200 early copies of the *Decretum*. At the time of this remark (1985), Weigand had not yet examined the pertinent text of the *Continuatio*. In fact, it reads: "Certain people say that the bishop committed simony, the monks did not, because they claimed their

---

atio, De cons. D.2 c.22 *pars in altari*: "Dicit Bar. quod ipse vidit in hac civitate hoc fieri a quodam sacerdote qui duas partes [sc. eucharistie] sumebat et terciam reservabat, ut siquis repente casus emergeret circa infirmantes haberet quod morientibus dare posset. Ergo hoc antiquatum non est ut dicunt doctores cum hodie observetur" (Montecassino 396, p. 187b); also C.23 q.3 c.7 *Non inferenda* (Montecassino 396, p. 139a; Paris 15397, fol. 47vb): "ut dicit Augustinus in glosa quam habet Bar. in libro suo." That the Continuatior was in direct contact with Gandulph is evident from C.23 q.5 c.12 *Similiter et de his*: "Gan. adhuc in ea opinione est," ed. F. Gillmann, AKKR 92 (1912), 367. For interpolated passages dealing with opinions of "bar.," see also Appendix II below.

143. *Summa* C.1 q.3 c.4 *sub cuius redemptione* (ed. R. Weigand, "Huguccio," 511; MS Klosterneuburg 89, fol. 128ra–b).

right. We do not deny [*non negamus*] that simony occasionally can be committed by one party only. But here it is different. For here simony is committed by both parties, as is argued in the decretal MATHEUS."[144]

As Professor Weigand has indicated to me, this is the sole occurrence of a decretist passage corresponding to what Huguccio called the "notula bar." Granted that, the adherence of the Continuator to the same view (*negamus*) almost invites us to identify him with Bazianus.

And there is more. A second suggestive parallel is provided in a study by Antonio Padoa Schioppa on the medieval doctrine of direct representation (proctorship). Padoa Schioppa shows that the prohibition of this institution in Roman law met with the opposition of certain decretist teachers. As the French apparatus *Ecce vicit leo* (ca. 1202) asserted, proctors could indeed bind clients, on whose behalf they acted in legal transactions. The contemporary apparatus of Alanus Anglicus, *Ius naturale* (second recension; ca. 1205), went even further and identified the original proponent of this opinion as Bazianus.[145] Padoa Schioppa did not find any earlier evidence of Bazianus's statement and concluded that it must have been developed not much before his presumed death in 1197. Surprisingly, however, the quotation of Bazianus in *Ius naturale* repeats word for word a passage already to be found in the *Continuatio* fifteeen years earlier.[146]

Finally, another argument in favor of Bazianus as the author of the *Continuatio* can be made, it seems, on the basis of a text that treats the problem of how the Eucharist is transsubstantiated once it has entered the human body. The Continuator first introduces Bazianus's

---

144. *Continuatio,* C.1 q.3 c.4 *simoniace pravitatis usus*: "Dixerunt quidam episcopos committere simoniam, monachos non. Nam ius suum redimebant. Non negamus simoniam quandoque ex una parte tantum committi posse. Sed hic non sic. Nam ab utraque parte committitur hic simonia, ut ar. in extra: MATHEUS [JL 14547]" (MS Paris 15396, fol. 104vb; collated with MS Montecassino 396, p. 128a–b).

145. *Ius naturale,* C.1 q.7 c.9 s.v. *et per te*: "Ar. quod per alium alii potest promissio fieri. Quod verum est si mandatarius sit. bar." (cited by A. Padoa Schioppa, "Sul principio della rappresentanza diretta nel diritto canonico classico," *Proceedings Toronto* [Vatican City, 1976], 107–31 at 114–15).

146. *Continuatio,* C.1 q.7 c.9 s.v. *per te*: "Quod per alium alii potest fieri promissio. Quod verum est [et] si fit mandatarius cui promittitur" (Paris, lat. 15396, fol. 106vb).

doctrine: "Bazianus says that as soon as it enters the mouth it ceases to be matter and does not enter the stomach; . . . Consequently, nobody can be fed by the Eucharist. There is talk about a certain St. Johannes who intended to eat nothing except the body of Christ and became so weak that he could barely survive." A little later, the Continuator refers back to the teaching of Bazianus in this fashion: "But when we say [*dicimus*] it ceases in the mouth, that seems to be contrary to this chapter. . . ."[147] Here again, the anonymous author of the *Continuatio* adopts the expression "dicimus" to point to a previous statement of "bar.," in what appears to be an indication not just of converging views but even of identity.

This, of course, would go too far. There is, to be sure, a series of other remarks related to "bar.," which curiously repeat comments already made by the *Continuatio*.[148] Others are rather inconspicuous

147. Both texts appear at De cons. D.2 c.23 s.v. *commiscere*, MS Montecassino 396, p. 188a.

148. C.1 q.3 c.14 *altare decimas*: "Decimas vendere autem non licet. [Ius: P] decimarum vel aliarum [altarium: P] fructus [aut ipsos *add.* P] licet vendi ei [ipsi: P] qui nullum ius in eis habet. Utrum [Quod: P] autem transigi super decimis possit dicere [*om.* P *male*] videtur Alexander in extra: STATUIMUS [JL 14191]. Sed Bar. contradicit [Bar. contradicit statuimus quis: P *male*]." (Montecassino 396, p. 130a; Paris 15396, fol. 105va, the latter offering a very corrupt text). Bazianus's critique of the decretal STATUIMUS coincides with the opinion the Continuator had expressed immediately before. C.24 q.1 c.39 *a clericatu*: "Per hoc capitulum probat Bar. contra aliorum opinionem et etiam [*om.* P] Gratiani [in gratiam: P] quod sententia lata ab heretico in subiectum suum tenet" (Montecassino 396, p. 162a; Paris 15397, fol. 54rb); cf. *Continuatio prima*, C.24 q.1 p.c.39 *in detestatione*: "Distingue: sententia heretici ligando vel solvendo nichil facit quia dum solvere vult ligat et econverso. Alias vero sententia eius tenet dummodo rite procedat et tales sunt quibus iure [iura *add.* P] discernat. Hanc sententiam approbat bar." (Montecassino 396, p. 162a; Paris 15397, fol. 54rb). De cons. D.1 c.48 *eadem hora cruci.*: "Sexta autem hora revera crucifixus est Christus a Romanis ut dicit Bar." (Montecassino 396, p. 181b); cf. ibid.: "Ex sequenti videtur capitulo quod hora vi cantari possit a sensu contrario. Et verum est. Nam et tunc passus est. Similiter nona quia tunc mortuus est [sc. Christus]." Four other texts likewise repeat statements made in *Continuatio prima*. They do not, however, appear in all of the MSS: C.1 q.1 c.108 *Si quis potuerit probare se nescire*: "Bar. legit de dampnatis per sententiam et dicit ordinatos hoc nescire quia tempore sententie non essent presentes. Et quod sequitur *pro catholicis habebantur* dicit ipse verum ab ipsis scilicet ordinatis" (Montecassino 396, p. 124b; *om.* Paris 15396, fol. 103va); C.1 q.1 c.111 *Si statim*: "Nota quod Bar. dicit mensem utiliter computandum. Unde si hodie posset et cras non ei preiudicaretur" (Montecassino 396, p. 125a; *om.* Paris 15396, fol. 103vb); C.1 q.7 c.23 *Si lapsus post baptismum*: "Bar. intelligit hoc de adulterina fornicatione vel incestuosa vel de publica ubi scandalum timetur, ut infra: De his; vel quando in examinatione tacuit se esse criminosum vel mentitus est se non esse cri-

and do not call for critical comment.[149] But for the rest, the commentary contains numerous references to Bazianus that prove that the author is another individual. Some explicitly state doctrinal agreement with Bazianus.[150] There are also glosses opposing him outright.[151] As a result, identity between the Continuator and Bazianus can be ruled out, although there must have been very close ties between their learned activities.[152]

---

minosum" (Montecassino 396, p. 133a; *om.* Paris 15396, fol. 106va); C.23 q.3 c.11 *pre multitudine*: "Baza. dicit quod populus si iniuste aliquis dampnaretur potest eum defendere contra imperatorem vel principatum alterum" (Montecassino 396, p. 139a; *om.* Paris 15397, fol. 47vb).

149. Those are: De cons. D.2 c.28 *vii diebus* (MS Montecassino 396, p. 188b); C.1 q.3 p.c.11 *Res ecclesie* (ibid., p. 130a; MS Paris, B.N. lat. 15396, fol. 105rb); C.23 q.3 c.7 *Non inferenda* (Montecassino 396, p. 139a; Paris 15397, fol. 47vb; ed. above, n.142); C.24 q.1 c.14 *iudicio quod* etc. (Montecassino 396, p. 158a; Paris 15397, fol. 53ra); C.24 q.1 p.c.39 *In detestatione* (Montecassino 396, p. 162a; Paris 15397, fol. 54rb); C.24 q.3 c.6 §1 *peremptorio* (Montecassino 396, p. 166a; Paris 15397, fol. 55va); C.24 q.3 c.17 *episcopale iudicium* (Montecassino 396, p. 167b; Paris 15397, fol. 55vb; ed. above, n.134); De cons. D.1 c.3 *Omnes* (Montecassino 396, p. 176b); De cons. D.2 c.17 *a quibusdam* (Montecassino 396, p. 187a). The passages appear consistently in the MSS and are well integrated into the context.

150. C.23 q.5 c.11 *absque eo ubi* etc.: "Bar. aliter legit sic: 'absque eo' etc. inclusive i.e. nec in eo etc., ut xxxv [xxv: P *male*] q. iii Porro [c.22], i.e. et ibi non licet propria manu perire ubi castitas etc. Et quidem preter et nisi sepe [frequenter: MC] inveniuntur [*om.* MC] accipi inclusive sed absque raro, ut in Canticis sponsus ad sponsam: 'Oculi tui columbarum absque eo quod intrinsecus latet'; acsi diceret in his duobus casibus non licet mortem [modo rem: MC *male*] arripere. Ergo in nullo casu. Nam de istis magis videtur" (Montecassino 396, p. 149a; Paris 15397, fol. 50va); *Continuatio prima* later agrees with the interpretation of "bar." C.24 q.1 c.40 *Si quem*, ed. above, n.132. By arguing against the opinion of Huguccio and Gandulphus, the Continuator finally gives support to Bazianus's view, ibid.: "Sed numquid debeo accipere de manu heretici eucharistiam a catholico confectam? Dico quod non."

151. De cons. D.2 c.22 *pars in altari*; ed. n.142 above. C.26 q.2 c.10 *Si de area*: "Item queritur utrum sit peccatum vesci azimis Iudeorum. Dico quod sic quia distinguunt cibos et quia nostris non utuntur nec nos illorum cibis uti debemus ne per hoc inferiores eis esse videamur. Vel potest dici quod sicut in odium Iudeorum prohibemur comedere acima eorum ita in odium ydoli et ydolatrie prohibemur ydolatrium comedere, ut di.xxx Si quis carnem [c.13], et xxxii q.iiii Sicut satius [c.8]. Dicit tamen Bar. quod ipse comederet. Nam in primitiva ecclesia propter hominum infirmitatem prohibitum est. Sed melius est ut dicamus quia in tempore apostoli licebat. Unde illud: 'Omnia munda mundis,' modo non licet" (Paris, B.N. lat. 15397, fol. 57vb). De cons. D.1 c.35 *Si quis*: "Similiter de laicis potest dici qui audiunt missas in capellis civitatis quod in maioribus festis ad maiorem sedem deberent confluere. Et hoc attendens dicit Bar. quod tale oratorium non est ecclesia. Est inde locus religiosus. Sed potest dici quod hic vocat capellas oratoria, non ut supra" (Montecassino 396, p. 180b). Another

e. The Author

Like the majority of contemporary legal commentators, the Continuator did not reveal his identity. This is not to say, however, that he consciously avoided all personal remarks. On the contrary, we have already noted the unusual frequency with which he hinted at current events and mentioned the prominent personalities of his scholarly environment. The commentary also shows a particular inclination to enrich the discourse by including lively narratives and other details. The text repeatedly cites Arnold of Brescia, the memorable leader of heretics, who ended being hung on "a very tall oak."[153] Further references to Bolognese and papal politics abound, so that it would be suprising if the Continuator had not included certain clues as to his own origin and predilections as well.

Twice, the *Continuatio* contains the mention of a Spanish custom, indeed an uncommon occurrence among the early Bolognese canonists.[154] But to associate the author for that reason with Spain would

instance is omitted from one of the MSS, C.1 q.7 c.23 *Nec ulla necessitas:* "Bar. aliter legit" (Montecassino 396, p. 135a; *om.* Paris 15397, fol. 47vb).

152. Cf. also the evidence given n.142 above. The Continuator should therefore be considered as a reportator of some of Bazianus's teachings, as was first suggested by T. Lehnherr, *Exkommunikationsgewalt,* 226. Interestingly, the anonymous *Summa* in MS Aschaffenburg (cf. n.121 above) again shares this characteristic. It contains two (not clearly legible) passages which seem to indicate that the author elaborated on lecture materials of Bazianus, see C.12 q.2 c.29 *Cognovimus:* "Et est ar. pro sententia Car. qui dicebat omnes decimas esse dandas intuitu personarum, sicut diligenter notavimus post bat. (!), infra xvi," Aschaffenburg, Perg. 26, fol. 221ra); C.12 q.1 c.8 §2 *faciendis por.:* "Ar. quod communiter viventes puta monachi, regulares canonici tunc tenentur ad separationes quartarum vel ad decimas prestandas; ar. ad idem supra, cap. Duo sunt [c.7]. Immo generalius de quibuslibet clericis utrum hoc verum sit necne nos plane notavimus in secundam [sequentem?] causam secundum bar. Ug. tamen contrarium dicit ut ibidem Deo volente ostendemus" (ibid., fol. 225vb). "Reportationes" of lectures held at the various medieval law schools have been discussed comprehensively by F. Soetermeer, "Une catégorie de commentaires peu connue. Les 'commenta' ou 'lecturae' inédites des précurseurs d'Odofrède," *Rivista internazionale di diritto commune* 2 (1991), 47–67, at 48–57.

153. C.23 q.4 c.39 *de imperio suo:* "Arnaldus tamen Brixiensis a papa Adriano degradatus suspensus fuit in altissima quercu et postea concrematus" (Montecassino 396, p. 144b). In the context of the *Cause hereticorum,* the *Continuatio* speaks of this event seven times.

154. C.23 q.4 c.51 *non defuerunt tales:* "Hic est ar. contra quandam consuetudinem yspanorum, ubi pro certa iniuria iniuriatus certos ictus infert iniurianti" (Leip-

be the wrong conclusion, considering that the references are of little weight compared to bulk of passages dealing with Rome and southern Italy. As later with the *Summa, Continuatio prima* often mentions, for instance, the legateship conferred by the pope on the kings of Sicily. But unlike Huguccio, who considered the political consequences of this ecclesiastical privilege in the hands of a layman harmful, the Continuator had no such reservations.[155] Does that imply a subject's loyalty to his Norman king? The *Continuatio* is also well acquainted with Rome and its environs and speaks of the wooden altar in the Lateran Church as well as the *Pincio,* an insignificant hill next to today's *Piazza di Spagna.*[156] Particularly striking, however, are his repeated hints at customs observed in Campania. The name of this province occurs no fewer than four times, of which one case, revealing the author's knowledge of the local vernacular, deserves special mention.[157] Very likely, the anonymous canonist's origins were in the south of Italy, more specifically Campania.

As with other twelfth-century canonists whose identity has remained a riddle, only a systematic study of the numerous glosses to Gratian's *Decretum* might result in the attribution of a name. Of course, such a task would go far beyond the present study. The few suggestions that follow are, therefore, restricted to the research done by others. The consultation of scholarly literature soon leads to the

zig 985, fol. 240vb); cf. C.23 q.5 c.8 *nisi forte:* "Et est ar. contra predictam consuetudinem Ispanorum qui certos ictus pro iniuria propria inferunt" (fol. 241vb). De cons. D.1 c.50 *elemosinis:* "Nota quod ante cibum debent fieri elemosine. Quod bene faciunt yspani" (Montecassino 396, p. 181b).

155. E.g. *Continuatio,* C.23 q.8 c.22 *tributum:* "Debet autem ecclesia tributum imperatori, ut tuetur pacem et quietem ipsius. Si quid autem plus velit concedere ei sicut et regi Siculo concessit potest" (Montecassino 396, p. 155a). The author of the *Summa* D.63 c.23, instead remarked on a similar occasion: "Sicut hodie est in persona regis Apulie: Sed male!" (MS Admont 7, fol. 91va).

156. C.23 q.4 c.30 *principis:* "Quidam codices habent 'pincis.' Et est locus Rome" (Montecassino 396, p. 143a). For other remarks on Rome, see C.23 q.8 c.7 *Igitur;* C.24 q.2 c.6 *dipticis;* De cons. D.1 c.18 *superflua;* De cons. D.1 c.20 *Si tamen;* De cons. D.1 c.42 *vestimenta;* also n.139 above.

157. De cons. D.1 c.17 *Encenia:* "Enceniare enim est in vulgari Campanie aliquid ad novum usum assumere" (Montecassino 396, p. 178a); direct contact with the province is also suggested by De cons. D.1 c.48 *eadem hora:* "In Campania non cantatur missa nisi hora tertia, in Italia mane" (p. 181b). For further mentions, cf. C.23 q.1 c.4 *dominandi;* C.23 q.8 c.29 *Sepe principes.*

perplexing discovery that, some decades ago, Alfons Stickler was confronted with a similar problem.[158] He also searched for a canonist who wrote during the late 1180s, often reflected Huguccionian doctrine, and betrayed a great concern for matters related to southern Italy and Campania. With these biographical data he attempted to identify a canonist who had composed not the *Continuatio* but another decretist commentary known as the *Summa Reginensis*. On the basis of coincidences between this anonymous work, composed between 1187 and 1192, and several decretist glosses signed "p.," Stickler tentatively suggested that Petrus Beneventanus might have been the author.[159]

Since then, nobody has tried to examine Stickler's preliminary assertions in more depth. They are now further complicated by the *Continuatio*, which, despite its identical features, was written by yet another author. Perhaps the *Summa Reginensis* drew much of its material from the Continuator, so that Stickler's references to southern Italy would turn out to be second-hand? Or did both texts draw on the teachings of a third canonist? A separate study would be required to determine these relationships more precisely.

The present reassessment of the *Continuatio* has elaborated on the results obtained by former research. It has demonstrated that the transmission of the text in combination with Huguccio's *Summa* has led to overstating its dependency on the latter. In truth, the *Continuatio* emerged from a different set of circumstances, unconnected with the genesis of the *Summa*. Composed in 1185/86 by an anonymous canonist of probably south Italian origins, the *Continuatio* reflected the teaching of Bazianus rather than Huguccio, who even seems to have disapproved of the former's great influence on canonistic circles. Contrary to the traditional view, which has stressed the overall indebtedness of the Continuator to Huguccio, it is more

158. In his study "Decretisti Bolognesi dimenticati," SG 3 (1955), 375–410, revised Italian version of "Vergessene Bologneser Dekretisten," *Salesianum* 4 (1952), 481–503.

159. For the date of the *Summa Reginensis*, see especially ibid. (1955), 391–92; parallel "p."-glosses are printed ibid., 406–7, and their attribution to Petrus Beneventanus is proposed ibid., 408–9. But Petrus, later to be the author of *Compilatio tertia* (1210), is not known to have composed glosses on Gratian's *Decretum*.

appropriate to see his work as a product that appeared simultaneously with the *Summa*. All in all, therefore, we have good reason to restore to the *Continuatio* the title of *Summa Casinensis,* proposed by Kuttner at a time when he had not yet realized its ties to the textual tradition of Huguccio's commentary.

Huguccio's Use of Roman Law

WHEN THE canonists established their new discipline in the 1140s, they largely modelled it on the somewhat older scholastic branch of Roman law. In two ways their indebtedness became particularly apparent. First, the successors of Gratian gathered at Bologna, which was already enjoying considerable fame as a center of secular jurisprudence. Second, Gratian's idea of creating a comprehensive textbook to serve as the reference work for teaching certainly owed much to the example provided by Justinian's *Corpus iuris civilis*. The combination of the factors proved decisive. Once the *Decretum* had ensured a textual basis for canonistic studies, legal scholarship both canonistic and civilian rapidly developed and grew side by side.[1]

During the second half of the twelfth century, decretist learning also acquired considerable influence on the shaping of ecclesiastical law. It often drew inspiration from teachings first proposed by the professors of civil law (legists). This was not surprising, because Master Gratian himself had given indirect support to such tendencies. He had put forward a principle recommending recourse to Roman law

1. See the general introductions by P. Legendre, *La pénétration du droit romain dans le droit canonique de Gratien à Innocent IV (1140–1254)* (Paris, 1964); G. Le Bras, "Introduction aux sources," *Histoire du droit et des Institutions de l'Église en Occident 7: L'âge classique (1140–1378). Sources et théorie du droit*, ed. G. Le Bras (Paris, 1965), 30–37; C. Lefebvre, "Formation du droit canonique," ibid., 167–74.

in matters left undefined by the canons (D.10 p.c.6).[2] The early canonists steadily extended the use of Gratian's guideline. The conceptual development, as well as certain legal institutions (especially procedure), showed great susceptibility to the impact of Romanization.[3] As a result, close ties between the two major branches of legal learning were an undeniable fact by the time Huguccio came on the scene.

For a full assessment of Huguccio's attitude toward Roman law, several aspects need to be distinguished. To measure his acquaintance with Roman legal thought, we must analyze not only the theoretical foundations set forth in the *Summa* with regard to the relationship between both laws, but also give an illustration of how Huguccio actually adapted Roman doctrine. A brief discussion of those passages in the *Summa* that refer to views held by certain "legiste" will serve the latter purpose. But prior to that, Huguccio's contribution to each of these aspects has to be placed in the proper historical context.

I. THE DECRETIST BACKGROUND

Modern legal historians have pointed out that by 1200 the leading canonists had abandoned all restraint in quoting Roman sources and teachings.[4] Apparently, they welcomed secular jurisprudence as an

2. "Ecce quod constitutiones principum ecclesiasticis legibus postponende sunt. Ubi autem evangelicis atque canonicis decretis non obviaverint omni reverentia digne habeantur." Despite these favorable assertions, only twenty-one excerpts of Roman law, drawn from intermediary canonical collections (listed by A. Vetulani, "Gratien et le Droit romain," RHD 24/25 [1947], 14; repr., with "addenda et corrigenda," in idem, *Sur Gratien et les Décrétales,* ed. W. Uruszczak [Aldershot, 1990], n.3), had formed part of the original *Decretum,* whereas the bulk of texts entered the work in the form of later supplements; surveyed by S. Kuttner, "New studies on the Roman law in Gratian's Decretum," *Seminar* 11 (1953), 19; idem, "Additional notes on the Roman law in Gratian," *Seminar* 12 (1954), 67–74: both reprinted with further "Retractationes iv–v" in idem, *Gratian*; cf. also J. Rambaud, "Le legs de l'ancien droit: Gratien. Le legs de droit romain," ed. G. Le Bras, *Histoire du droit,* 119–29.

3. The earliest stages of this development have been studied in particular by P. Legendre, *La pénétration,* 97–115; C. Munier, "Droit canonique et droit romain d'après Gratien et les décrétistes," *Études dediées à G. Le Bras* (Paris, 1965), 2.943–54; A. Bernal-Palacios, *La "Concordia utriusque iuris" de Pascipoverus* (Valencia, 1980), 41–46; R. Weigand, "Romanisierungstendenzen im frühen kanonischen Recht," ZRG Kan. Abt. 69 (1983), 200–49. Also still useful is the older account of F. Maassen, "Beiträge," 67–84.

4. As is evident from the statistics presented by P. Legendre, *La pénétration,* 112–

additional tool that made a stock of weighty arguments available to them. Although a general theory admitting Justinian's *Corpus* as a subsidiary textbook was never proposed, recourse to it grew rapidly.[5] However, this tendency became manifest only in the period after Huguccio. Before the appearance of his *Summa,* the use of noncanonical materials developed in a rather inconsistent and hesitant fashion.

Some studies have connected the weaker influence of Roman law among the earliest decretists (ca. 1140–80) with a series of contemporary conciliar enactments that forbade the spread of secular learning into the houses of regular clergy. Besides medicine, the prohibitions also excluded the study of the *Corpus iuris civilis* from monastic and chapter halls.[6] As the driving force behind this legislation, some have identified a strong faction of "monastic" reformers in the papal curia, which counted Bernard of Clairvaux (d. 1153) among its most eloquent leaders.[7] The same group, they argued, influenced a number of teachers during the initial phase of the Bolognese canon

13. G. Fransen, " 'Utrumque ius' dans les 'Questiones Andegavenses,' " in *Études G. Le Bras,* 2.901, has found the strongest expressions for the watershed mark represented by Huguccio and his *Summa:* "Après lui le droit romain est invoqué de façon massive, on a envie d'écrire: brutale." See further n.33 below.

5. The nature of this reception has been discussed by P. Legendre, *La pénétration,* 59–65, who denied that the decretists ever admitted to Roman law an overall supplementary validity; see also Chr. Lefevbre, "Formation"; contra: A. van Hove, "Droit Justinien et droit canonique depuis le Décret de Gratien (1140) jusqu'aux Décrétales de Grégoire IX (1234)," in *Miscellanea van der Essen* (Brussels, 1948), 1.257–71.

6. First in the council of Clermont 1130 (c.5); then, in the presence of Saint Bernard, at Reims 1131, can. 6; reinforced by Lat. II (1139) can. 9, and the council of Tours 1163, can. 8 "Non magnopere" = 1 Comp 3.37.2 = X 3.50.3: S. Kuttner, "Retractationes x," *The history of ideas and doctrines of canon law in the middle ages* (London, 1980), 45. R. Somerville, "Pope Innocent II and the study of Roman law," *Revue des études islamiques* 44 (1976), 105–14, reprinted in idem, *Papacy, councils, and canon law in the 11th–12th centuries* (Aldershot, 1990), has argued that Gratian's neglect of Roman law in the *Decretum* might have resulted from the Lateran legislation, which forbade its use to monks. Huguccio saw the canon of Tours 1163, "Non magnopere," as directed alone to the regular clergy, and interpreted it rather leniently, *Summa* C.15 q.2 p.c.1 s.v. *Hoc autem:* "Non videtur multum approbanda talis solutio cum monachi non debeant exire claustrum vel causa legendi leges vel fisicam vel causa advocandi vel alicuius negotii nisi hoc exposcat utilitas monasterii. Et hoc de imperio abbatis, ut in extra: NON MAGNOPERE; et xvi q.i Monachi [c.35]" (Klosterneuburg 89, fol. 231va). The same rules were extended to other groups of clerics when Pope Honorius III issued SUPER SPECULA in 1219 (n.9 below).

7. P. Legendre, *La pénétration,* 42; S. Chodorow, *Christian political theory,* 47–64, has made Gratian's affiliation with this group the centerpiece of his thesis; but cf. the review by R. Benson, *Speculum* 50 (1975), 97–106.

law school. Similar assertions, however, overlook the fact that none of Gratian's commentators ever spoke of a dramatic tension between the impact of Roman principles on the one hand and "monastic" legislation on the other. To the contrary, the papal chancery under Alexander III (1159–81) and Lucius III, his successor (1181–85), issued decretals that recommended the use of Roman law in the church courts according to the principle of subsidiarity.[8] Critical remarks occurred only several decades later, when Pope Honorius III published SUPER SPECULA in 1219.[9] That decretal extended the ban on secular studies to almost all clergy directly engaged in the care of souls. Yet it hardly affected future canonistic curricula, which continued to require of students some expertise in Roman law.[10]

What, then, accounted for the slow acceptance of secular legal elements among the decretists preceding Huguccio? General political considerations, such as Frederick Barbarossa's perennial struggle for supremacy in northern Italy, may have played a role, considering that the emperor's frequent encroachments on ecclesiastical liberty were carried out under reference to Roman legal principles. However, resentment against such practice cannot be traced in the succinct writings of the decretists. Also, it certainly took time for the canon lawyers to acquire the skills necessary to integrate doctrines from outside of their own textbook. As Pierre Legendre has proved in his introductory work on the penetration of Roman law after Gratian (1964), progress in this respect initially depended very much on the personal preferences of a given author.[11] In a statistical survey, he

8. Cf. Alexander III's letter to the archbishop of Uppsala (JL 12117), which included a paraphrase of Gratian's *dictum* D.10 p.c.6 (n.2 above). For Lucius III, see n.19 below.

9. X 3.50.10: S. Kuttner, "Papst Honorius III. und das Studium des Zivilrechts," in *Festschrift für Martin Wolff,* ed. E. v. Caemmerer (Tübingen, 1952), 79–101, reprinted in S. Kuttner, *The history of ideas,* along with "Retractationes x," 43–47; P. Legendre, *La pénétration,* 44–50.

10. As asserted unanimously by leading thirteenth-century canonists such as Hostiensis, *Lectura super X* (ed. Strasbourg, 1512), X 3.50.10 s.v. *ampliari,* vol. 2, fol. 196rb–va; and Guilelmus Durantis, *Speculum iudiciale,* 2.2 de disp. et alleg. Porro. Sed numquid (ed. Lyons, 1521), fol. 145rb–va. SUPER SPECULA nevertheless favored the subsequent appearance of monographs on the *Casus legum,* by which clerics could circumvent the direct consultation of Roman law sources; cf. M. Bertram and M. Duynstee, "Casus legum sive suffragia monachorum," TRG 51 (1983), 326–29.

11. P. Legendre, *La pénétration,* 102–8. The fact that simple references to Jus-

illustrated how references to the legists and their *Corpus* varied in frequency throughout the decades between Rufinus (ca. 1164) and Huguccio (1188–90).

More recently, two investigations by Ronald Knox (1980) and Herbert Kalb (1983) have proposed that these inconsistent attitudes reflected a fundamental disagreement among contemporary canonists as to the general suitability of secular legal reasoning in the ecclesiastical courts.[12] Both authors point to the conflicting views that the leading teachers of their days, Rufinus of Bologna and Stephan of Tournai (1165/66), cherished on that matter. Kalb gathered from Rufinus's *Summa* a number of passages hostile to, or subtly biased against, Roman law, and he contrasted them with the more sympathetic tone adopted by Stephan of Tournai. Knox presented a similar theory. Likewise focusing on Rufinus's and Stephan's works, he detected diametrically opposed notions of ecclesiastical law and its purpose behind what seems to be the same juristic terminology. In closely examining Rufinus's treatment of questions such as the nature of ecclesiastical punishment, Knox showed that Rufinus's principal concern was that the judgment of the Church on earth should anticipate the ultimate sentence of God. His ideas consequently tried to make the decisions of the ecclesiastical tribunals conform to those of the *forum internum* and strengthened the moral categories at the expense of legal ones. Not so Stephan. He maintained that a public trial should be governed by rules different from those of private confession, and he found a much more satisfactory basis in the principles of Roman law. As Knox aptly summed up, Stephan shaped his order on the external, Rufinus on the internal forum. Kalb instead was content to point vaguely to the political setting and Rufinus's possible adherence to the "monastic" party around Bernard of Clairvaux.

---

tinian's *Corpus* gradually replaced the longer excerpts (*casus*) and the doctrinal treatises of the older decretist writings attests to the increasing familiarity with Roman law all through the second half of the twelfth century; cf. ibid., 97–102.

12. R. Knox, "The problem of academic language in Rufinus and Stephan," *Proceedings Berkeley* (Vatican City, 1985), 109–23, a paper based on his unpublished dissertation, *Rufinus and Stephan on church judgment* (1976); H. Kalb, *Studien zur Summa Stephans von Tournai* (Innsbruck, 1983), 31–64; and again in "Bemerkungen zum Verhältnis von Theologie und Kanonistik am Beispiel Rufins und Stephans von Tournay," ZRG Kan. Abt. 72 (1986), 338–48.

Although the findings of Kalb and Knox are not necessarily wrong, they present in some ways inadequate attempts to verify their premises. According to them, Rufinus was the last to give expression to a traditional notion of an ecclesiastical law that formed part of the penitential system. Stephan, on the other hand, foreshadowed a new, legalistic approach, which tended to dissolve the former linkage between the rules governing inner church discipline and those regulating the Christian conscience. Both Kalb and Knox concentrated on a few isolated texts from Rufinus and Stephan, disregarding the fact that their commentaries have to be understood within a larger intellectual setting. Actually, canonistic doctrine always was, and long continued to be, a mixture of penitential and "legalistic" elements; it would thus be easy to make other decretists champions of either cause as well. Regarding the question of Roman law, moreover, the neglect of the scholastic context and of contradictory evidence within the writings of Rufinus and Stephan is soon apparent. To reconstruct the real issues at stake among Huguccio's predecessors (ca. 1140–90) about the fundamental relationship between ecclesiastical and imperial law, we must survey the comments they produced on the foremost *sedes materie, Distinctio* 10 of Gratian's *Decretum.*[13]

In *Distinctio* 10, Gratian had set forth a quite straightforward view of the limits of the two legal systems.[14] In his usual manner, he first lined up canons arguing for and against the application of Roman principles in the courts of the Church. He then reconciled them in a single sentence, to the effect that secular laws not contradictory to canonical rules could serve as the basis for arguments before eccle-

13. C. Munier, "Droit canonique," 943–54, reprinted in idem, *Vie conciliaire et collections canoniques en Occident, ive–xiie siècles* (London, 1987), has gone over the same ground, but did not pay attention to the controversial nature of the decretist glosses on D.10 prior to Huguccio's *Summa;* the same is true of A. Stickler, "Imperator vicarius papae," MIÖG 62 (1954), 171–76, in his discussion of the French decretist glosses on D.10; only P. Bellini, *L'obbligazione da promessa con oggetto temporale nel sistema canonistico classico, con particolare riferimento ai secoli xii e xiii* (Milan, 1964), 297–300, has briefly noted the disagreement between Rufinus and Huguccio. The treatment of J. Portemer, *Recherches sur les "Differentie iuris civilis et canonici" au temps du droit classique de l'Eglise* (Paris, 1946), 36–39, offers no more than a sketch.

14. His key *dicta* are D.10 a.c.1: "Constitutiones vero principum ecclesiasticis constitutionibus non premineant sed obsecuntur"; and D.10 p.c.6 (n.2 above). A good analysis of Gratian's thought is in C. Munier, "Droit canonque," 943–47.

siastical judges. He thus asserted the complete independence of the spiritual judiciary from secular encroachments and at the same time did not object to possible, subsidiary use of the *leges*.

The first generation of commentators saw little reason to modify this position and was satisfied to paraphrase it.[15] But, after two decades of tacit agreement, the teachings of Rufinus were to spark an unexpected and highly controversial discussion of *Distinctio* 10, which lasted for a quarter of a century. With the appearance of Rufinus's widely read *Summa*, Gratian's position suddenly appeared in a dubious light. As a matter of fact, Rufinus expressed himself in a way absolutely atypical of the "anti-legalistic" stand attributed to him by Knox and Kalb:[16]

15. Among them, the paraphrase of Paucapalea (ca. 1148), *Summa* D.10 a.c.1 s.v. *Constitutiones*, ed. J. F. v. Schulte, *Die Summa des Paucapalea über das Decretum Gratiani* (Giessen, 1890), 15, later found the greatest acclaim. It was copied by the anonymous author of the Summa *Sicut vetus testamentum* (ca. 1148–59), Florence, B.N. Conv. soppr. G IV 1736, fol. 3va; and by Rufinus (n.16 below), lines 1–9; slightly modified, it later entered the influential *Summa* of Johannes Faventinus (n.21 below), whence Huguccio literally incorporated it into his *Summa*, ibid., MS Admont 7, fol. 10rb.

16. H. Kalb, *Studien,* 35 n.12, included Rufinus's text in his study, but overlooked the challenge it might represent to his main thesis: *Summa* D.10 a.c.1: "*Constitutio vero principum* etc. Quoniam de imperatorum legibus supra mentionem fecerat et quia de ecclesiasticis negociis necessarie sepe esse videntur, an ecclesiasticis premineant constitutionibus, merito queritur. Si ergo leges principum constitutionibus ecclesiasticis in aliquo negocio contrarie sunt, omnino postponende sunt; at ubi evangelicis et canonicis decretis non obviaverint, omni reverentia digne habeantur et in ecclesie adiutorium assumantur. Illud autem, quod in subiecto capitulo dicitur, quod 'lex imperatorum iura dissolvere non potest' [c.1], non omnino indistincte pretereundum est. Sciendum ergo est quod ius ecclesiasticum aliud est merum solummodo, sc. ex divina constitutione vel patrum sanctorum descendens, ut ius decimationum, diocesum et huiusmodi; aliud adiunctum vel mixtum, sc. quod ex constitutione humanarum legum propendet, ut ius prescriptionis et si qua similia. Mera itaque iura ecclesiastica leges imperatorum nulla ratione, nec in totum nec in partem, valent dissolvere; ea vero iura ecclesiastica, que de imperatorum constitutionibus pendent, aliqua quidem sunt, que lege imperatorum in totum et in partem credimus quod possent convelli: que quidem magis in odium quorundam, quam in generalem favorem ecclesie instituta sunt, ut predictum ius prescribendi. Hoc enim ius ecclesie in partem cotidie dissolvitur, quando aliqua ecclesia ab imperatore privilegium impetrat, ne adversus eam ecclesia alia prescribat. In totum etiam putamus quod ius hoc posset extingui; si enim imperator legem daret, ut omnis et omnium prescriptio quantumvis longi temporis de cetero cessaret, ex tunc et deinceps nec ecclesia ullo modo prescribere posset" (ed. H. Singer, 26–27; cf. C. Munier, *La pénétration,* 947–48; J. Portemer, *Recherches,* 37 n.3; P. Bellini, *L'obbligazione da promessa,* 297 n.1b).

1 Since [Gratian] above has mentioned the laws of the
emperors, and because these often appear necessary in
ecclesiastical proceedings, one rightly asks if they
excel the constitutions of the Church. If in certain
5 cases the laws of secular lords contradict
ecclesiastical constitutions, they must be completely
discarded. But where they do not oppose evangelical and
canonical decrees, they shall be treated with all due
reverence and be accepted in support of the Church. What
10 is said in the chapter below, though, that "the law of
the emperors cannot dissolve [ecclesiastical] rights"
[c.1] is not to be accepted without further distinction.
Note therefore, that ecclesiastical law is partly pure,
i.e. originating from divine precepts or those of the holy
15 fathers, such as the law of tithes, dioceses, and the
like; in part it is mixed or adjunct, i.e. it depends on
human constitutions, such as the laws of prescription and
similar ones. This means that the pure laws of the Church
cannot be changed by any means through imperial
20 legislation, neither entirely nor in part. Among the
ecclesiastical laws, however, which derive from imperial
legislation, there are some that, I believe, can be
abolished by the emperor, in part as well as entirely;
those, of course, that have been passed against certain
25 people rather than those generally in favor of the
Church, as for instance the above-mentioned law of
prescription. This law of the Church, namely, is infringed
upon almost daily, whenever a particular church requests
a privilege from the emperor, lest another church
30 prescribe against it. Also, I believe that this law might
be completely invalidated, if the emperor issued a law
that would nullify all of the prescriptions, regardless
of their length. Then, the Church could not prescribe any
longer, either.

Rufinus copied the initial parts of his gloss (lines 1–9) from an older
decretist, Paucapalea. He then introduced a major modification to the
argument followed ever since Gratian by distinguishing between
"pure" and "mixed" ecclesiastical laws (lines 9–27). Eventually, he
came to deny ecclesiastical autonomy in the latter category. One
might speculate on Rufinus's motives for proposing such a theory,

which a century after the Gregorian reform may seem to have been all but reactionary. After all, Gratian's *Decretum* (C.11 q.1) had already expounded a similar doctrine in dealing with the question of jurisdictional competence over churchmen. One of Gratian's *dicta* (p.c.26) suggests that clerics were under imperial jurisdiction whenever a legal matter would be governed by Roman law. This view, of course, was eventually discounted by Gratian (p.c.31 §1) as well as by Rufinus. "Actor sequitur forum rei," they both concluded.[17] In his discussion of *Distinctio* 10, however, Rufinus proposed an extended sphere of imperial legislation in order to adapt canonistic thought to a situation prevailing de facto. He clearly stated that the ecclesiastical laws of prescription were daily (*cotidie*) circumvented by imperial privileges (lines 27–34), a phenomenon not accounted for by Gratian's straightforward teaching. The cause of Rufinus's concern can be traced in the series of surviving imperial privileges. Emperor Frederick Barbarossa had in fact issued several charters granting churches exemption from the ecclesiastical rules of prescription. This seems to have been the expression of a deliberate policy, since these grants were confined to the years 1159–60 and 1163, and only to churches in northern Italy.[18] To explore Frederick's policy and motives goes

17. Cf. C.11 q.1 p.c.26: "Clerici ex offitio sunt subpositi episcopo, ex possessionibus prediorum inperatori sunt obnoxii. . . . Quia ergo ut predia possideantur inperiali lege factum est patet quod clerici ex prediorum possessionibus inperatori sunt obnoxii," and Gratian's final rejection of this view, at p.c.31 §1: "Sacris enim canonibus et forensibus legibus tam in civili quam in criminali causa clericus ad civilem iudicem pertrahendus negatur." My thanks to Prof. Peter Landau (Munich) for bringing these passages to my attention. Rufinus agreed to Gratian's treatment at the end of his commentary to C.11 q.1 a.c.1: "Si causa civilis atque forensis fuerit, tunc generaliter illa regula observabitur ut actor forum rei sequatur," *Summa*, ed. H. Singer, 309.

18. According to a survey of Frederick's charters for the years 1152–67, ed. H. Appelt, *Friderici I diplomata* (MGH-Diplomata regum et imperatorum Germaniae 10.1–2; Hanover, 1975–79), the emperor overrode ecclesiastical prescription in the following cases: Document n.249 (1159, to S. Gennaro di Lucedio), n.251 (1159, to San Solutore in Torino), n.252 (1159, to the bishop of Torino), n.255 (1159, to Casale Monferrato), n.267 (1159, to Fruttuaria), n.275 (1159, to S. Pietro in Rome), n.278 (1159, to S. Pietro in Modena), n.301 (1160, to the bishop of Modena), n.309 (1160, to the church of Mantua), n.314 (1160, to the church of Reggio Em.), n.315 (1160, to the church of Ravenna), n.413 (1163, to S. Pietro near Perugia), n.414 (1163, to the church of Perugia), n.422 (1163, to S. Zeno in Verona). These acts were already implied in Frederick's general legislation at Roncaglia, 1154 and 1158, ibid., nn.91, 241. J. Petersohn, "Das Präskriptionsrecht der Römischen Kirche und der Konstanzer

beyond the scope of this present chapter, but these charters point up an interesting relationship between canonistic doctrine and current political events. Writing around 1164, Rufinus offered an immediate, learned response to these developments, creating an intellectual turbulence among his colleagues that was to last for several decades.

Rufinus's successors quickly realized that this solution of the problem posed a fundamental question of ecclesiastical sovereignty. His oddly "legalistic" teachings thus did not receive a sympathetic treatment at the hands of Stephan of Tournai. Indeed, if we compare Stephan's views to Rufinus's on this point, the positions of the two almost seem to be reversed. In his *Summa,* the founder of the French decretist school totally disregarded Rufinus's new distinction and reasserted the opinion of Gratian. Stephan did this by including in his comment a phrase of Justinian himself (Novella 83 c.1), in which the emperor had expressed his high esteem of the canons: "Our laws do not disdain the imitation of the sacred canons."[19]

Stephan's intervention, however, did not succeed in settling the dispute. Instead, canonists struggled with Rufinus's theory for another quarter century. From an examination of later decretists and their glosses on *Distinctio* 10, Johannes Faventinus emerges as the canonist

---

Vertrag," in *Ex ipsis rerum documentis. Beiträge zur Mediävistik. Festschrift für H. Zimmermann zum 65. Geburtstag,* ed. K. Herbers, H. Kortüm, and C. Servatius (Sigmaringen, 1991), 307–15 at 311 n.28, has compiled a similar list of rescripts, in which Emperor Frederick modified the rules of prescription in favor of particular churches. Petersohn, however, did not pay attention to the contemporary canonistic debate regarding these imperial acts. For a general sketch of the impact of political reality on other areas of decretistic thought, see E. Hehl, *Kirche und Krieg,* 174–87.

19. "Leges nostre non dedignantur imitari sacros canones," Stephanus, *Summa* D.10 a.c.1 s.v. *Constitutiones principum,* ed. J. F. v. Schulte, *Die Summa des Stephanus Tornacensis über das Decretum Gratiani* (Giessen, 1891), 19; ed. H. Kalb, *Die Summa,* 35 n.13. Of the other commentaries not affected by Rufinus's new teachings, the *Summa Parisiensis* (1160/70), D.10 c.1 s.v. *Leges,* ed. T. P. Mc Laughlin (Toronto, 1952), 9, restated Gratian's position in terms equally independent from Stephanus's gloss. Not so the *Summa Coloniensis* (ca. 1169), ed. G. Fransen and S. Kuttner, MIC A 1.1 (New York, 1969), 19; *Iuditiorum instrumenta* (n.24 below); and Sicardus, *Summa* (n.22 below). They both quote Justinian's Novella in the context of D.10 a.c.1. Finally, Justinian's maxim reappeared in an official pronouncement of Pope Lucius III (1181–85), who furnished with it one of his decretals. In a statement very much in favor of the use of Roman law in the ecclesiastical courts, he wrote: "Quia vero sicut humane leges non dedignantur sacros canones imitari, ita et sacrorum statuta canonum priorum principum constitutionibus adiuvantur (JL 15189 = 2 Comp 3.26.3 = X 5.32.1)."

who played a key role in prolonging the debate. Although his *Summa,* composed around 1171, consisted of little more than a transcription of Rufinus's and Stephan's works, it nevertheless soon eclipsed the older literature. Thanks to the compilatory character of Johannes's commentary, Rufinus's terminology of "pure" and "mixed" legislation reappeared therein alongside Stephan's citation of the imperial Novella. Yet in copying from Rufinus, Johannes took care to signal his disagreement with him through a number of textual manipulations.[20] At the end of his excerpt, he further modified the position held by Rufinus and his partisans in a comment of his own:[21]

This is what certain people think. Yet to me it seems that despite their origins in civil law, the ecclesiastical laws cannot at all be abolished through the emperor, save for those persons who are his subjects. This applies when the law has already found its expression in the canons and has been confirmed by the universal use of the Church. But if the law has been approved by use alone, it can still be modified by the emperor. In this way, the laws governing patronage, prescription, and all the other ones forming part of the civil laws, can be changed by the emperor and the pope alike, but by both only with regard to their own subjects.

Johannes's influential commentary on *Distinctio* 10 made the situation more complicated than the decretists up to Stephan would ever have suspected. Instead of sorting out the materials contradicting his own view, he first handed on the plain teachings of Gratian, then

20. It is interesting to note the mosaic fashion in which Johannes put together the texts of his predecessors. He was careful to express his dissent by way of departing from Rufinus's original on several occasions. Given here in the form of an apparatus (for line numbers, cf. n.16 above), the most important variants were the following ones (MSS Paris, B.N. lat. 14606, fol. 5va; Vatican, Borgh. lat. 71, fol. 8va–b):   6 postponende sunt.] Non enim dedignantur imitari sacros canones *add. ex Summa Stephani*   16 in partem] videntur quibusdam convelli *add.*   20 In totum etiam] putant *add.*   20 si enim] ut aiunt *add.* It is evident that the few variants serve the sole end of setting apart Johannes's own opinion from that held by Rufinus and others ("putant," "aiunt").

21. "Ita quidam sentiunt. Nobis autem non videtur ius ecclesiasticum licet habuerit a iure civili exordium per imperatorem nisi circa eas personas quibus preest in aliquibus capitulis posse abrogari, cum iam sit in canones redactum et universali ecclesie consuetudine corroboratum. Si vero ius illud solo usu ecclesie comprobatum est, prorsus commutari potest ab imperatore. Potest ergo ius patronatus et prescriptio et reliqua similia que iuri civili ammixta sunt tam ab imperatore quam ab apostolico commutari, sed ab utroque tantum circa personas sibi subiectas," Johannes Faventinus, *Summa* D.10 a.c.1 s.v. *Constitutiones vero principum,* MSS Paris, B.N. lat. 14606, fol. 5va; Vatican, Bibl. Ap. Borgh. lat. 71, fol. 8vb; Bamberg, Can. 37, fol. 5vb.

those of Rufinus's circle, identified as "quidam," and finally his own distinction on the question of imperial interference in ecclesiastical legislation. Obviously, Johannes was unwilling to accept the reduction of church autonomy to the "pure" laws alone. Yet at the same time he accorded to the secular lord a certain degree of authority within the spiritual realm. As Johannes asserted, the emperor could pass new laws for the clergy wherever these superseded older, unwritten custom. In this fashion, he did put all of the positive rules issued by the church out of secular reach, but in the end departed only halfway from Rufinus's conception of a "mixed" sphere of competence.

For some time, the canonistic debate continued to draw inspiration from the remarks of Johannes. The literature prior to Huguccio regularly reported his and Rufinus's distinctions. An exception was Sicardus of Cremona, whose plain reading of Gratian rather stood in the tradition of Stephan.[22] Meanwhile, the *Note Atrebatenses* (ca. 1171–79), the *Summa Monacensis* (ca. 1175–78), *Tractaturus magister* (ca. 1182–85), and the *Summa Lipsiensis* (ca. 1186) all repeated the notions of *ius scriptum* and *ius non scriptum* as an adequate borderline of secular competence.[23] The *Summa Monacensis* supplied a

---

22. Sicardus, *Summa*, MSS Munich, Staatsbibl. lat. 4555, fol. 3vb; lat. 8013, fol. 7v: "In dignitate quoque differunt constitutio forensis et ecclesiastica. Quia forensis cedit ecclesiastice. Nam forensis constitutio quandoque convenit ecclesiastice et tunc omni reverentia digna habeatur, ut d.x Si in adiutorium [c.7]; quandoque obviat et tunc penitus obsequatur quia sacre leges non dedignantur imitari sacros canones [Nov.83], ut in matrimonio; quandoque eam non contingit et tunc est in auctoritatem laicis et clericis in exemplum, nisi ab ecclesia confirmetur vel per subscriptionem vel per ratihabitionem ut d.xcvi c.i; et c.xi q.i Continua [c.5]." Sicardus obviously did not think it worthwhile to devote a single line to all the speculation that had emerged in the wake of Rufinus's teachings. This made him the first decretist who silently challenged them even in the modified form proposed by Johannes Faventinus. The French Summa *Reverentia sacrorum canonum* (ca. 1184–91), MS Erfurt, Stadtbibl. Amplon. qu.117, fol. 117vb, as well as the author of the *Summa Reginensis* (c.1187/92), MS Vatican, Bibl. Ap. Reg. lat. 1061, fol. 2rb, later embraced the same attitude. In a manner foreshadowing Huguccio's definitive gloss on D.10, the two Summe, *Et est sciendum* (Stuttgardiensis), and *De iure canonico tractaturus* (see n.26 below), instead turned to an open attack against the constantly growing number of new distinctions.

23. *Note Atrebatenses*, MS Arras, B.M. 271, fol. 149rb; in the *Summa Monacensis* (MS Munich, lat. 16084, fol. 3ra; printed by A. Stickler, "Imperator vicarius papae," 173 n.31), the possibility of imperial interference is only implied: "*Leges imperatorum* Constitutio alia ecclesiastica alia forensis vel secularis. Item secularis alia in scriptura redacta alia solo usu ecclesie comprobata. Que in sacram scripturam est redacta inter

third distinction. It gave the emperor the right to extend concessions made to a church in a former rescript, but not to revoke them.²⁴ To be sure, Rufinus's opinion was not forgotten along the way, but it met with almost unanimous disapproval. Only a small number of canonists still adhered to his view. One was the anonymous writer of the Summa *Antiquitate et tempore* (ca. 1170). His interpretation of D.10 managed to blend Stephan's reference to Novella 83 c.1 into a doctrinal framework basically provided by Rufinus. Meanwhile, the position taken by Simon of Bisignano (ca. 1177–79) was not quite as clear. Although his treatment of D.10 accorded the notions of "pure" and "mixed" laws no more than the status of possible arguments, he was not reluctant elsewhere to endow each of the supreme rulers in Church and State with the same authority to intervene in "mixed" affairs.²⁵

canones conputatur neque ab imperatore mutari potest"; but cf. next note. *Summa Tractaturus magister*, MS Paris, B.N. lat. 15994, fol. 4ra–b; *Summa Lipsiensis*, MS Rouen, B.M. 743, fol. 4rb–va.

24. *Summa Monacensis* (in continuation of the text given n.23 above): "Item ius ecclesiasticum aliud merum aliud mixtum i.e. seculari annexum. Merum ecclesiasticum tantum apostolico est concessum vel commissum. Quod seculari est annexum ab utroque potest mutari, ut prescriptio, ius patronatus; ab utroque, sed circa personas sibi subiectas. Item refert an lex sit omnibus communis an talis que solius ecclesie contineat privilegium. Legem omnibus communem imperator mutare potest, puta ut usucapio non triennio sed quadriennio compleatur, ut iniuriarum accusatio non sit temporalis sed perpetua. Privilegium vero ecclesie a suis predecessoribus inductum in melius quidem reformare, non autem in deterius potest, cum sit ipse quasi pupille tutor cuius conditionem meliorem quidem, deteriorem autem facere non potest. Tutor enim intelligitur quamdiu res bene amministretur, non cum pupillam rebus spoliat aut privilegiis nudare presumit, xvi q.iii Placuit [c.8]. Illud autem sc. ut mutari possint de illis maxime legibus intelligendum est que in canonicam scripturam traducte non sunt." The French Summa *Iuditiorum instrumenta* (ca. 1178) combined its adherence to Stephan's opinion with a hint, otherwise unrecorded, to still another distinction circulating at decretist schools: "Unde dicit Ysidorus: 'Constitutio imperialis si fuerit contra decreta et canones nullius esse momenti.' Hoc ecclesia tenet sicut et in ipsis legibus continetur: 'Sacre leges non dedignantur imitari sacros canones [Nov.83].' Sed quidam dicunt quod tantum de decretis, non de canonibus hoc intelligitur," MS Munich, Staatsbibl. lat. 16084, fol. 28v.

25. *Summa Antiquitate et tempore* (MS Göttingen, Univ. bibl. 2 Cod. Jurid. 159, fol. 13ra–b), D.10 a.c.1: "*Constitutiones vero principum* Subsequenter ostendit quod etiam seculares constitutiones cedere debent ecclesiasticis quod multorum auctoritatibus declaratur et etiam conditor legum attestatur qui ait: 'Non dedignantur nostre leges sacros imitari canones'"; ibid., D.10 c.1: "*imperiali iudicio non possunt iura ecclesiastica dissolvi* Iura ecclesiastica dicuntur duobus modis. Primo sunt ea que modo obtinentur solummodo divina vel ecclesiastica institutione puta ius decimarum,

None of these speculations, to be sure, rested on a firm legal basis. Rufinus and Johannes had both argued without offering references that would have tied their views to any authoritative source. And yet, a whole generation of canonists had to work its way through the glosses piling up around *Distinctio* 10 before their unfounded character became evident. This clarification was perhaps prepared by the critical remarks found in less well known works such as the *Summa Stuttgardiensis* (ca. 1181–85).[26] Eventually, however, it received its

---

prebendarum et ius determinatarum diocesum, de quo in presenti capitulo fit mentio. Secundum ea que ex quacumque institutione ad res ecclesiarum spectant sicut est ius prescriptionis et huiusmodi. Priora ergo iura ecclesiastica imperiali iudicio convelli numquam possunt. Posteriora vero in aliquibus casibus possunt. Verbi causa: Si nunc imperator legem faceret ut nulla de cetero futura prescriptio temporis alicui rem alienam possidenti subveniret et deinceps ecclesia contra ecclesiam vel quemlibet nec xxx annis prescribere valeret, licet modo ita se habeat ius ecclesiasticum." The position held by Simon of Bisignano cannot be grasped as easily from the lapidary comment of his *Summa* on D.10 c.1: "*Imperium nostrum* etc. *usque que sacerdotibus Domini solis conveniant in his* sc. quorum cognitio et dampnatio ad solos clericos pertinet, ut in meris ecclesiasticis. Unde videtur quod contra mixta iura imperator possit legem constituere" (Bamberg, Can. 38, p. 5a; Augsburg, Stadtbibl. 1, fol. 2rb). Evidence from other parts of Simon's work shows, however, that he did not hesitate to use Rufinus's argument, e.g. in a gloss on C.33 q.2 p.c.5, ed. J. Juncker, "Die Summa des Simon von Bisignano und seine Glossen," ZRG Kan. Abt. 13 (1926), 364: "*gladium* Supra di.x c. De capitulis [c.9] contra. Sed hic de legibus, que contradicunt canonibus agitur, ibi vero de illis que canonice consonant equitati; vel hic de meris rebus ecclesiasticis, ibi de mixtis. S⟨imon⟩" (= *Summa* C.33 q.2 c.6 s.v. *legibus*). According to a text published from the *Summa decretalium questionum* (MS Reims, B.M. 689, fol. 38) by M. Pacaut, *Alexandre III. Étude sur la conception du pouvoir pontifical dans sa pensée et dans son oeuvre* (Paris, 1956), 349 n.5, Edward of Ypres (ca. 1181) may also count among Rufinus's late followers.

26. MS Stuttgart, Hist. fol. 419, fol. 35ra, D.10 a.c.1 s.v. *Lege imperatorum* (ed. F. Gillmann, "Codex Stuttgart," 235. The Summa *De iure canonico tractaturus* of Honorius (ca. 1188–90) is contemporary with Huguccio's *Summa,* but still expresses its critique of Rufinus in the opponent's own terms of "mixed" and "pure" laws: D.10 c.1 *non in omnibus*: "Hinc distinguitur secundum quosdam dicentes hoc verum passim esse de me⟨ri⟩s, utpote que processerint de constitutionibus sanctorum patrum. Nam secus de mixtis, ut prescriptione quam si tollat vel immutat princeps immutabitur etiam in ecclesia, quia ecclesia non invenit sed approbavit. Nobis videtur hoc verum de utrisque esse. Nec enim si tollet princeps prescriptionem ideo minus ecclesia uteretur prescriptione. Est enim ius ecclesiasticum. Princeps ergo circa suos posset tantum tollere vel immutare, papa similiter circa suos. Sed numquid princeps laicos a iure patronatus posset suspendere ecclesia hoc acceptum non habente? Respondetur sic secundum quosdam. Nam universitatem posset auferre. Unde et ius patronatus. Aliis videtur in contrarium. Licet enim ex universitate pendeat tamen ratione universitatis non potest vendicari, sed ratione canonum tantum, ut xvi q.v Cause [c.2]. Unde circa

strongest formulation in Huguccio's *Summa* (1188–90), which dismissed the doctrinal aberrations of twenty-five years one by one. By analyzing his lengthy gloss, we turn to the more specific question of Roman law and its place in Huguccionian thought.

2. THE ROLE OF SECULAR JURISPRUDENCE IN CANON LAW: HUGUCCIO'S THEORETICAL VIEW

Modern scholarship has described the *Summa decretorum* as the first work of synthesis since Johannes Faventinus. In an almost encyclopedic approach, Huguccio assembled the best he could find in previous canonistic literature and set his penetrating mind to the task of arriving at well-balanced conclusions. To illustrate his technique, the argument he adopted in the context of *Distinctio* 10 offers an example as good as any. It not only presents a summary of the preceding discussion but also indicates the doctrinal path that later decretist treatments were to follow:[27]

---

ius patronatus utpote quidem est merum spirituale nil potest mutari nisi quantum canones concedunt" (MS Laon, B.M. 371bis, fol. 85rb).

27. Translation: "Others make useless distinctions at this point, saying that the ecclesiastical law is partly pure, i.e., deriving from ecclesiastical legislation only, such as the law of tithes, donations, dioceses, the establishment of a church and the like; partly it is mixed, i.e., originating from secular legislation, such as the law of patronage, prescription, usucaption, etc. They say that an imperial constitution cannot change pure ecclesiastical laws, but mixed laws it can. Others distinguish differently: Ecclesiastical laws are partly written, partly unwritten. The emperor cannot change the written laws, yet the unwritten ones he can change. But neither distinction is authoritative, nor do they deserve any credit. And therefore I reject each of these distinctions. For the emperor cannot determine or change anything concerning the property or the rights of the Church, as is argued here and D.96 c.1 and C.16 q.7 c.23. If, in other words, the emperor wishes to change the laws of prescription, or to remove them entirely, he can do so only for his own subjects, because whatever the emperor statutes, his constitutions do not bind the clergy, as is expressed here and C.33 q.2 c.6. Although the laws of prescription may have their origins in secular law, they nevertheless have been received by the Church and found general approval. Hence, they have turned into ecclesiastical law, and the emperor can change laws affecting the Church only as far as his own subjects are concerned. If the emperor decreed that prescriptions should cease to exist, the Church would nonetheless continue to prescribe against other churches and against laymen. But laymen could no longer prescribe against any church. In sum, secular laws never do or can prevail, unless the Church herself passes a law to that effect."

1 Hic inutiliter distinguunt quidam dicentes ius
ecclesiasticum aliud merum sc. quod tantum ex
constitutione ecclesie descendit, ut decimarum,
oblationum, diocesum, in constituendas ecclesias et
5 huiusmodi, aliud mixtum sc. quod ex constitutione seculari
habuit initium, ut ius patronatus, ius prescriptionis,
usucapionis et huiusmodi. Dicunt isti quod merum ius
ecclesiasticum non potest dissolvere constitutio
imperialis, sed mixtum potest. Alii aliter distinguunt ius
10 ecclesiasticum aliud est scriptum aliud non scriptum.
Scriptum imperator non potest immutare, non scriptum
potest. Sed neutra distinctio est de auctoritate nec etiam
verba videntur esse alicuius auctoritatis. Et ideo
utramque distinctionem reprobo, quia imperator de rebus
15 vel iure ecclesie nil potest statuere vel immutare: ar.
hic et di. xcvi Bene quidem [c.1]; et xvi q.vii Non
placuit laicis [c.23]. Si ergo imperator ius
prescriptionis velit immutare vel ex toto removere, non
potest nisi tantum circa suos subditos. Quicquid enim
20 imperator statuat ecclesiam talis constitutio non ligat,
non constringit, ut hic dicitur et xxxiii q.ii Inter hec
[c.6]. Licet enim ius prescribendi forte initium habuerit
a iure seculari, tamen receptum est ab ecclesia et
approbatum et iam ius ecclesiasticum, et circa ecclesiam
25 in nullo potest immutari nisi quoad subditos suos. Si enim
imperator statueret ut nulla de cetero curreret
prescriptio, non ideo minus prescriberet ecclesia contra
ecclesiam et contra privatum, sed privatus non
prescriberet. Item si statueret quod nulla prescriptio
30 curreret contra ecclesiam, non ideo minus ecclesia
prescriberet contra ecclesiam, sed laicus contra ecclesiam
non prescriberet. In nullo ergo secularis constitutio
preiudicat vel potest preiudicare nisi ab ecclesia hoc
statuatur: ar. hic et xxxiii q.ii Inter hec [c.6]; et de
35 con. di.iii Celebritatem [c.22]; et xi q.i Continua [c.5],
Sacerdotibus [c.41]; et ii q.vi Non ita [c.18]; et xxiii
q.viii Convenior [c.21]; et di.i Ius quiritum [c.12].

Notes. The text has been taken from the *Summa* D.10 c.1 s.v. *iuditio*, MSS Vatican, lat. 2280, fol. 9rb–va; Klosterneuburg 89, fol. 13ra–b; Admont 7, fol. 10rb–va (no major variants); cf. C. Munier, "Droit canonique," 951 n.27, who transcribed (with errors) lines 1–17 from MS Paris, B.N. lat. 3892, fol. 10ra; also P. Bellini, *L'obbligazione da promessa*, 297 n.1b, 298 n.2: lines 9–12, 12–15, 17–21, 22–25, 25–34, cited from MS Vatican, lat. 2280, and Vatican, S. Pietro C.114, fol. 11va.   **1–9** *quidam dicentes . . . mixtum potest* Behind this distinction one recognizes the authorship of Rufinus (above n.16, lines 11–21), which Huguccio probably came to know through the *Summa* of Johannes Faventinus (n.21 above).   **9–12** *Alii . . . non scriptum potest* As first proposed by Johannes Faventinus (above n.21, lines 1–7). Huguccio simplified the terminology by rendering "ius in canones redactum" (line 5) as "ius scriptum" and "ius solo usu ecclesie comprobatum" (line 7) as "ius non scriptum." Earlier the *Note Atrebatenses* (n.23 above) had spoken of "lex redacta in scriptis," while the expression "non in scriptis redacta," employed by the *Summa Lipsiensis* (n.23 above), corresponded to the original formula "solo usu."   **12–13** *Sed . . . auctoritatis* Huguccio's key argument, which was to conclude the entire debate (cf. nn.22–25 above).   **15** *nil potest statuere* Cf. Honorius (n.26 above): "nil potest mutari."   **17–25** *Si ergo . . . subditos suos* Returns to Rufinus's distinction (above lines 1–8) and rejects it. The wording of Huguccio's critique echoes that of Johannes Faventinus (n.21 above, lines 1–5).   **25–32** *Si enim . . . prescriberet* Known to him via Johannes (n.21 above), Huguccio finally opposes Rufinus's interpretation of the *prescriptio* (above n.16, lines 22–29) as an example of "ius mixtum." As to his own conclusion, cf. Johannes (above n.21, lines 5–7), the principal source for Huguccio's comment, and the often strikingly similar formulations (see also above, line 15) by his contemporary Honorius (n.26 above).   **32–37** *In nullo . . . Ius quiritum* The long chain of allegations attests to the central importance of this gloss for Huguccio's theory on the relationship between the two laws. In this fashion, it offers the point of departure for the subsequent, closer analysis of his thought.

Huguccio's detailed explanation would appear completely out of proportion if it did not reflect the intent to restore order after a long and confused debate. In substance, he tried to achieve little more than to render explicit the *Libertas Ecclesie* in matters of jurisdiction. Already foreshadowed by Gratian, his position is perfectly clear: The emperor can accomplish nothing (*nil*) in the ecclesiastical sphere, unless being called upon to do so by the Church itself. Aside from this succinct statement, Huguccio devoted a great deal of space to rejecting the "useless" distinctions of Rufinus, Johannes, and others. Their weakness principally derives from the lack of support by the canons, which deprives them of all true authority. With a few strokes of his pen, the author of the *Summa* thus ended a debate that had frustrated so many intellectual endeavors of the preceding generation. As a result, the older opinions formulated in the wake of Rufinus's dissent altogether disappeared from decretist commentaries after 1190.

In line with the categorical denial of all secular interference in canonical legislation, Huguccio also proposed a simplified set of rules to govern the relationship between imperial and ecclesiastical jurisdiction in general. Most importantly, his critique of Rufinus had the effect of rendering Roman law irrelevant for clerics, unless some kind of ecclesiastical approval accorded to its precepts the status of what was soon to be called *leges canonizate*. This reception by the Church did not necessarily depend on a formal act, and Huguccio made no objection to laws that were applied due to tacit consent only.[28] To put it differently, the sole fact that a law proved noncontradictory to any canonical rule might imply its acceptance by ecclesiastical authorities. If disagreement should arise, however, the pope alone was to decide whether the law in question conformed to the canons. Like most of his fellows, Huguccio employed a whole range of images to describe the elevated position of the Roman pontiff as supreme head presiding over ecclesiastical jurisdiction. For example, he compared papal and imperial authority by attributing to both the plenitude of power in their respective spheres.[29] To enhance papal authority, Hu-

---

28. *Summa* D.1 c.12 s.v. *in eos solos*: "Item quid de clericis? Numquid et ipsi ligantur legibus Romanis? Sic. Illis que approbantur ab ecclesia et non obviant canonibus. Sed non ideo quia sunt promulgate ab imperatoribus, sed quia sunt confirmate a domino pape" (MS Lons-le-Saunier 12.F.16, fol. 5rb; full gloss printed by G. Catalano, *Impero*, 61–62). Similar statements abound. Huguccio, however, rarely attempted an exact definition of how secular laws were to be confirmed by the Church. Yet in one instance, he made an equation between the conformity of a Roman maxim and its presumed approval by the Church, see *Summa* D.96 c.1 §5 *a laicali*: "Sed numquid omnes leges que de rebus vel personis ecclesiasticis facte sunt quia a laicis facte sunt debent irritari? Non, quia omnes leges que canonibus non obviant intelliguntur esse confirmata a papa et corroborate" (MS Klosterneuburg 89, fol. 109va). Such an assumption of ecclesiastical approval Huguccio called "tacit" at C.6 q.4 c.3 *legibus nostris*: "i.e. a nobis [that is, the pope] tacito saltem consensu confirmatis et receptis scil. quandocumque non obviant canonibus" (P. Bellini, *L'obbligazione da promessa*, 326 n.19a; Paris, B.N. lat. 15396, fol. 144rb); and again, in dealing with custom, *Summa* D.4 p.c.3 *abrogate*: "non interveniente consensu pape vel imperatoris non possunt constitui quia populus respondet ei et in eum omne ius et potestatem consensit, ut Inst. De iure naturali. Sed et quod [Inst. 1.2.6]; ita nec infirmari vel abrogari. Idem dicendum est de canonibus quia sicut sine auctoritate pape non possunt constitui ita nec irritari. Sed interveniente consensu istius vel illius vel leges vel canones possunt abrogari contraria consuetudine. Consensu ideo expresso vel tacito quia hoc quod papa vel imperator scit contrariam consuetudinem esse et non reprobat tacito consensu videtur eam confirmare" (MS Lons-le-Saunier 12.F.16, fol. 6va); cf. C. Munier, "Droit canonique," 953.

29. *Summa* D.4 p.c.3 *moribus utentium*: "Omne enim ius condendi leges vel canones populus contulit in imperatorem et ecclesia in apostolicum. Unde intelligitur

guccio obviously did not hesitate to draw appropriate formulas from both canonical and Roman sources.

From a modern viewpoint, the exact dividing line between secular and spiritual jurisdiction remained, of course, blurred. Besides the personal status of the litigants, there were other factors determining the competence of the courts. In certain cases, such as those concerning marriage, the Church had long claimed an exclusive right to pass judgment, although the question affected laymen rather than clergy. In the same vein, usury represented a crime that the Church wished to wrestle from the imperial courts; hence, Huguccio vigorously attacked secular laws against usurers and condemned them as "unjust" and too lax.[30] Despite his dualist convictions, he obviously could adopt quite expansionist views wherever secular indifference fostered un-Christian and immoral acts. But in the absence of such disputed areas, the *Summa* supported the perfect autonomy of the temporal order.[31] This is also clear from the fashion in which the

---

uterque plenitudinem potestatis habere quoad hoc; ar. viiii q.iii Conquestus [c.9], Ipsi [c.16], Cuncta [c.18], Nunc vero [c.20]; et ii q.vi Decreto [c.11]; et Instit. De iure naturali, Sed quod principi placuit [Inst. 1.2.6]" (MSS Admont 7, fol. 5vb, Lons-le-Saunier 12.F.16, fol. 6vb). Other examples of decretist imagery in P. Legendre, "Le droit romain, modèle et langage," in *Études dediées à G. Le Bras* (Paris, 1965), 2.921–25; for literature treating Huguccio's theory of papal monarchy within the ecclesiastical realm, cf. Introduction, nn.31–32 above.

30. *Summa* D.10 c.1 *obviare*: "Ut in usuris que prohibentur lege Dei permittuntur lege fori. Et in matrimoniis que hodie reguntur iure poli non fori" (MS Admont 7, fol. 10ra). Huguccio's comments make clear that he wished to make all cases involving usury subject to ecclesiastical jurisdiction; see D.10 c.2 *contra divina mandata*: "Ar. contra leges que usuras permittunt exigi, cum sint contra Deum et ita contra ius. Non dic 'leges' vel 'iura' cum ius dicatur quia iustum est, et lex quia legitime agere doceat, ut di.i Ius generale [c.2]. Auctoritate ergo canonica et divina omnes tales leges abrogate sunt" (Admont 7, fol. 10vb); cf. also Introduction, n.30 above.

31. The strongest statements to that effect the *Summa* included at D.10 c.1 *preiudicium*: "Sed in canonibus dicitur quod appellatio potest esse et ante et post sententiam, in legibus tantum post, ut ii q.vi Non ita [c.18]. Sed non idcirco fit preiudicium canonibus per leges vel legibus per canones quia utrumque obtinet nec in hoc lex contradicit canoni vel canon legi, quia quod in canonibus dicitur non est generaliter institutum, sed tantum in causis ecclesiasticis. Similiter quod in legibus dicitur non est generaliter statutum sed tantum in causis secularibus" (MS Admont 7, fol. 10vb); and again on the same subject at C.2 q.6 c.18 *recedere*: "Sed quero: Si causa ecclesiastica sit commissa laico an ante sententiam possit appellari. Et dico quod potest quia residet non tamquam iudex secularis sed tamquam iudex ecclesiasticus. Et e converso si secularis sit delegata ecclesiastico iudici a principe vel alio iudice seculari non licet ibi

numerous disagreements between Roman and canon law are handled. Huguccio assembled them in a long list of *differentie,* similar to those that later came to be elaborated into a self-standing literary genre.[32]

As to the use of arguments from Justinian's *Corpus* in the church courts, we have already noted how boldly Huguccio restated the assertions made by Gratian in his *dicta* on *Distinctio* 10. Throughout the *Summa,* Huguccio applied the same principles again and again. Accordingly, Roman law provided a stock of weighty arguments for accusers and defendants, unless these proved contradictory to the canons. This meant further that Roman laws were especially suitable when canonical legislation was deficient. In that case, the judge could base his decision on civil sources.[33] But to present a complete picture

---

appellari ante sententiam quia tamquam secularis iudex residet. Et tunc in utroque casu apellandum est ab illo vel illo ad delegantem" (MS Klosterneuburg 89, fol. 143rb). On the distinctiveness of the two jurisdictions in ordinary cases, cf. also the bibliography cited in the Introduction, nn.23, 26 above.

32. C.2 q.6 c.18 *si necesse est*: "Hic habetur quod ecclesiastica negotia differunt a secularibus in appellatione. Differunt etiam in pene impositione quia ibi imponitur pena sanguinis hic numquam, ut iii q.iiii Hi qui [c.9]; et xxiii q.viii His a quibus [c.30]; et xxxiii q.ii Inter hec [c.6]. Item in sacramenti de calumpnia prestatione quia ibi semper prestatur saltem in causa civili et per principalem personam, hic autem non, ut in extra: INHERENTES [JL 7401]; LITTERAS [JL 9654]; IN PERTRACTANDIS [JL 9506]. Et in matrimonio clericorum, quia secundum leges soli cantores et lectores possunt ducere uxores, secundum canones vero omnes infra subdiaconatum existentes, ut xv q.iii Cum autem [p.c.4]; et di.xxxii Placuit [c.13]; Seriatim [c.14]. Item in coniunctione consanguineorum quia secundum leges etiam in secundo gradu coniuncti non separantur, ut xxxv q.iii Quedam [c.20]. Item in separatione matrimonii quia secundum leges preter causam fornicationis separantur causa religionis etiam coniuncti carnaliter altero invito. Quod canones contradicunt, ut di.x Lege [c.1]; et xxvii q.ii Sunt qui dicunt [c.19], Agathosa [c.21]. Item in usura que ex toto prohibetur in canonibus. Et in prescriptione ubi secundum canones exigitur bona fides continua. Item in priorum vel posteriorum prepositione quia secundum leges posteriora preiudicant prioribus. Quod non ita generaliter obtinet in canonibus, ut di.l Domino [c.28]. Item in retractatione sententie. Nam secundum leges non retractatur sententia lata ordine iuris a qua non appellatur nisi protextu falsi usque ad xx annos. Secus in canonibus, ut xxxiii q.v Quod Deo [c.4]; et xxxv q.ix Quia ergo [p.c.2]; et xi q.iii Episcopus presbiter [c.65]. Item in testimonio et accusatione quia secundum leges non repelluntur a testimonio vel accusatione bigami vel vitiati corpore vel criminosi nisi notati per sententiam. Sed secundum canones repelluntur, presertim contra clericos. Et in multis aliis differunt quia in multis alia est ratio secularium causarum et alia ecclesiasticarum, ut de con. d.iii Celebritatem [c.22]" (MS Paris, B.N. lat. 15396, fol. 116va). Huguccio's extensive account on the *differentie* predates all of the material that J. Portemer, *Recherches,* has discussed in his general survey; see also P. Weimar, "Differentienliteratur," LMA 3 (1986), 1042–43.

33. *Summa* D.10 c.3 *constitutum ipsius*: "Dei i.e. ecclesie. Ar. quod in causis ec-

of the Huguccionian scheme, the most important element still needs to be addressed. Thus far, we have stressed the "legalistic" aspect of his teachings. Like most contemporary canonists, however, Huguccio showed an equal awareness of possible theological implications. To avoid the impression that Roman Law might ever gain preponderance over canonical rules and the principal moral goal of ultimate salvation, he admonished lawyers not to forget the ultimate superiority of *equitas canonica* in all the administrative acts of the Church.[34] Every rule, in other words, had to pass the test of *equitas* before it could be used in the courts. Not surprisingly, as a true medieval catholic Huguccio did not hesitate to make Christian equity the basic guideline for everyone, including secular judges. In this connection, his views on public order took on an almost hierocratic turn:[35]

In those cases that do not concern criminal charges, if the secular law states something and the canons do not contradict, it is presumed to be licit. . . . Not so in cases which belong to the category of crimes. For in these the permission of human laws is insufficient unless divine law permits the same. This is also true provided that the divine laws do not envisage a prohibition in explicit terms. . . . When therefore some sort of crime is committed, the defendant is excused from all guilt if it is allowed by laws and canons alike.

---

clesiasticis pocius sunt allegandi canones quam leges, ar. ii q.vi Non ita [c.18]; et de con. di.iii Celebritatem [c.22]; et xi q.i Continua [c.5]. Si tamen leges consonent canonibus, licite et ille allegantur, ut infra c. Si in adiutorium [c.7]; et iii q.viiii Dignum est [c.9]; et xi q.iii Summopere [c.70]. Sed in sententia in nullo modo est recedenda a canonica allegatione propter legalem. Sed et ubi canones deficiunt licite leges allegantur dummodo rationi canonice non obvient; ar. di.xvii Nec licuit [c.4]; xxiii q.v Principes [c.20]" (MS Admont 7, fol. 10vb). Considering the simplicity of these guidelines, it would be tempting to strike a parallel between them and the generally extended use of Roman law among the canonists after Huguccio (cf. n.4 above). After all, canonistic quoting habits took a turn toward consistent growth once the issue of imperial legislative powers within the ecclesiastical sphere, brought to the fore through the intervention of Rufinus and others (nn.16, 20–22, 23–24 above), had been settled in favor of the traditional view, adopted by Gratian and Stephan (nn.19, 22, 25–26). Does this imply a correlation?

34. For bibliographical information about *equitas canonica*, cf. Introduction, nn.29–30 above.

35. *Summa* C.33 q.2 c.6 s.v. *numquam constringit* (MS Klosterneuburg 89, fol. 314ra): "In his enim que non sint de genere criminum si lex aliquid dicit et canon non contradicit presumitur esse licitum. . . . Secus in his que sunt de genere criminum. In his enim non sufficit permissio legis humane nisi et hoc permittatur in lege divina, licet specialiter non inveniatur prohibitum. . . . Cum ergo aliquid fit quod est de genere criminum, si hoc permittitur a lege et a canone, excusatur quis a pena et a peccato. Si a lege et non a canone, excusatur a pena legis sed non a peccato."

Yet if it is allowed by the laws and not by the canons, he is excused from legal punishment, but not from sin.

Elsewhere, Huguccio expressed in more specific terms how he envisioned the *equitas canonica* to play a decisive part in bringing about perfect harmony between pastoral demands on the one hand and those of legislation on the other. Once, noting that Roman lawyers did not require good faith on the part of someone who wanted to base a property claim on prescription, he deplored their disregard of *equitas* at this point. The rules governing Roman *prescriptio,* he wrote, promote sinful behavior, because they presuppose continuous possession but do not expect the litigant to meet the moral qualifications of good faith and just title:[36]

What we have said about the salvation of the souls with regard to usucaption, we can safely repeat according to canonical equity: In every prescription a just title is indispensable. This can be inferred from below, ch.10; and, *ex negativo,* from ch.8; and so is good faith, as is argued in C.34 q.2 c.5; and in C.14 q.6 c.1; and in extra: VIGILANTI. Also, someone sins if he is conscious of another one's property and does not return it. Nor can the passing of time save him from sin. Because the length of time does not diminish his fault, but rather adds to it, as in extra: NON SATIS; and in C.24 q.1 c.34. And I would be glad to see the injustice of the secular jurists being led back to the same degree of equity.

Having outlined Huguccio's theory of how Roman law should be handled by the clerical judges, it is interesting to explore his actual use of secular jurisprudence in the *Summa*. As the following chapter will

36. *Summa* C.16 q.3 a.c.1 *Quod autem prescriptione* (MS Klosterneuburg 89, fol. 243ra): "Sed sicut diximus de usucapione secure quantum ad salutem animarum secundum canonicam equitatem dicimus quod in qualibet prescriptione exigitur iustus titulus, quod potest colligi infra e. q. Si sacerdotes [c.10]; et ex contrario sensu illius cap. infra e. q. Placuit huic [c.8]; et bona fides continua, ar.xxxiiii q.ii Si virgo [c.5]; xiiii q.vi Si res [c.1]; et in extra: VIGILANTI [JL 14186]. Item ex quo quis habet conscientiam rei aliene peccat nisi reddat et a peccato defendi non potest temporis diuturnitate. Nam temporis diuturnitas peccatum non minuit sed auget, ut in extra: NON SATIS [Conc. Turon. (1163) c.6]; et xxiiii q.i Scisma [c.34]. Et vellem ut ad hanc equitatem iniustitia legistarum reduceretur." The text continues with a longer invective against the legists: "Sed quia difficile videtur quod diutius prohibetur et ordo lucri bonus est ex re qualibet illis in sua iniustitia relictis dicimus quod nulla res ecclesiastica sine continua bona fide prescribitur" (ed. by F. Maassen, "Beiträge," 70–71; L. Scavo-Lombardo, *Il concetto di buona fede nel diritto canonico* [Rome, 1944], 65–66; N. Vilain, "Préscription et bonne foi du Decret de Gratien [1140] à Jean d'André [+ 1348]," *Traditio* 14 [1958], 139 n.8).

demonstrate, its impact, though visible on each folio, reached dimensions as undramatic as the general attitude of our canonist toward Roman law.

3. ROMAN LAW IN THE *SUMMA DECRETORUM*

Huguccio strongly opposed all tendencies that seemed to diminish the sovereignty and self-sufficiency of the Church. To defend ecclesiastical liberty against any possible encroachment by secular powers, he insisted upon the complete separation of their respective spheres of legislation. Naturally, such a view did not fail to leave an imprint on his practical use of civil law as well. Huguccio certainly agreed that as long as materials drawn from the *Corpus* did not contradict the canons, canonists could use them freely in order to bolster their own reasoning. At the same time, he saw no obligation for them to study Roman doctrine for its own sake. This prompted him to choose a middle path between both extremes. On the one hand, he revealed little eagerness to impress readers with abundant references to Justinian's compilation. Compared to the later gloss-apparatuses of the French decretists, this restraint is very evident.[37] On the other hand, the *Summa* included quotations from Roman law whenever necessary. Side by side with long stretches of text in which they were thinly spread, the *Summa* frequently cited the *Corpus* in dealing with legal concepts that canon law had originally taken over from Roman jurisprudence. In so doing, Huguccio simply followed a practice long established by his predecessors. There is no reason to describe their treatment of the civil sources in terms other than those of selectiveness, gradual progress, and moderation.[38]

37. An example of the restricted application of Roman legal concepts is the use of "lese majesty" by Huguccio and his predecessors: V. Piergiovanni, "La lesa maestà nella canonistica fino ad Uguccione," *Materiali per una storia della cultura giuridica* 2 (1972), 55–88.

38. As pointed out by P. Legendre, *La pénétration,* 112–13. Concerning the legal education of clerics, Huguccio did not think that a bishop had to be particularly familiar with Roman law, cf. *Summa* D.23 c.2 *in lege Dei*: "i.e. in utroque testamento, in iure canonico, quod non solum verbotenus sed scrutabiliter scire tenetur, ut di.xxxviii Omnis [c.6]. Et nota quod dicit 'lege Dei' et non lege seculi. Non ergo exigitur ab episcopo ut sit exercitatus in lege seculari" (MS Admont 7, fol. 27va). See also n.6 above.

To illustrate these general observations, Huguccio's occasional remarks on the opinions of his secular counterparts, the civilians, offer a case in point. A comprehensive survey of all the pertinent passages in the *Summa* fully attests to the deliberate and moderate use Huguccio made of secular legal doctrine. Take, for instance, the following statistical considerations: While the overall number of texts referring to legists is very low (about 25), several among them include extensive reports on views held by eminent civilians. Besides a single reference to "dominus Aldricus," teachers such as Wernerius (Guarnerius) (5), Martinus (5), Placentinus (6), Bulgarus (7), and Johannes Bazianus (11) receive multiple mentions.[39] Sometimes, their names appear in clusters (7), lined up by Huguccio as participants in a debate among contemporary Roman lawyers. Likewise low in comparison is the number of passages in which Huguccio speaks of the "legiste" as an anonymous group (8).[40] In the search for motives that may have induced him to incorporate these digressions, however, we must move beyond our quantitative analysis to an examination of the contents.

Measured in numbers, the *Summa* hardly suggests that Huguccio had a strong interest in the intellectual disputes fought out at the neighboring schools of the legists. His scattered reports form an exception to the normal routine of his glossing of Gratian's textbook.

39. Aldricus (cf. J. Fried, *Zur Entstehung*, 187–88): *Summa* C.12 q.1 c.13: "*Expedit* usque *non sunt proprie* Cuius est ergo dominium vel proprietas rerum ecclesiasticarum? Dominus Aldricus dicebat quod est ipsius ecclesie i.e. ipsius loci sacrati conclusi a parietibus ecclesie qui in nullius bonis est" (MS Paris, B.N. lat. 15396, fol. 175vb; ed. C. Gross, *Das Recht an der Pfründe* [Graz, 1887], 100–101; E. Cortese, "Per la storia di una teoria dell'arcivescovo Mosè di Ravenna (m. 1154) sulla proprietà ecclesiastica," *Proceedings Salamanca* [Vatican City, 1980], 122 n.18; the name of "Guarnerius" appears at D.51 c.3 *verum etiam in sacerdotio constituti*; D.54 c.20 *episcopalis dignitas* (same context, see n.41 below); and in the texts nn.1 (identification uncertain) and 6 (twice), printed below, Appendix III; for Martinus, see the texts nn.1, 5 (twice), 6, 7 (twice), below, Appendix III; Bulgarus: *Summa* C.16 q.1 c.64 *non debent*; C.17 q.4 c.21 *novies*; plus the passages nn.1–2, 5–6, 7 (twice), edited below, Appendix III; Placentinus: cf. below, Appendix III, nn.1, 2, 6, 7 (twice), 8–9; Johannes Bazianus: *Summa* C.35 q.6 c.4 *vel ipsi*; and nn.1–4, 5 (twice), 6, 7 (twice), 9, below, Appendix III. The figures are based on an examination of MS Admont 7.

40. *Summa* D.1 c.2 *quia iustum est*; D.1 c.7 *violentie* (ed. S. Kuttner, *Kanonistische Schuldlehre von Gratian bis auf die Dekretalen Gregors IX.* [Vatican City, 1935], 338 n.2); D.29 a.c.1 *Sed notandum*; C.11 q.1 p.c.9 §1 *non flagitetur*; C.14 q.5 c.13 *A parte* (cf. n.43 below); C.22 q.4 c.22 *opprobium*; C.35 q.2/3 a.c.1 *Quia ergo*; and n.9 below, Appendix III.

In most cases, they were uninspired by the immediate context of the *Decretum*. In fact, only a small group of passages, discussing variant readings to be found in the authoritative sources, directly contributed to an improved understanding of Gratian's work. These instances, containing clarifications of a philological nature (4), all highlight the existence of intruded glosses in Justinian's *Novellae*, which Huguccio habitually attributed to "Guarnerius."[41] Yet the majority of references owed its inclusion in the *Summa* to Huguccio's own intellectual curiosity.

At times, the *Summa* interrupts the flow of the canonistic argument to venture a brief excursion into the legistic realm of thought. In a few cases, this occurs for purely illustrative purposes, as when Huguccio decided to present a legal definition or maxim.[42] Their overall number is relatively low, however, compared to those instances in which Huguccio deliberately pointed to a doctrinal difference between the two laws. In this latter group of texts, soon to develop into a literary genre of its own (*differentie*), the educational goal was to throw into particular relief a rule of canon law by juxtaposing it with the often contradictory principle prevailing in the civil sphere. As is witnessed by the *Summa*, Huguccio made occasional use of this propaedeutical tool in his lectures. He thereby addressed the "legiste" as a whole group rather than singling out one of them.[43] Still, he did not employ *differentie* to any great extent. Instead, his accounts of

---

41. E.g. *Summa* D.54 c.20 *episcopalis dignitas*: "Sed nonne sacerdotium precedens liberat? Utique, ar. supra e. Ex antiquis [c.9], Frequens [c.10]. Ergo episcopalis ordo non liberat. Dicunt quidam quod hoc non invenitur in corpore Autenticorum et ita male appositum fuit a Guarnerio vel alio. Sed in corpore Autenticorum invenitur. Unde hoc expresse colligitur, sc. in t. de scis. epis. § Sed hec quidem [Nov. 123 c.4], ubi hec verba inveniuntur: 'Post ordinationem vero servili et inscriptitia fortuna episcopos liberos esse precipimus' etc. Dicatur ergo hoc dictum esse secundum leges que nolunt sacerdotium liberare a servitute. Secundum canones hoc non potest esse" (MS Lons-le-Saunier 12.F.16, fol. 75vb). Huguccio had already addressed the same textual problem in his comment on D.51 c.3 *verum etiam in sacerdotio constituti*. Philological concerns are further treated at C.11 q.1 p.c.9 §1 *non flagitetur*.

42. On "furtum": C.14 q.5 c.13 *A parte*; a Leonine verse ("Ordine turbato succedis, Bulgare, nato"), attributed, like other ones included in the *Summa Coloniensis*, ed. G. Fransen and S. Kuttner, (MIC A 1.2; Vatican City, 1978), 161, to Bulgarus: C.16 q.1 c.64 *non debent*; on "iuramentum": C.22 q.4 c.22 *opprobrium*; for further casual remarks, see also C.17 q.4 c.21 *novies*; C.35 q.6 c.4 *vel ipsi*.

43. Similar digressions, dealing with doctrinal differences between the laws (cf. n.32 above), appear in the texts printed above (n.36) and below n.9, Appendix III.

the learned controversies among Roman lawyers represent the most conspicuous group of references to the legists.

The *Summa* includes ten of these reports on disputed points of doctrine, which secular lawyers soon came to collect and publish in separate monographs known as *Dissensiones dominorum*.[44] They are all concentrated in the commentary on part ii of Gratian's *Decretum,* where the influence of Roman jurisprudence was strongest. But this is not to say that Huguccio drew them from older decretist material.[45] As the edition and analysis of each of these texts in appendix III shows, it was rarely the works of his decretist predecessors that sparked Huguccio's interest. His decision to incorporate the *Dissensiones* rather attests to personal concerns and represents glimpses of his genuine, intellectual curiosity in the current teachings at the Bolognese schools of Roman law. Thanks to the encyclopedic range of his mind, the *Summa* preserves several monuments of Roman legal teaching prior to Azo, in what is probably its most significant contribution to the early history of secular jurisprudence.

To conclude this survey of Huguccio's doctrine on the relationship between canon and Roman law, it is illustrative to return to the works of Knox and Kalb.[46] Contrary to some of Kalb's claims, our evaluation of the decretist comments on *Distinctio* 10 of Gratian's *Decretum* has demonstrated that Rufinus went much farther than other decretists in allowing secular interference in ecclesiastical jurisdiction. This clearly challenges his allegiance, suggested by Kalb, with monastic and conservative ideals, yet it does not mean that Kalb altogether misrepresented Rufinus's critique of certain Roman legal in-

44. Edited by G. Haenel, *Dissensiones dominorum* (Leipzig, 1834); V. Scialoja, "Di una nuova collezione delle Dissensiones dominorum con l'edizione della collezione stessa," *Scritti giuridici* (Rome, 1934), 2.327–413. An update on the more recent research has appeared in P. Weimar, "Dissensiones dominorum," LMA 3 (1986), 1120–21.

45. Of the texts printed in Appendix III, only nn.6–8 seem to elaborate on earlier decretist references to the legists: N.6 (lines 1–4) on one by the *Summa Lipsiensis* (MS Leipzig, U.B. 986, fol. 142ra); n.7 on a comment by Stephan of Tournai, *Summa,* ed. J. F. v. Schulte, 228, also transmitted by the *Summa Lipsiensis* (MS Leipzig, U.B. 986, fol. 185vb); n.8 on the *Summa* of Sicardus, C.3 q.7, ed. K. W. Nörr, *Zur Stellung des Richters im gelehrten Prozess der Frühzeit: "Iudex secundum allegata non secundum conscientiam iudicat"* (Munich, 1967), 46.

46. Cf. above, at nn.12, 16. For the following, see Rufinus's comment on *Distinctio* 10 (n.16) and Huguccio's critical response (n.27).

stitutions. He only overstated his case when he saw in Rufinus's rejection of, for instance, Roman prescription and marital laws an exceptional principle involved. Huguccio actually agreed with much of what Rufinus had to say about prescription. At the same time, he became his fiercest opponent in expounding the legislative theories of *Distinctio* 10, which prompted him to assert the complete independence of the ecclesiastical laws from imperial authority. It is therefore evident that later canonists (including Huguccio) repeated Rufinus's rejection of uncanonical elements in Roman law, even though most of them did not share the views he had formulated in the context of *Distinctio* 10.

Returning, finally, to the argument of Knox, this essay does not challenge his analysis of several legal concepts employed by Rufinus and Stephan. Knox has argued convincingly that Rufinus's terminology carried connotations derived from the *forum internum,* whereas Stephan of Tournai tried to conform canon law to the rules of secular jurisprudence. Nevertheless, it seems that Knox overstressed the importance of Stephan's approach for the future development of canonistic doctrine and wrongly characterized Rufinus as backward and conservative. Actually, it is probably more accurate to see them as representing a wider spectrum of doctrinal alternatives. As we have seen, the succeeding generations of canonists did not lose sight of Rufinus's pastoral concerns. Twenty-five years after Rufinus and Stephan, Huguccio still insisted on *equitas canonica* as the ultimate criterion of ecclesiastical rules. He thus emphasized a tension that has always constituted one of the basic characteristics of the discipline—before and after the *Summa decretorum.*

Epilogue
The *Rigor Huguccionis*

THE PRECEDING pages have attempted to offer an illustration of Huguccio's lasting contribution to European legal history. They contain references to the modern scholarship on his doctrinal views; they have outlined the stages of his successful career as a teacher and ecclesiastical administrator; and they have surveyed the textual tradition of his *Summa* as it survives in the libraries all over Europe. The last chapter has examined a particular aspect of Huguccio's teachings, that of the applicability of Roman law in ecclesiastical jurisdiction. The treatment of this issue has served as an example of Huguccio's intellectual and argumentative skills. It has attested to his comprehensive grasp of older decretist doctrine and his great ability to transform a complex and disputed issue into coherent and clear-cut doctrine. These were the chief characteristics of Huguccio's accomplishment, which modern scholars have cited, with appreciation, as "a moment of synthesis."

Due to the lack of a printed text and other editorial tools, an exhaustive analysis of the *Summa* remains impossible.[1] There are, on the other hand, numerous detailed monographs on certain aspects of decretist doctrine that illustrate Huguccio's extraordinary ability to distill substance from the overwhelming mass of older canonistic dis-

1. Questions of method have been discussed by A. Stickler, "Sacerdotium et regnum," 575–80; summarized in B. Tierney, "Some recent work on the political theories of the medieval canonists," *Traditio* 10 (1954), 594–625, at 595–96; repr. in idem, *Church law*, n.i.

course. They also point up in his argument recurrent themes and fundamental notions. These underlying principles obviously served Huguccio as a sure guide, helping him to integrate the most intricate juridical problems into the powerful "synthesis" he had in mind. At the same time, they gave his conclusions an air of austerity and reflected a fundamentalist attitude that did not escape the attention of his contemporaries. Since the days of Johannes Teutonicus (fl. 1215), the "rigor Huguccionis," Huguccio's rigor, has acquired almost proverbial status.[2]

Huguccio's rigor came to the fore in numerous contexts. Johannes Teutonicus, for example, referred to it while discussing the use of weapons by clerics. The clerical garb, he agreed, prohibits the use of violence as a matter of course. Huguccio, however, carried this obligation to the utmost extreme, forbidding clergy the right to resort to potentially harmful weapons in self-defense. If a cleric killed the attacker, he not only sinned mortally, but should also face a temporal sanction. As a murderer, he had to be barred from promotion.[3] Elsewhere, Huguccio appeared just as unwilling to admit the threat of death as a valid excuse, psychologically or legally. Particularly interesting is his verdict of the famous ancient heroine Lucretia, who had chosen rape over death in order to denounce the rapist to her husband the next morning. In Huguccio's eyes, Lucretia did not deserve praise for her conduct. Due to her insufficient resistance to the rapist, she had committed a mortal sin. Treating the juridical consequences of

---

2. *Glossa ordinaria*, D.50 c.6: "H⟨uguccio⟩ tamen cum suo rigore dixit quod in nullo casu homicida potest promoveri," cited by S. Kuttner, *Kanonistische Schuldlehre von Gratian bis auf die Dekretalen Gregors IX. (1140–1234)* (Studi e testi 64; Vatican City, 1935), 369 n.4.

3. "Mihi videtur quod mortaliter peccat qui repercutit ferientem se iuste vel iniuste . . . nisi faceret hoc auctoritate iudicis. . . . Peccat tamen mortaliter unde repellitur a promotione. . . . Debemus enim . . . a nobis removere non repercutiendo sed opponendo et pretendendo aliquod obstaculum." *Summa* D.1 c.7 s.v. *violentie*, similarly D.50 c.6 s.v. *defendendo*: S. Kuttner, *Kanonistische Schuldlehre*, 351–53, 364–65; E. Hehl, *Kirche und Krieg*, 194–96, 236–37; also H. Maisonneuve, *Etudes*, 83–88; the analysis of Huguccio's thought in F. Russell, *The just war in the Middle Ages* (Cambridge, 1975), 86–126, does not sufficiently distinguish texts of the *Summa* from those of the *Continuatio prima* (*Summa Casinensis*), cf. E. Hehl, *Kirche und Krieg*, 191 n.745; as to "irregularitas" impeding clerical promotion, see F. Gillmann, "Zur Geschichte der Ausdrücke 'irregularis' und 'irregularitas,'" AKKR 91 (1911), 49–86, at 61–67; V. Piergiovanni, *La punibilità degli innocenti nel diritto canonico dell'età classica I: La discussione del problema in Graziano e nella decretalistica* (Milan, 1971), 176–80.

her case, Huguccio's interpretation remained relentless. The marital vows, he concluded, obliged Lucretia to preserve her chastity regardless of necessity. Since she had failed to do so, her husband could go to court and bring a charge of adultery.[4]

As in the case of Lucretia and the cleric in self-defense, the *Summa* treats questions of liability in an uncompromising fashion. The analysis focuses exclusively on the obligations of the marital and clerical status, which derive their binding effects from free consent.[5] Huguccio was anxious to disregard intervening factors. According to him, they could not modify the validity of the original contract.[6] To establish this principle, he did not distinguish clearly between the competences of the spiritual and the temporal court, and he treated sin and guilt as a continuum rather than as separate standards. Like the confessor, the judge of the external forum should focus on one's inner disposition to act against the rules of Christian conscience.[7]

4. The decretist debate on Lucretia, departing from *Summa* C.32 q.5 c.4 §2, has been examined in my article "Lucretia," 13–32.
5. The central role of mutual consent in the formation of marriage is emphasized at *Summa* C.27 q.2 (printed by J. Roman, "Summa d'Huguccio sur le Décret d'après le manuscrit 3891 de la Bibliothèque Nationale: Causa XXVII, Questio II [Théories sur la formation du mariage]," RHD 27 [1903], 745–805): for a good summary, M. Hussarek Ritter von Henlein, *Die bedingte Eheschliessung. Eine canonistische Studie* (Vienna, 1892), 82–87, whose treatment of conditional marital consent (69–82) is partly superseded by R. Weigand, *Die bedingte Eheschliessung im kanonischen Recht I: Die Entwicklung der bedingten Eheschliessung in kanonischen Recht. Ein Beitrag zur Geschichte der Kanonistik von Gratian bis Gregor IX.* (Munich, 1963), 203–18; cf. also idem, "Die Durchsetzung des Konsensprinzips im kirchlichen Eherecht," ÖAKR 38 (1989), 301–14. On intercourse, see in particular *Summa* D.13 a.c.1, C.32 q.2 c.4 s.v. *sed et alia plura sunt*: R. Abellán, *El fin y la significación sacramental del matrimonio desde S. Anselmo hasta Guillermo de Auxerre* (Granada, 1939), 17–25; R. Weigand, "Die Lehre der Kanonisten des 12. und 13. Jahrhunderts von den Ehezwecken," SG 12 (1967), 445–78, at 470–73; J. Brundage, *Law, sex, and Christian society in medieval Europe* (Chicago/London, 1987), 260–62, 281–82.
6. His outspoken criticism of recent papal legislation (JL 15176) to that effect is well known, *Summa* C.27 q.2 p.c.45 §3 s.v. *Sed concedatur* (ed. J. Roman, "Summa," 799–801; cf. R. Weigand, "Durchsetzung," 305–7), where Huguccio states that "papa etiam Lucius [III.] fuit in hac pessima opinione."
7. For Huguccio's understanding of sin, *Summa* D.40 c.5, De pen. D.5 c.1, and its theological background, S. Kuttner, *Kanonistische Schuldlehre,* 22–28; J. Gründel, *Die Lehre von den Umständen der menschlichen Handlung im Mittelalter* (Münster, 1963), 225–34 (with ed.). His concept of guilt, see also *Summa* D.25 p.c.3, D.81 c.1, shows parallel origins: S. Kuttner, *Kanonistische Schuldlehre,* 3–62. Criminal capacity and the capacity to sin coincide as well and can be presumed from age seven onward, *Summa* C.30 q.2 pr., De cons. D.4 c.76: F. Gillmann, "Die 'anni discretionis' im

Huguccio's refusal to divide strictly the realms of Christian morality (internal forum) and law (external forum) were, in turn, conditioned by his evaluation of the fundamental concepts of sin and guilt. Unlike most of his fellow canonists and theologians, Huguccio adhered to the Abelardian view, which measured both by taking into account solely the intention of the wrongdoer. This ruled out the existence of intrinsically bad acts, assuming instead that the focus of the confessor and judge should be on one's inner disposition to act against confessional and legal principles. In spelling out another, radical implication of the Abelardian theory, Huguccio also denied that the circumstances of an act could affect the degree of responsibility on the part of those who performed it. Accordingly, a Christian accepting rebaptism in the face of death proved to be just as ill-intentioned as another one who did so without any external threat.[8]

Whereas the theological premises of this doctrine had already been introduced into the canon law by Rufinus (fl.1164) and Sicardus (fl.1181), Huguccio surpassed them, as well as his successors, in his determination to extend their applicability into the legal sphere.[9] Of course, the ascertainment of each, guilt and sin, took place in a distinct forum and employed a different set of procedural principles. Huguccio recognized this fact by asserting that God alone had full cognizance of sinful intentions. Man's judgment depended instead on some sort of externalization, which rendered the misinterpretation of signs of wrongful behavior more likely.[10] The greatest degree of cer-

---

Kanon 'Omnis utriusque sexus' (c.21 conc. Lat.IV)," AKKR 108 (1928), 556–617, at 583–97; S. Kuttner, *Kanonistische Schuldlehre,* 124–29.

8. The case of forceful re-baptism offered one of the paradigms (*sedes materie*) for the decretist discussion of sin and guilt and their relationship, *Summa,* De cons, D.4 c.118 s.v. *coactos:* S. Kuttner, *Kanonistische Schuldlehre,* 301–7.

9. Similarities with the older views of Rufinus have been noted by J. Gründel, *Die Lehre,* 233–34; the analysis of R. Knox, "Academic language," 109–23, also suggests, despite contrary assertions (111), that Huguccio's notion of liability is closer to Rufinus's definition than to that of any other decretist.

10. This is recognized in priestly absolution, which Huguccio understood as valid before God provided it had not been given erroneously, *Summa,* De pen. D.1 c.88: F. Gillmann, "Clave non errante?" AKKR 110 (1930), 451–65, at 456–58. He also made a clear distinction between divine judgment and excommunication. The Church might pass a formally valid sentence condemning a person innocent before God, as in the case of an interdict, *Summa* D.90 c.21, or of someone related to the excommunicate, *Summa* C.1 q.4 p.c.9, C.9 q.3 c.103: V. Piergiovanni, *La punibilità,* 109–12, 139–

tainty could be attained in confession. It offered the Christian sinner an opportunity to reveal his innermost intentions without fear of legal consequences. Everything said was to be kept secret and could not be used as evidence in civil or criminal action. These principles, designed to secure forgiveness for the repentant Christian soul, clearly established the procedural autonomy of the internal forum.[11]

While accepting the distinctiveness of sin and guilt with regard to procedure, Huguccio treated them as a continuum whenever he was confronted with questions of liability and punishment. The peculiarities of this approach emerge nowhere more clearly than in his discussion of vows. Against prevailing canonistic opinion, Huguccio held that the obligation to fulfill a promise did not derive from any formal consideration. Other canonists had required certain formal qualifications in order to guarantee the sincerity of a vow. In their view, only "solemn" vows, such as those of priestly or monastic celibacy, ought not to be broken or modified under any circumstance. For Huguccio's intransigent voluntarism, it was instead intention alone which created the permanently binding effects of a vow, before God as well as man. As a result, a simple agreement between two persons on the streets enjoyed the same mandatory status as a ceremonial promise made to a priest in front of the altar.[12]

Having reduced the substance of a promise to the expression of intention alone, Huguccio saw little reason to distinguish the legal from the spiritual effects. Both the temporal and the confessional court were called upon to guarantee that Christians did not endanger their souls by falling short in any type of contractual obligation. Building on older canonists, Huguccio translated this principle into

---

48; due to error or because of insufficient cause, *Summa* C.11 q.3 pr. s.v. *Sed ponatur* usque *queritur* (see Introduction, n.28 above).

11. Cf. B. Kurtscheid, *Das Beichtsiegel in seiner geschichtlichen Entwicklung* (Freiburg, 1912), 71–73, citing *Summa* C.22 q.5 c.8; S. Kuttner, "Ecclesia de occultis non iudicat. Problemata ex doctrina poenali decretistarum et decretalistarum a Gratiano usque ad Gregorium PP.IX," *Acta congressus iuridici internationalis, Romae 1934* 3 (Rome, 1936), 225–46, at 238–43: citing D.50 c.6 s.v. *peccati.*

12. *Summa* C.17 q.1 a.c.1: "Sed numquid non tenetur quis de simplici promissione? Utique. Non enim voluit dominus differentiam esse inter communem loquelam et iuramentum, ut xxii q.v Iuramentum [c.12]," cited by A. Scharnagl, *Das feierliche Gelübde*, 153, and J. Brundage, *Crusader*, 53; other key passages in Huguccio's treatment of vows have been mentioned in the Introduction, n.42 above; for the corresponding evaluation of simple promises, see nn.13–14 below.

a theory that had no precedent in the Roman law of contracts. Instead, it was based on a biblical maxim, Mt. 18.15–17, which decretist doctrine formed into its own, procedural instrument, the *Denunciatio evangelica*.[13] Unlike Roman contractual theory, which admitted only claims that would formally fit into a rather limited set of actions, the *denunciatio* allowed a plaintiff to bring a suit before the episcopal court without complicated, formal requirements. The pertinent passages of the Gospel demanded that every Christian "tell the Church" if a fellow believer threatened to depart from a promise he had made in the presence of two or three witnesses. Canonists following Huguccio used the biblical instance to assert that such informal agreements could be legally enforced, thereby adding to the list of legal actions provided by Roman law. They were clearly concerned that a whole range of contracts might otherwise not be protected by the law. While this may reflect the legalization of an evangelical teaching, it is in stark contrast with the attitude of Huguccio, who elaborated exclusively on the spiritual dangers involved in going against former intentions. For him, the *denunciatio* rather served as a corrective tool in the interest of those who might break their promise. Huguccio made a sharp distinction between ordinary civil actions and the *denunciatio* by insisting that the latter obliged the offended party to put forward its claim. This mandatory character of the *denunciatio* he based on the duty of every Christian to help ensure the spiritual well-being of his fellow believers.[14]

13. The term refers to the evangelical precept, Matt. 18.15–17, to which the *Decretum* alludes at C.2 q.1 c.19 and C.22 q.5 c.8. On the canonistic *denunciatio* see P. Bellini, *L'obbligazione da promessa*, of which only part ii, chaps. 1 and 3 (195–256, 393–516) has been reprinted, slightly revised, in idem, *Denunciatio evangelica et denunciatio iudicialis privata. Un capitolo di storia disciplinare della chiesa* (Milan, 1986). The pertinent texts from Huguccio's *Summa* (next note) are quoted most extensively in J. Roussier, *Le fondement de l'obligation contractuelle dans le droit classique de l'Eglise* (Paris, 1933) appendix 1.

14. *Summa* C.2 q.1 c.19 s.v. *dic ecclesie*: "i.e. accusa coram ecclesiastico iudice non ad penam ordinariam sed denuntiando ad penitentiam. Est enim preceptum nec loquitur de accusatione ad penam ordinariam ad quam nullus cogitur invitus nisi casualiter. Sed loquitur de denuntiatione ad penitentiam ad quam quilibet precepto artatur, ar. i q.i Quisquis [c.5], ii q.vii Quapropter [c.47]" (Paris, B.N. lat. 15396, fol. 110vb); see also C.12 q.2 c.66 s.v. *oportebit absolvere*: P. Bellini, *L'obbligazione da promessa*, 195–213, 281–85, 409–12. The first canonist to equate *denunciatio* with an ordinary legal action was, apparently, Laurentius Hispanus, cf. ibid., 257–94, 393–

Huguccio's treatment of the vow and of simple contracts sufficiently indicates the underlying assumptions of his "rigor." Departing from an understanding of sin and guilt that values intention to the exclusion of intervening factors, he adopts a radically voluntaristic approach in evaluating questions of liability. Throughout the *Summa,* this approach appears with systematic consistency, suggesting Huguccio's resolve to treat secular offenses as just another manifestation of sinful behavior and a mere extension of spiritual concerns. Modern scholarship has supplied more illustrations of the same, fundamentalist attitude touching a wide variety of legal issues. Huguccio's strong appreciation of voluntary commitments thus emerges again in his doctrine of excommunication. In its most extreme form, the sanction prohibits all personal contacts with the excommunicate, including the members of his kin and family. Canonists, to be sure, exempted votive obligations from this rule, leaving, for example, the marital bond fully intact. Huguccio, however, went even farther than that in order to comply with his theoretical appreciation of informal promises. He concluded, accordingly, that every contract remained unaffected by excommunication, to ensure that the punishment would not cause any spiritual damage for the contracting partner who remained within the Church.[15]

Some aspects of Huguccio's use of *bona fides* (good faith), which also attests to the overlapping of confessional and legal concepts in his thought, were discussed in chapter III. There it was shown that the *Summa* required continuous good faith not only in prescription, but also in usucaption.[16] Huguccio was obviously very uncomfortable with the idea that someone might take advantage of the law without acting in good conscience, and vice versa. The impact of *bona fides* appears again when he explores the legitimacy of children born and

443. After Laurentius, "ex nuda promissione actio oritur" became a generally accepted principle. Huguccio's insistence on the obligation to enforce a promise was considered "too harsh," *nimis rigida,* by the author of the *Glossa Palatina,* C.2 q.1 c.9 (ca. 1215), and as *dura opinio* by Goffredus of Trano, *Summa titulorum* X 5.1.30, a generation later (ca. 1243): quoted after P. Bellini, *L'obbligazione da promessa,* 235 n.85, 237 n.89 = idem, *Denunciatio* 54 n.90, 57 n.94.

15. E. Vodola, *Excommunication,* 63–64, 130, 219–20 (ed.), citing *Summa* C.11 q.3 c.103, and C.15 q.6 c.4 s.v. *fidelitatem.*

16. Bibliographical references and the text of *Summa* C.16 q.3 a.c.1 s.v. *Quod autem prescriptionis,* have been given above, chap. III, n.36.

raised by parents who were presumably married. For Huguccio, the offspring enjoyed all the benefits of a regular marriage, as long as the marital partners believed that they were married canonically. Moreover, the same subjective standard of good conscience continued to prevail over law when only one of the spouses acted in good faith. Even then, Huguccio argued, the children could not be stripped of their right to become legitimate heirs of the respective parent.[17]

As perhaps the most surprising consequence of his "voluntarism," Huguccio also discussed the case of a man who, to avoid starvation, took food belonging to someone else.[18] Huguccio showed great originality in the way he denied that this incidence involved any unlawful violation of the rights of ownership. The task was further complicated by his resolve to rule out, too, that such a theft in necessity amounted to any degree of sin. As Huguccio argued, the cited case did, properly speaking, not constitute theft at all. Considering the minimal role his analysis of guilt and sin attributed to circumstance, he could not, of course, base his reasoning on the maxim "necessitas non habet legem," necessity knows no law. Instead, he resorted once again to his "voluntaristic" analysis, concluding that hunger rather than sinful greed or avarice represented the motive of the starving man.[19] Prevention of death, to be sure, did not necessarily prevail over another person's rights. Huguccio had demonstrated this in his treatment of Lucretia, in which he valued the marital obligations toward her husband more highly than her life. Consequently, the *Summa*

17. *Summa* C.34 q.1/2 c.5, C.35 q.7 c.5: A. Albisetti, *Contributo allo studio del matrimonio putativo in diritto canonico. Violenza e buona fede* (Milan, 1980), 22–23, 194–95, who cites Huguccio after S. Galgano, "Violenza nel consenso e matrimonio putativo," *Rivista di diritto civile* 13 (1921), 438–94, at 468–75.

18. *Decretum*, C.12 q.2 c.11, De cons. D.5 c.26: G. Couvreur, *Les pauvres ont-ils des droits? Recherches sur le vol en cas d'extrême nécessité depuis la Concordia de Gratien (1140) jusqu'à Guillaume d'Auxerre (m.1231)* (Analecta Gregoriana 111; Rome, 1961), 45–154. B. Tierney, "Natural rights language," 638–44, has also noted the significance of this case for the canonistic treatment of conflicts between objective laws and subjective rights.

19. *Summa* C.12 q.2 c.11 s.v. *ex inopia*: "Ego tamen credo quod non peccet quis in tali casu sc. cum utitur re alterius propter urgentem necessitatem famis": G. Couvreur, *Les pauvres*, 84–85. The notion of "necessitas non habet legem," which appears in the *Decretum* several times (e.g. C.1 q.1 p.c.39, De cons. D.1 c.11) was alien to Huguccio's concept of guilt. He vigorously denied the existence of absolute necessity (*perplexio*), as in *Summa* D.13 a.c.1: S. Kuttner, *Kanonistische Schuldlehre*, 257–70; G. Couvreur, *Les pauvres*, 66–80.

went on to prove that the rights of property occasionally ranked lower than the preservation of one's life. After all, canonists did not view property as guaranteed by natural law. It was rather an invention of society and reflected human sinfulness.[20] Huguccio developed this line of argument into a powerful obligation on the part of the property holder, who, in order to avoid sin, had to dispose of possessions in a socially responsible fashion. This implied that since it was actually the owner's own intention not to bring harm to any of his fellow Christians in need, a starving man could avail himself of the necessary food and presume the owner's automatic approval.[21]

It would be easy to add further illustrations of how Huguccio applied his "voluntaristic" premise to a whole range of confessional and legal matters. Repeating the basic evaluation of sin and guilt, they offer proof of an extraordinary consistency. Still, canon law included certain elements that could not possibly be reconciled with Huguccio's principal approach. Theological and formal considerations actually imposed a number of absolute limits on any attempt to evaluate canonical institutions by focusing exclusively on inner intentions. Huguccio himself was aware that these intentions could never be measured objectively by human judges, as they depended on some kind of externalization. While this merely expressed scepticism with regard to the ascertainment of sin and guilt, the rules of procedure provided more tangible restraints. Huguccio fully respected the principle that information obtained in a confessional situation could not be used in the external forum. This formed a concrete obstacle to his analysis of the human will, which separated sin from guilt in at least one respect.[22] Huguccio was, moreover, imbued with a sense of pro-

20. On the dispensability of property laws, G. Couvreur, *Les pauvres,* 119–54, and the literature cited in the Introduction, n.42; for Lucretia, see n.6 above.
21. "Nec committit furtum quia credit aut debet credere dominum esse permissurum, arg. di.lxxxvi Non satis [c.14], Pasce [c.21], quo casu non committitur furtum, ut Inst. de obl. que ex delicto nascuntur § Placuit tamen [Inst. 4.1.7]": *Summa* C.12 q.2 c.11 s.v. *ex inopia*; cf. D.47 c.8 s.v. *unius est criminis*: G. Couvreur, *Les pauvres,* 80–106, 293–96 (ed.). *Denunciatio evangelica* (nn.13–14 above) provided the poor with the appropriate procedural instrument to claim this right, ibid., 106–9. Huguccio's conclusions have elicited among modern authors the most favorable comments. They derive, however, from principles considered "rigoristic" in other contexts.
22. The problem of evidence admissible in the judicial courts was expounded by Huguccio at *Summa* C.3 q.7 c.4, C.30 q.5 c.11 s.v. *cuncta rimari* (cf. app. III, n.8):

cedural fairness. Like other decretists, he was constantly reminded of the idea by Gratian's quote of the Golden Rule (Matt. 7.12) in the opening passages of the *Decretum*. As a result, the *Summa* offers a systematic exposition of canonical procedure, which deals efficiently with the checks and balances of litigation. It gives an unprecedented account of the safeguards against any abuse of judicial authority, such as those restricting the use of evidence in court or guaranteeing the rights of the defendant. Modern studies have also observed that Huguccio went further than contemporaries in his concern for the judicial capacities and rights of Jews and women.[23] Apparently, he was ready to place his somewhat radical analysis of liability in a strictly formal procedural framework.

The greatest tension between voluntaristic and formal factors, between intention and circumstance, resulted, however, from Huguccio's doctrine of the sacraments. At the time he was writing the *Summa*, sacramental theology was still in its formative phase. An unmistakable indication of this was the decretal AD ABOLENDAM of Pope Lucius III (1184), which first included the willful misinterpretation of the sacramental tenets among the heretical offenses.[24] The

---

K. Nörr, *Zur Stellung des Richters,* 36–65; see also his treatment of presumptions, *Summa* C.11 q.1 c.25: R. Motzenbäcker, *Die Rechtsvermutung im kanonischen Recht* (Munich, 1958), 117–22.

23. G. Minnucci, *La capacità,* 107–20; W. Pakter, *Medieval canon law and the Jews* (Ebelsbach, 1988), 51–55 and passim, who states that Huguccio "often proposed the most equitable solution possible under contemporary canonical rules" (55). For further literature dealing with Huguccio's procedural views, see Introduction, nn.27–28, 30–35, chap. III, n.36 above, and app. III, n.1 below; also K. Neumeyer, *Die gemeinrechtliche Entwicklung des internationalen Privat- und Strafrechts bis Bartolus,* 2 (Munich, 1916), 110–16; A. Van Hove, "La territorialité et la personnalité des lois en droit canonique depuis Gratien (vers 1140) jusqu'à Jean d'Andreae (m. 1348)," RHD 3 (1922), 277–332; K. Weinzierl, *Die Restitutionslehre der Frühscholastik* (Munich, 1936); W. Onclin, "La contribution du Décret de Gratien et des décrétistes à la solution des conflits des lois," SG 2 (1954), 115–50; P. Landau, *Die Entstehung des kanonistischen Infamiebegriffs von Gratian bis zur Glossa ordinaria* (Cologne/Graz, 1966), passim; idem, "Ursprünge und Entwicklung des Verbotes doppelter Strafverfolgung wegen desselben Verbrechens in der Geschichte des kanonischen Rechts," ZRG Kan. Abt. 56 (1970), 124–56; H. Schmitz, *Appellatio extraiudicalis. Entwicklungslinien einer kirchlichen Gerichtsbarkeit über die Verwaltung im Zeitalter der klassischen Kanonistik* (Munich, 1970), 38–43. Respect for "rational" procedure is expressed, finally, in Huguccio's total rejection of the trial by ordeal, *Summa* C.2 q.5 c.20, and c.22: J. Baldwin, "The intellectual preparation for the canon of 1215 against ordeals," *Speculum* 36 (1961), 613–36, at 624–26.

24. JL 15109 = 1 Comp 5.6.11 = X 5.7.9; cf. W. Hageneder, "Der Häresiebe-

exact number of the proper ecclesiastical sacraments was just about
to be established at seven, thanks to the influence of the *Libri iv sen-
tentiarum* of Peter Lombard (ca. 1150). From the time of Stephan of
Tournai (ca. 1166), the decretists gradually adopted this teaching, yet
there remained major uncertainties regarding the finer points of doctrine.[25] Huguccio himself exceeded all of the other canonists in his
contribution to doctrinal development. None of them devoted as
much energy to exploring the ramifications of a debate that was still
ongoing.

Not surprisingly, the conclusions Huguccio formulated were again
heavily influenced by "voluntaristic" ideas. His treatment of penance
offers a primary example of this.[26] He made its sacramental effects
almost entirely dependent on the inner disposition of the sinner to
repent. Full contrition also involved for him the readiness to exter-
nalize it in the form of oral confession. Interestingly, however, Huguccio put little emphasis on the necessity to obtain the remission of
sin through priestly mediation. Instead, he argued that the choice of
the confessor might alter with the situation. Laymen, too, could receive penance and absolve from mortal sin, provided that a priest was
not available. In fact, he considered failure to take recourse to the
ordinary priest detrimental only insofar as it might reflect the sinner's
contempt for the Church (*contemptus ecclesie*) and call into question
the sincerity of his intention to repent.[27] Huguccio even seemed willing to eliminate priestly authority altogether from the sacramental
process. The priest's role as the ordinary administrator of abso-

griff," 82–83; and, for more recent literature, P. Diehl, "'Ad abolendam' (X 5.7.9)
and imperial legislation against heresy," BMCL 19 (1989), 1–11.

25. Details in F. Gillmann, *Die Siebenzahl der Sakramente bei den Glossatoren des
gratianischen Dekrets* (Mainz, 1909), including a discussion of texts from Huguccio's
Summa (24–37).

26. P. Anciaux, *La théologie du sacrement de pénitence au xiie siècle* (Louvain/
Gembloux, 1949), 360–61, 374, 443–47; regarding Huguccio's contribution to theology, see also above, Introduction, n.21.

27. *Summa,* De pen. D.1 c.62 s.v. *penitentia exterior,* De pen. D.1 p.c.87 s.v. *si
quam est iubendi,* discusses briefly the importance of contrition and externalization,
following Gandulphus; as to the need of priestly participation, see next note; the extraordinary recourse to lay confessors, *Summa* D.25 p.c.3 §4 s.v. *alterutrum,* De pen.
D.1 c.88, De pen. D.6 c.1: A. Teetaert, *La confession aux laiques dans l'église latine
depuis le viiie jusqu'au xive siècle* (Wetteren/Bruges/Paris, 1926), 220–26; P. Anciaux,
La théologie, 588–89.

lution was, as he concluded, based only on an ecclesiastical constitution.[28]

The tension between Huguccio's analysis of the will on the one hand, and proper sacramental form on the other, emerges no less dramatically in his discussion of marriage. As mentioned earlier, Huguccio categorically rejected the idea of the French decretist school, that the conjugal bond was formed in the two successive acts of marital consent and carnal consummation. Instead, he argued that the wedding vows alone created marriage with all its sacramental blessings. Although ensuing intercourse made it more difficult for the spouses to separate without mutual agreement, consensus already ruled out divorce.[29] This interpretation may well reflect Huguccio's

28. "Ad quid ergo postquam peccatum est dimissum per cordis contritionem precipitur et est necessaria exterior confessio et satisfactio? Responsio: . . . ne homo in aliud peccatum incidat, scil. in contemptu Ecclesie, que constituit ut homo confiteatur et satisfaciat," *Summa*, De pen. D.1 pr. s.v. *His breviter decursis,* De pen. D.1 c.1 and c.5: P. Anciaux, *La théologie,* 443–47. When Huguccio speaks of a *constitutio ecclesiastica,* he thinks of it as a divinely inspired, indispensable principle. An example is *Summa* D.64 c.5 s.v. *nec unus solus ordinare;* D.66 c.2 s.v. *archiepiscopus,* where he analyzes the origins of the episcopal *ordo.* For Huguccio, the order itself was instituted *inspiratione divina,* whereas the administration of confirmation became an episcopal prerogative only through a statute of the Apostles: *Summa* D.93 c.24–25, D.95 c.1 s.v. *concedimus.* Like a number of other sacramental regulations, it could consequently be revoked by the apostolic successor, the pope: F. Gillmann, *Spender der Firmung,* 4–13; idem, *Spender und äusseres Zeichen der Bischofsweihe nach Huguccio* (Würzburg, 1922), 1–5; R. Stenger, "The episcopacy as an ordo according to the medieval canonists," *Medieval studies* 29 (1967), 67–112, at 76–82, 86–89; also M. Ríos Fernández, "El primado," 7.144–49; again, Huguccio treated the prohibition to ordain women as based on an ecclesiastical constitution, *Summa* C.27 q.1 c.23 s.v. *ordinari,* implicitly allowing, therefore, papal dispensation: F. Gillmann, "Weibliche Kleriker nach dem Urteil der Frühscholastik," AKKR 93 (1913), 239–53, at 246–49; I. Raming, *Der Ausschluss der Frau vom priesterlichen Amt. Gottgewollte Tradition oder Diskriminierung?* (Cologne/Vienna, 1973), 102–9 (Engl. trans. by N. Adams, *The exclusion of women from the priesthood* [Metuchen, N.J., 1976], 61–64); finally, a *constitutio* is responsible, in Huguccio's mind, for the clerical vow of celibacy, which does not form an essential part of the higher orders, *Summa* D.27 pr. s.v. *Quod autem,* D.28 c.1 s.v. *approbata:* F. Liotta, *La continenza,* 114–25; *Summa* D.34 c.18: ed. S. Kuttner, "Pope Lucius III and the bigamous archbishop of Palermo," *Medieval studies presented to Aubrey Gwynn, S.J.,* ed. J. A. Watt et al. (Dublin, 1961), 409–54, at 442–43 (ed.), repr. with "Retractationes" in: S. Kuttner, *The history of ideas and doctrines of canon law in the Middle Ages* (London, 1980), n.viii.

29. The only exception was divorce on grounds of the "Pauline privilege," cf. above, chap. I, nn.26–33; marital consent also prevailed over the rights of ownership of a lord, who could neither invalidate it nor separate married slaves without their

association of sin with all sexual activity and offers another illustration of his respect for voluntary commitments. Difficulties arose, however, as soon as Huguccio went on to explore the intentions underlying marital consensus, which he analyzed with his usual rigidity. True consensus existed, properly speaking, only when the partners agreed to live in accordance with the nature of marriage. The constitutive elements of the institution included, above all, the ideas of permanence, exclusiveness, and the purpose of procreation. Any positive intention to exclude them from taking effect would, theoretically, nullify the marital agreement.[30] This conclusion reveals clearly the radical implications of Huguccio's "voluntaristic" approach. Modern scholars have often pointed out its impracticability in the courts. But to be sure, Huguccio was himself fully aware of the destabilization marriage would suffer if a spouse could revoke his consent by simply asserting that he had lacked proper intention in the first place. He consequently refrained from the full application of the voluntaristic principle. The respect for the sacrament, Huguccio warned, ought not to be diminished through the frivolous and preposterous assertion of tacit reservations against it. Presumed intentions, as expressed in the form of the wedding vows, should prevail over all doubts regarding their sincerity.[31]

---

agreement, *Summa* C.29 q.2 c.8 s.v. *Dictum est*: P. Landau, "Hadrian's Dekretale 'Dignum est' (X 4.9.1) und die Eheschliessung Unfreier in der Diskussion des 12. und 13. Jahrhunderts," SG 12 (1967), 511–53, at 534–36; J. Gilchrist, "The medieval canon law on unfree persons: Gratian and the decretist doctrines, ca. 1141–1234," SG 19 (1976), 271–301, at 289–92.

30. *Summa* C.27 q.2 c.10 s.v. *quia nullum divortium* (ed. J. Roman, "Summa," 758–59), C.32 q.2 c.6 s.v. *Solet* (discussed next note); for literature regarding the principal purposes of marriage, see n.5 above.

31. *Summa* C.27 q.2 c.2 s.v. *frustrantur* (ed. J. Roman, "Summa," 751): "Sed ecce isti sic contrahunt: 'Accipio te in meum' et econverso, sed animo non consentiunt. Quere ergo si sit matrimonium inter istos? Respondeo et dico quod re vera non est ibi matrimonium cum non sit ibi consensus. Ex quo tamen constat de verbis cogit eos esse simul, cum de intentione verborum eorum certificari non possit. Quod si illi confiteantur? Respondeo: non est credendum confessioni eorum. Possent enim hoc facere in fraudem matrimonii et sic quilibet posset separari ab uxore sua"; cf. F. Gillmann, *Die Notwendigkeit*, 33–38; following M. Hussarek Ritter von Henlein, *Bedingte Eheschliessung*, 74–78, the text has been disregarded by R. Weigand, *Bedingte Eheschliessung*, 203–18, who again cites *Summa* C.32 q.2 c.6 (cf. last note) to show that Huguccio, due to his "extreme Willenstheorie" (211), attributed an invalidating, "ehevernichtend" (214), effect to intentions incompatible with the nature of marriage. Hu-

Huguccio's emphasis on intention affected marriage and penance much more than the remaining sacraments. In dealing with them, he encountered a canonical tradition that rather stressed form and the mediation of the Church as essential for the attainment of salutary effects. When he discussed the validity of baptism, the Eucharist, and ordination, Huguccio in fact stated that the observation of proper form offered sufficient grounds for presuming the existence of proper intention. The resulting legal rights and obligations rested exclusively on the correct performance of the sacramental act.[32] Having proposed this absolute equation of form and intention, Huguccio systematically drew the doctrinal consequences. They emerge, for example, in his subtle analysis of the famous distinction between the capacity to exercise sacramental powers (*potestas ordinis*) and the actual right to do so (*potestas iurisdictionis*), conferred by ordination and ecclesiastical appointment, respectively.[33] The implications are further spelled out in Huguccio's treatment of forcefully administered baptism. In evaluating the legal effects of the act, he employs the same

---

guccio's statement: "Ego autem dico quod non est (matrimonium) . . . ubi non est consensus animorum," remains, however, without legal consequences, considering that he is quick to add: "licet probari non possit." Such inner dispositions against the marital union cannot be proven in court.

32. The validity of baptism, the Eucharist and ordination was discussed most specifically by the decretists in connection with simony, cf. *Summa* C.1 q.1 c.17, c.30 s.v. *Si fuerit iustus*, p.c. 39, c.73 s.v. *ratum*, p.c.97 §§2–5, C.9 q.1 pr. *Quod ordinatio*, also De cons. D.2 c.97 *non presumat*: H. Heitmeier, *Sakramentenspendung bei Häretikern und Simonisten nach Huguccio* (Analecta Gregoriana 132; Rome, 1964), 41–94; J. Weitzel, *Begriff und Erscheinungsformen der Simonie bei Gratian und den Dekretisten* (Munich, 1967), 134–48; T. Lehnherr, "Der Begriff," 372–79, 401–15 (ed.). The formal act of ordination, for example, immediately ended the state of servitude, regardless of the lord's consent, *Summa* D.54 c.9 *nec privilegia ecclesiarum*, cited in P. Landau, "Frei und Unfrei in der Kanonistik des 12. und 13. Jahrhunderts am Beispiel der Ordination der Unfreien," *Die abendländische Freiheit vom 10. zum 14. Jahrhundert*, ed. J. Fried (Sigmaringen, 1991), 177–96 at 188–91. Concerning baptism, see also n.34 below.

33. Huguccio clarified both terms through the use of a third concept, "potestas executionis," which has been thoroughly studied by T. Lehnherr, "Der Begriff," esp. 369–72; cf. R. Benson, *The bishop-elect*, 116–33; H. Heitmeier, *Sakramentenspendung*, 124–66; also, concerning "ordo," "iurisdictio," and "potestas clavium," Huguccio's interpretation of the "power of the keys": L. Hödl, *Die Geschichte der scholastischen Literatur und der Theologie der Schlüsselgewalt 1: Die scholastische Literatur und die Theologie der Schlüsselgewalt von ihren Anfängen bis zur Summa Aurea des Wilhelm von Auxerre* (Münster/W., 1960), 548–49; P. Anciaux, *La théologie*, 548–49.

concept of conditional as opposed to absolute coercion as in his discussion of votive obligations. But whereas, in the latter case, the binding effects were determined by subjective will, the validity of baptism was based on the objective standard of proper administration. Accordingly, a person resisting baptism had to avoid by all means that the sacramental act was performed on him. If he failed to do so, he was to be considered a Christian.[34]

Huguccio's voluntaristic understanding of guilt played a central role in his thought. Focusing on inner intentions at the expense of circumstantial factors, his assessment of liability took on an unusual rigidity. His appreciation of vows, contracts, and promises was strong enough to form a constitutional element in his ecclesiology. Neither papal command nor necessity could suspend the resulting legal obligations, which bound Christian conscience before God rather than man.

It is important to note, finally, that Huguccio's teachings reflect the full range of doctrinal options available to twelfth-century canonists. Gratian's *Decretum* had provided many excerpts from older canonical collections and contained numerous contradictory statements. Huguccio's predecessors had already noted the traditional coexistence of constitutional and absolutist elements in ecclesiastical government, of intention and circumstance in the evaluation of guilt and sin, and of penitential and disciplinary objectives in the various forms of punishment. To solve these tensions, they had also been forced to formulate their own dogmatic preferences. As mentioned, research has suggested that Sicardus of Cremona (fl. 1181) and Rufinus (fl. 1164) anticipated much of Huguccio's voluntaristic analysis of guilt,

34. "Si absoluta coactione quis baptizetur puta unus tenet eum ligatum et alius superfundit aquam . . . si tamen baptizetur sacramentum accipit quia sive volens sive nolens sive vigilans sive dormiens quis baptizetur in forma ecclesie sacramentum accipit," *Summa* D.45 c.5 s.v. *adsociatos, unctos corpore domini participes*; also C.1 q.1 p.c.58 s.v. *mos est sacerdotibus*, De cons. D.4 c.31 *explorarem*: F. Gillmann, "Notwendigkeit," 33–44; M. Condorelli, *I fondamenti giuridici della tolleranza religiosa nell'elaborazione canonistica dei secoli xii–xiv* (Milan, 1960), 52–58. Baptism conferred on someone who is held involuntarily is valid, although Huguccio suggests that he might not be compelled to live as a Christian, *Summa* D.45 c.5: "Sed si coacti fidem suscepissent et numquam postea consensissent, non essent cogendi vivere secundum ritum Christianorum"; similarly, forceful baptism of Jews was valid, but nevertheless rejected by Huguccio, *Summa* C.28 q.1 c.11 s.v. *Iudeorum*: W. Pakter, *Jews*, 322–23; on the absolutely binding nature of votive obligations, see n.12 above.

whereas Stephan of Tournai put emphasis on procedural questions and thus came to distinguish sharply between sinful and criminal conduct. Canonists after Huguccio continued to develop their own conceptual hierarchies and gradually moved away from Huguccio's rigid voluntarism. They soon admitted that circumstance could modify intention in the form of the Roman concept of *metus*, fear, allowed numerous dispensations from vows and contracts, left the enforcement of simple promises to the discretion of the damaged party, and undermined the validity of marriage by consent only. In this way, they gave in to a more realistic appreciation of changing situations. By abandoning the austere simplicity of Huguccio's extreme voluntarism, however, they also lost sight of his accomplishment as a systematic thinker. History proved that the *Summa* represented only "a moment" of synthesis.

A Cumulative List of *Extravagantes*
Cited in the *Summa*

At least from the time of Simon of Bisignano and the appearance of his *Summa* (1179–81), it was common among the decretists to include in their comments authoritative texts transmitted outside (*extra*) of Gratian's *Decretum*. In Huguccio's *Summa,* mentions of "extra(vagantes)" or, in his language, "extra(vagantia)," appear numerous times. The present inventory provides an alphabetically ordered index of these references. Each entry is analyzed in rubrics, indicating:

a. the incipit used by Huguccio
b. the JE-, JK-, JL-, WH- or Po.- number (if applicable)
c. the appropriate reference to the *Compilationes antique*
d. the appropriate reference to the *Liber extra*
e. quotes from the *Summa* relevant for identification (including varying incipits).

The list cannot claim completeness. While some omissions are due to oversight or identical incipits, others go back to terminological inconsistencies for which twelfth-century canonists were themselves responsible. Technically speaking, every legal text not included in the *Decretum* could be termed "extra." However, decretists often preferred to distinguish these materials according to varying forms of transmission. As his older colleagues had done, Huguccio addressed as "paleae" texts known to have been integrated into the *Decretum* sometime after Gratian had completed the work. He also treated as distinct those chapters that had been supplied from the *Decretum* of Burchard of Worms. They were obviously available to Huguccio through separate lists, because he cited them as: "B.⟨urchardus⟩ l.⟨iber⟩ iii Si quis" and the like.[1] The present index shows further that the *Summa* is rather spe-

---

1. F. Gillmann, *Paucapalea und Paleae bei Huguccio* (Mainz, 1908), revised version of an article in AKKR 88 (1908), 466–79, 783, also repr. in R. Weigand (ed.), *Schriften Franz Gillmann,* 1, n.7, has assembled from Huguccio's *Summa* references to "paleae"; the use of "paleae" and quotations from Burchard in older decretist glosses have been examined by R. Weigand, "Burchardauszüge in Dekrethandschriften und ihre Verwendung bei Rufin und als Paleae im Dekret Gratians," AKKR 158 (1989), 429–51; idem, "Paleae und andere Zusätze in Dekrethandschriften mit dem Glossenapparat 'Ordinaturus Magister,'" AKKR 159 (1990), 448–63; also P. Landau, "Vorgratianische Kanonessammlungen bei Dekretisten und in frühen Dekretalensammlungen," *Proceedings San Diego* (Vatican City, 1992), 93–116.

cific about the origins of conciliar enactments, particularly those from Tours (1163) and Lateran III (1179): "In conc.⟨ilio⟩ Rom.⟨ano⟩," "in conc. Turon⟨ensi⟩." The expression "extravagantia" therefore seems to exclude items that reached Huguccio under a heading other than *Collectio extravagantium*.

The texts deriving from interpolations in *Decretum* manuscripts, from Burchard, or recent councils were outnumbered by the steadily increasing output of papal legislation. Canonists anxiously assembled the new papal decretals in order to keep their curricula up to date. From insignificant beginnings in the form of appendices to the *Decretum,* this material soon developed into separate *Collectiones extravagantium,* ever growing in size and sophistication of arrangement. On the eve of Bernard of Pavia's *Compilatio prima,* the first collection to be accepted generally (1191), Huguccio and his colleagues had a wide range of similar works at their disposal. These works offered them fresh legal arguments, to which they referred indiscriminately as "extra."[2]

However, the divisions between the various categories of "extra" were not always strictly observed. The *Summa* shows that the term was employed not only in a narrow but also in its broader sense. There are instances in which conciliar texts, excerpts from Burchard, or "paleae" are likewise cited as "extra." There are even cases in which Huguccio addressed the same passage once as "extra" and once as a regular chapter of the *Decretum.*[3] This makes it necessary to apply Huguccio's own, subjective standards in order to determine which material has to be included in the present inventory. As a result, "paleae" and Burchardian texts are omitted as long as they do not appear as "extra" in the *Summa.*

The following list would be much more deficient without the kind collaboration of Charles Duggan (London). Besides identifying some of Huguccio's references to "extra," he also suggested that the author of the *Summa* must have had access to a source similar to the *Collectio Lipsiensis* (Lips.). Certain observations may illustrate, in conclusion, that Duggan's hypothesis deserves further study. In fact, a significant number of Huguccio's quotations can be traced to Lips.[4] The strongest evidence comes from two decretals, CUM CLERICI, and QUESITUM (JL 15176), which so far have been found only in this

2. For a comprehensive account of twelfth-century decretal collections and their development, see P. Landau, "Die Entstehung der systematischen Dekretalensammlungen und die europäische Kanonistik des 12. Jahrhunderts," ZRG Kan. Abt. 65 (1979), 120–48; a full inventory of the surviving texts can be found in W. Holtzmann, *Studies,* xx–xxxi (with further bibliography).

3. DE ILLIS offers an illustrative case. Huguccio cited it as "extra" at D.81 c.8, as "B. l.xi De illis (c.45)" and "palea" (= C.6 q.3 c.5) at C.6 q.3 c.4 (ed. F. Gillmann, *Paucapalea,* 5 [470]); VIDUAS AUTEM (= C.27 q.1 c.8) appears as "extra" at C.20 q.1 c.4, elsewhere, at C.27 q.1 c.3 (ed. Gillmann, *Paucapalea,* 15 n.11 [483]), as a regular chapter of Gratian"s *Decretum.*

4. The abbreviations used in the following for twelfth-century decretal collections correspond to those given by W. Holtzmann, *Studies* (n.2 above).

collection (31.17, 59.16). Similarly, RELIGIOSI (Lips. 59.12) was not available in any other compilation of Huguccio's time. In several instances, Lips. figures among the very few Italian compilations Huguccio may have consulted, as in the case of CONSTITUTUS (1.19; also surviving in Cus. 36), or EX LITTERIS DILECTI (Lips. 59.42 and Cus. 23). Again, Lips. (31.18) is unique among the Italian sources in matching literally the incipit of EGO PE-TRUS, quoted by the *Summa*.

On the other hand, Lips. does not cover all of Huguccio's references to "extra." A number of them remain yet to be identified (CUM B. IUVENIS, EX ORDINE ROMANO, GRATUM, QUANDO, VIDETUR TIBI). The *Summa* itself seems to be the oldest testimony to the status of ESTOTE (from Lk 6.36–37) as "extra." It cannot be ruled out, therefore, that Huguccio supplied the materials of Lips. by taking recourse to additional compilations. He may have had on his desk several primitive Italian collections which preserve unusual "extravagantia." This is indicated by rare incipits such as IAM TERTIO (Cus. 37), IN EXCEPTIONIBUS (Flor. 50.ii, Ambr. 29.i.), and VIDETUR NOBIS (Ambr. 20; not cited as "palea" [= C.35 q.6 c.2] by Huguccio). The eighth-century *Dionysio-Hadriana* was probably also within his reach, since SI QUIS CONTRA SUAM (Dion., Conc. Carthag. 13) and PLACUIT UT SI QUISQUAM (ibid. 119) are not known to have made their way through intermediary collections. That Huguccio's acquaintance with recent legislation went beyond a single compilation somewhat akin to Lips. is attested, finally, by his citation of CON-SULUISTI SI CAUSA in connection with IN EMINENTI (Lips. 47.40). He did not notice that both incipits referred to identical passages in one and the same decretal (JL 14350). CONSULUISTI SI CAUSA points to a version that did not circulate widely. Today, it survives only in the French *Collectio Brugensis* (47.22).

(a)	(b)	(c)	(d)
ACCEPISTI	—	1 Comp 4.16.1	X 4.15.1
(e) C.33 q.1 c.3: "Spatium duorum mensium statutum est coniugatis frigidis."			
ACCEPTA	JL 13984	1 Comp 2.9.2	X 2.13.3
(e) C.3 q.1 a.c.1: "Non est audienda exceptio . . . nisi ei obiciatur ab adversario exceptio iuramenti vel facti."			
ACCESSIT AD PRESENTIAM	JL 13887	1 Comp 4.2.6	X 4.2.5
(e) C.3 q.7 p.c.1: "Filii nati tunc cum credebatur esse matrimonium . . . legitimi sunt reputandi."			
AD AUDIENTIAM	JL 14034	1 Comp 1.20.2	X 1.28.1
(e) C.2 q.5 c.20: "Ar. quod interpretatio vel exceptio que non habetur in canone non est admittenda."			

(a)	(b)	(c)	(d)

AD AUDIENTIAM · JL 13304 · 1 Comp 2.17.3 · X 2.24.7

(e) C.15 q.6 c.4: "Nam et usure que ex toto sunt indebite videntur persolvi . . . si iuramento sint promisse."

[AD AUDIENTIAM · see AD NOSTRAM NOVERITIS]

AD AURES · JL 13876 · 2 Comp 2.19.6 · X 2.28.33

(e) C.2 q.6 c.16: "Si autem non tenet [appellatio] potest excommunicari."

AD AURES · JL 13163 · 1 Comp 4.13.2 · X —

(e) C.27 q.2 p.c.30: "Alex. sic distinguit: . . . Si [quis] . . . attinentem [uxori sue] in tertio gradu vel ulteriori [cognoscit] . . . reddere et debet [debitum]."

AD AURES · JL 14158 · 1 Comp 3.33.19 · X —

(e) C.16 q.7 c.23: "Venditione per se transferri non potest ius patronatus."

AD HEC · JL 13587 · 1 Comp 3.22.7 · X 3.5.13

(e) C.12 q.2 c.37: "Consuetudo est in quibusdam ecclesiis quod clericus moriens debet disponere de omnibus fructibus sue prebende . . . usque ad annum."

AD HOC · JL 14013 · 1 Comp 3.19.1 · X 3.23.1

(e) C.12 q.2 c.73: "Clericus moriens possit disponere de omnibus fructibus sue prebende percipiendis usque ad annum."

AD HOC CONTINGAT · JL 13949 · 1 Comp 2.10.1 · X 2.14.1

(e) C.3 q.9 a.c.1: "Si vero [reus] infra annum non venerit non audietur postea de possessione."

AD HOC IN BEATORUM · JL 12448 · 1 Comp 5.28.6 · X 5.33.5

(e) C.6 q.4 c.6: "Ar. quod quamvis iuret se obediturum sententie tamen potest appellare"; C.11 q.3 c.108: "Alex. dicit."

AD NOSTRAM · JL 14117 · 1 Comp 3.26.10 · X 3.30.10

(e) C.16 q.1 p.c.41: "Alexander sc. III . . . ex speciali favore Trecensis episcopi dixit."

AD NOSTRAM NOVERIS · JL 13854 · 1 Comp 3.27.8 · X 3.31.8

(e) C.17 q.2 c.1: "Quid enim si fiat sine probatione [episcopi]? Numquid non erit monachus? Utique."

AD NOSTRAM NOVERITIS · JL 13804 · 1 Comp 2.17.3 · X 2.24.7

(e) C.10 q.2 c.2: see CONQUESTUS; cf. D.27 c.6: AD AUDIENTIAM.

AD NOSTRAS AURES · JL 13865 · 1 Comp 2.20.3 · X 2.28.3

(e) C.11 q.1 c.38: "Coercio monachorum spectat ad abbatem."

AD PETITIONEM · JL 13972 · 1 Comp 3.27.1 · X 3.32.8

(e) D.32 c.14: "Compellenda est ut intret monasterium si vir eius efficitur monachus vel conversus."

(a)	(b)	(c)	(d)

APOSTOLICAM   JL 8272   1 Comp 5.35.2   X 3.43.2

(e) C.1 q.1 c.48: "Ibi presbiter vocatur ab Alexandro de solo facto."

ATTENDENTES   JL 13427   —   X —

(e) C.16 q.3 p.c.15: "Non ergo . . . laicis concedi possunt [decimi] quoad iura, leprosis tamen causa paupertatis."

AUDITA   JL 14143   1 Comp 2.9.4   X 2.13.4

(e) C.3 q.1 a.c.1: see SICUT EX LITTERIS.

CAUSAM QUE   JL 14070   1 Comp 1.4.17   X 1.6.8

(e) D.61 c.13: "Alexander . . . videtur contradicere in illo extra . . . ubi monache Sancte Magarete stare compelluntur electioni episcopi."

CAUSA QUE VERTITUR   JL 14010   1 Comp 2.13.19   X 2.20.19

(e) C.35 q.2/3 c.20: "Si dubitetur de tenore alicuius rescripti eius interpretatio a principe est expetenda."

CLERICI IN SACRIS   —   1 Comp 1.28.1   X 1.37.1

(e) D.81 c.23: "In concilio Romano (c.12)."

CLERICOS   JL 14093   1 Comp 4.2.4   X 3.2.4

(e) D.81 c.23: "Honore privetur si admonitus non dimittit cohabitationem feminarum"; C.27 q.1 c.17: "Alex. III scribens Salernitano."

COMMISSE   JL 11660   1 Comp 3.26.18   X 3.30.4

(e) C.16 q.1 p.c.41: "Episcopus contra privilegium pape nil potest facere."

CONQUERENTE NOBIS   JL 13795   2 Comp 2.7.1   X 2.13.7

(e) C.3 q.1 c.2: "Facta vero restitutione [spoliatorum] licite potest agere civiliter."

CONQUESTI SUNT   JL 17642   2 Comp 5.18.11   X 5.39.22

(e) C.17 q.4 c.5: "Alexander voluit alludere consuetudini hodierne: . . . Illi qui committunt sacrilegium . . . hoc ipso habentur excommunicati."

CONQUESTUS   JL 14167   1 Comp 4.18.1   X 4.17.1

(e) D.34 c.13: "Similiter . . . eam ducendo legitimat eos [proles]."

CONQUESTUS   JL 13979   1 Comp 5.15.10   X 5.19.8

(e) C.10 q.2 c.2: "Fructus debent computari tantum in sortem et non in usuram."

CONSTITUTUS   JL 14081   —   X —

(e) C.1 q.7 c.15: "Ar. quod lapsi etiam post penitentiam de iure restitutionem petere non possunt."

CONSULTATIONIBUS   JL 12636   1 Comp 3.33.23   X 3.24.4

(e) D.79 c.7: "Non enim licet alicui occupare locum viventis"; C.3 q.3 a.c.1 = 1 Comp 1.21.15 = X 1.29.10; C.27 q.2 c.22: PROPOSITUM = 1 Comp 4.7.1 = X 4.7.1.

(a)	(b)	(c)	(d)

[CONSULUISTI SI CAUSA   see IN EMINENTI]

CONSULUIT   JL 13790   1 Comp 4.19.2   X —

(e) D.81 c.5: "Consanguinei matrimonialiter coniuncti licet multo tempore steterint simul separandi sunt . . . Ar. contra . . . in extra"; C.35 q.6 c.1: "Alex."

CONSULUIT   JL 14025   1 Comp 5.34.8   X —

(e) D.90 c.5: "Si [quis] tamen antequam esset monachus vel canonicus regularis tale sacrilegium [sc. manus iniciendi in clericum] commiserit a papa est absolvendus."

CONSULUIT NOS   JL 14005   1 Comp 4.6.7   X 4.6.4

(e) C.33 q.4 c.10: "Cum ergo interdicto quod impedit matrimonium contrahendum et non dirimit contractum."

CONSULUIT NOS   JL 13740   1 Comp 3.33.18   X 3.38.15

(e) D.56 a.c.1: "Filii sacerdotum cum . . . geniti sunt de propriis uxoribus post sacrum ordinem . . . iure communi promoveri non possunt"; D.56 c.8: "Alex. III."

CONSULUIT NOS   JL 14071   1 Comp 2.20.18   X —

(e) C.11 q.3 c.27: "Ubi appellatio inhibetur ipsa appellatio interposita non valet."

CONTINEBATUR   JL 14033   1 Comp 3.9.2   X 3.10.2

(e) D.27 c.1: "Ar. taciturnitatem pro consensu haberi."

CONTINEBATUR   JL 13856   1 Comp 5.10.9   X 5.12.9

(e) D.50 c.39: "Omnis ludus inde prohibitus clerico qui potest esse occasio mali."

CONTINEBATUR   JL 14101   1 Comp 3.24.6   X 3.28.4

(e) C.13 q.2 p.c.8: "Omnes res illius qui intrat monasterium efficiuntur ipsius monasterii preter legitimam"; C.19 q.3 c.8: "Alex. III."

CUM AB ECCLESIARUM   JL 13936   1 Comp 1.23.3   X 1.31.3

(e) D.67 c.2: "Etiam plebanus ad tempus suspendit."

CUM APOSTOLUS SE   —   1 Comp 3.34.6   X 3.39.6

(e) D.34 c.1: "Credo quod venatio ex toto sit prohibita episcopis . . . in concilio Romano (c.4)."

CUM B. IUVENIS

(e) C.2 q.1 c.10: "Sepe appellans remittitur ad eundem a quo appellaverit sed volens"; C.27 q.2 p.c.45: "Urbanus in extra."

CUM CLERICI   JL 14056   —   X —

(e) C.16 q.1 c.54: "Consuetudo maiorum dummodo canonibus non obviet pro lege tenenda [est]."

CUM CHRISTUS   JL 12785   1 Comp 5.6.5   X 5.7.7

(a)	(b)	(c)	(d)

(e) D.19 c.1: "Peccant illi qui dicunt Christum non esse aliquid secundum quod est homo."

| CUM DE TUA | JL 12367 | 1 Comp 1.12.3 | X 1.20.2 |

(e) D.49 c.1: "Vitium [albuginiei] non repellat nisi nimiam inducat deformitatem."

| CUM ET PLANTARE | — | 1 Comp 5.28.3 | X 5.33.3 |

(e) C.16 q.7 c.32: "In concilio Romano (c.9)."

| CUM IN APOSTOLICA | JL 15729 | 1 Comp 4.1.20 | X 4.1.18 |

(e) C.28 q.1 c.16: "Videtur Urbanus dissentire ab Alexandro."

| CUM IN CUNCTIS | — | 1 Comp 1.4.16 | X 1.6.7 |

(e) D.47 c.4: "In quolibet prelato ecclesie necessaria est scientia. Aliter ordinari non debet, ut in concilio Romano (c.2)."

| CUM IN ECCLESIE | — | 1 Comp 5.2.8 | X 5.3.9 |

(e) D.94 c.3: "In concilio Romano (c.7)."

| CUM IN OFFICIIS | — | 1 Comp 3.22.4 | X 3.26.7 |

(e) D.70 c.2: "In concilio Romano (c.15)."

| CUM IN QUIBUSDAM | — | 1 Comp 5.3.2 | X 5.4.2 |

(e) C.21 q.2 c.5: "Non enim ibi constituendi sunt [decani vel archipresbiteri] aliter quam sub annuo pretio (Tours 1163, c.7)."

| CUM INSTITISSET | JL 13983 | 1 Comp 4.6.4 | X — |

(e) D.40 c.8: "Si ergo laicus de facto ordinetur in sacro ordine nil ordinis accipit."

| CUM INTER IO. | JL 14194 | 1 Comp 4.18.2 | X 4.17.2 |

(e) D.34 c.13: "Et est legitima [proles] ut tantum est ibi matrimonium."

| CUM NON IGNORETIS | JL 11665 | 1 Comp 1.22.1 | X 1.30.1 |

(e) D.93 c.26: see QUAMVIS SIMUS.

| CUM NOS TIBI | JL 13164 | 1 Comp 3.9.3 | X 3.10.3 |

(e) C.12 q.2 c.73: "Revocatur quod ab [episcopo] datur sine consensu clericorum."

| CUM NUNTIUS | JL 13249 | 1 Comp 2.13.11 | X 2.20.12 |

(e) C.14 q.2 c.1: "Aliter non repelluntur [canonici] quia sunt domestici."

| CUM VOS PLERUMQUE | JL 13822 | 1 Comp 1.23.4 | X 1.31.4 |

(e) C.9 q.3 c.8: "Mortuo episcopo res illius ecclesie debent esse in potestate yconomi."

| CUM SACROSANCTA | JL 12020 | 1 Comp 2.20.5 | X 2.28.5 |

(e) D.84 c.2: see REPREHENSIBILIS; C.2 q.6 c.16: "Alexandri."

| CUM SATIS SIT ABSURDUM | JL 13898 | 1 Comp 1.15.4 | X 1.23.4 |

(a)	(b)	(c)	(d)

(e) D.25 c.1: "Sed Alexander III dicit quod archidiaconus [non] . . . potest se defendere in danda cura animarum sine speciali mandato episcopi."

| CUM SECULUM | JL 13960 | 1 Comp 3.33.16 | X 3.38.13 |

(e) C.16 q.2 a.c.1: "Ex donatione laicorum tantum ius patronatus consequuntur monachi."

| CUM SIS PREDITUS | JL 13899 | 1 Comp 3.28.4 | X 3.32.4 |

(e) D.32 c.14: "Si iuvencula est compellenda est ut intret monasterium si vir eius efficitur monachus vel conversus"; D.77 c.6: "Alexander."

| CUM SIT ROMANA | JL 14126 | 1 Comp 4.22.1 | X 4.21.3 |

(e) D.34 c.20: "Sacerdotalis benedictio est sacramentum et ideo non debet iterari." D.65 c.9 = 1 Comp 5.2.9 = X 5.3.10; C.15 q.6 c.4 = 1 Comp 2.17.2 = X 2.24.6.

| CUM TU FILI | JL 13894 | 1 Comp 2.13.16 | X 2.20.16 |

(e) C.2 q.6 c.16: "Ar. quod excommunicatio post appellationem facta neminem ligat"; C.11 q.3 c.4: "Alex."

| CURA PASTORALIS | JL 13893 | 1 Comp 3.33.13 | X 3.38.11 |

(e) D.63 c.7: "Investitura . . . nullus debet recipere a laico . . . nisi postea consensu episcopi vel . . . ratione prescriptionis defendatur, ut in extra Alex."; C.16 q.7 c.12: "Ut Alex. III."

| DE FRANCIA | — | 2 Comp 4.1.1 | X 4.1.1 |

(e) C.27 q.2 c.51: "In matrimonio . . . non est certa forma statuta."

| DE HOC AUTEM | JL 14110 | 1 Comp 5.2.10 | X 5.3.11 |

(e) C.1 q.3 c.2: "Cui restituenda est pecunia simoniace recepta? . . . Ecclesie in cuius ignominiam data est . . . ar. in extra Alex. III"; D.30 c.17: DE HOC ETIAM.

| DE ILLIS | — | 1 Comp 5.14.1 | X 5.17.1 |

(e) D.81 c.8: "Non ergo clericus depositus tradendum est curie"; C.6 q.3 c.4: "Palea."

| DE ILLIS QUI | JL 13969 | 1 Comp 4.2.12 | X 4.2.9 |

(e) C.12 q.1 c.1: "Idem est de illis qui contrahunt sponsalia in minoritate"; C.30 q.2 c.1: "Alex."

| DE PEREGRINATIONIS | JL 13916 | 1 Comp 3.29.1 | X 3.34.1 |

(e) D.82 c.5: "Ar. quod una pena potest commutari in aliam et quod id quod tenemur facere aliud pro eo faciendo licite compensatur."

| DIGNUM | JL 10445 | 1 Comp 4.9.1 | X 4.9.1 |

(e) C.29 q.1 c.8: "Item Adrianus hoc dicit."

| DIGNUM EST | JL 13951 | 1 Comp 1.4.19 | X — |

(e) D.63 c.10: "Ex nuda electione . . . nil iuris acquiritur electo"; D.63 c.10: "Alex."

(a)	(b)	(c)	(d)

DILECTI FILI | JL 13934 | 1 Comp 2.20.1 | X 2.28.1

(e) C.11 q.3 c.36: "Hic non auditur postea de crimine sed de contumacia sive excommunicatione"; C.12 q.2 c.61: "Alex."

DILECTUS | JL 14023 | 1 Comp 3.26.6 | X 3.30.8

(e) C.16 q.1 p.c.41: "Que [monachi] colonis excolenda tradunt et tenentur dare decimas."

EA QUE HONESTATIS | JL 15171 | 1 Comp 3.8.3 | X —

(e) C.7 q.1 c.14: "Ar. quod de beneficio vel ecclesia non vacante licite potest fieri promissio. Sed prohibetur . . . in extra."

EGO PETRUS | — | 1 Comp 1.4.20 | X 2.24.4

(e) D.23 c.6: "Omnes . . . iurant fidelitatem pape."

EPISCOPUM | — | 1 Comp 5.22.1 | X 5.24.1

(e) D.34 c.1: see CUM APOSTOLUS; ibid.: "Palea."

ESTOTE | — | 1 Comp 5.37.7 | X 5.41.2

(e) D.21 c.9: "Sic de adulterio et furto et similibus que non possunt bene fieri."

EX CONQUESTIONE C. MULIERIS | JL 13766 | 1 Comp 4.21.2 | X —

(e) C.32 q.7 c.18: "Ar. quod nullus tenetur reddere dotem adultere."

EX LITTERIS | JL 13953 | 1 Comp 3.33.9 | X 3.38.7

(e) C.16 q.7 c.26: "Transfertur [ius patronatus] ratione universitatis . . . nisi specialiter excipiatur, ut Alex. III."

EX LITTERIS | JL 14129 | 1 Comp 2.4.2 | X 2.4.1

(e) D.96 c.5: see MIRAMUR.

EX LITTERIS DILECTI | JL 14187 | — | X —

(e) D.14 c.2: "Tollerabilius enim est ut non coniuncti coniungantur quam coniuncti separentur."

EX LITTERIS QUAS | JL 14142 | 2 Comp 2.14.1 | X 2.28.3

(e) D.63 c.24: "Non debet ei [excommunicato] parere vel prodesse appellationis diffugium."

EX LITTERIS QUAS NOBIS | JL 13793 | 1 Comp 4.1.6 | X 4.1.7

(e) C.22 q.5 c.11: "Secundum quod communiter sonant [verba] interpretabitur iuramentum."

EX LITTERIS VESTRIS | JL 14069 | 1 Comp 2.10.2 | X 2.14.1

(e) C.2 q.1 c.7: "Reus actori victus victori condempnandus est in expensis."

EX MULTIPLICI | JL 14144 | 1 Comp 3.26.17 | X 3.30.3

(e) C.16 q.1 p.c.41: see NOBIS IN EMINENTI.

EX ORDINE ROMANO

(a)	(b)	(c)	(d)

(e) D.75 c.7: "Sacros vero ordines . . . non licet alicui conferre extra constituta tempora nisi Romano pontifici."

| EX PARTE | JL 13955 | 1 Comp 2.13.23 | X 2.20.7 |

(e) C.12 q.5 c.4: "Clerici prohibentur . . . testari . . . ne sanctuarium Dei videatur iure hereditario possideri."

| EX PARTE | JL 13881 | 1 Comp 1.9.11 | X 1.17.11 |

(e) D.31 c.4: see VENIENS.

| EX PARTE | JL 11872 | 1 Comp 5.1.13 | X 5.1.11 |

(e) C.2 q.7 c.60: "Alex. III . . . dicit quod monachi non possunt accusare aliquem nisi abbatem."

| EX PARTE | JL 14317 | 1 Comp 1.2.2 | X 1.3.2 |

(e) C.27 q.2 c.20: see INTELLEXIMUS.

| EX PARTE | JL 14346 | 1 Comp 3.33.7 | X 3.38.5 |

(e) C.16 q.7 c.25: see RELATUM EST AURIBUS NOSTRIS.

| EX PARTE TUA | JL 13919 | 1 Comp 1.23.7 | X 1.31.5 |

(e) D.56 c.1: "Numquam est dispensandum . . . ut prelati ministrent in illis ecclesiis in quibus eorum patres"; C.17 q.4 c.29: "Alex."

| EX PUBLICO INSTRUMENTO | JL 13787 | 1 Comp 3.28.7 | X 3.32.7 |

(e) C.17 q.2 c.1: "Usque ad duos menses cogenda est monasterium intrare vel sponso adherere, ut Alex."

| EX QUERIMONIA | JL 13814 | 1 Comp 2.20.33 | X — |

(e) C.2 q.6 c.16: see AD AURES.

| EX PRESENTIUM LITTERIS | JL 13911 | 1 Comp 3.17.3 | X 3.21.3 |

(e) C.16 q.6 c.3: "Heres teneatur ex delicto defuncti."

| FALSIDICUS TESTIS | — | 1 Comp 5.16.2 | X 5.20.1 |

(e) C.3 q.9 c.16: "Falsus enim testis tres offendit sc. Deum, iudicem, proximum."

| FRATERNITATEM TUAM | JL 13873 | 1 Comp 3.26.8 | X — |

(e) C.16 q.1 p.c.41: "Alexander . . . ibidem et notat Adrianum" [see NOBIS IN EMINENTI].

| FRATERNITATIS | JL 14066 | 1 Comp 2.13.17 | X 2.20.17 |

(e) C.2 q.1 c.7: "Iurari enim debent [testes]"; C.2 q.6 c.38: "Alex."

GRATUM

(e) C.17 q.2 c.1: "Contraire voto etiam simplici est mortale peccatum . . . nisi maius vinculum superveniat"; C.27 q.1 a.c.1: "Alex. III."

| GRAVIS ILLA | JL 14007 | 1 Comp 3.14.2 | X 3.16.1 |

(a)	(b)	(c)	(d)

(e) C.10 q.2 c.2: "Videtur quod hoc onus [probandi contrarium] . . . incumbit [creditori]."

| IAM TERTIO | WH 541 | — | X — |

(e) C.14 q.4 c.6: "Debitor cogendus est ad restaurationem dampni."

| IN EMINENTI | JL 12411 | 1 Comp 5.33.3 | X 5.38.4 |

(e) D.21 c.4: "Non intelligitur absolvi ab isto episcopo sed ab illo qui imposuit ei penitentiam"; C.11 q.3 c.15: "Alex."

| IN EMINENTI | JL 13832 | 1 Comp 1.27.5 | X 1.36.5 |

(e) C.12 q.2 c.74: "Non enim predecessor . . . potest . . . facere ecclesiam censualem post mortem suam."

| IN EMINENTI | JL 14350 | 1 Comp 2.20.40 | X — |

(e) C.2 q.6 a.c.1: "Si . . . in litteris comissionis inhibeatur appellatio tunc non licet appellare nisi appellans priusquam citaretur iter arripuisset ad sedem apostolicam veniendi"; ibid.: CONSULUISTI SI CAUSA.

| IN EXCEPTIONIBUS | — | — | X — |

(e) C.2 q.8 a.c.1: "In exceptionibus enim non inscribitur."

| IN LITTERIS | JL 14219 | 1 Comp 4.22.2 | X 4.21.4 |

(e) C.2 q.2 p.c.7: "Papa potest remittere infamiam irrogatam per civilem iudicem . . . Alex. III . . . dicit"; D.12 c.2 = 2 Comp 2.12.5 = X 2.20.24; D.28 c.3 = 1 Comp 1.8.6 = X 1.14.5; D.50 c.25 = 1 Comp 2.9.5 = X 2.13.5; C.11 q.1 c.50 = 1 Comp 2.21.1 = X 2.30.1.

| IN OMNI | JL 6604 | 1 Comp 2.13.5 | X 2.20.4 |

(e) C.2 q.4 a.c.1: "Ar. quod principalis persona cum uno teste debet audiri."

| IN ORDINANDO | — | 1 Comp 5.2.1 | X 5.3.1 |

(e) D.16 c.9: "Ar. quod qui doctior in ecclesia ille preponi debet aliis."

| IN PARTIBUS TOLOSE | — | 1 Comp 5.6.10 | X — |

(e) C.1 q.4 c.6: "Ipsa exactionis pena compellatur ad rectitudinem festinare (Tours 1163, c.4)."

| IN PERTRACTANDIS | JL 9506 | 1 Comp 1.34.4 | X 2.7.3 |

(e) C.15 q.4 c.2: see LITTERAS.

| INDECORUM | JL 13820 | 1 Comp 1.8.4 | X 1.14.3 |

(e) D.60 c.2: "Adolescentibus i.e. infra annum xxv."

| INHERENTES | JL 7401 | 1 Comp 1.34.2 | X 2.7.1 |

(e) C.15 q.4 c.2: see LITTERAS.

| INSINUATUM | JL 13843 | 1 Comp 5.2.12 | X 5.3.13 |

(a)	(b)	(c)	(d)

(e) C.2 q.5 c.12: "Alex. dicit quod debet deponi tamquam actor sceleris."

INSINUATUM EST NOBIS   JL 13805   1 Comp 2.17.5   X —
(e) C.10 q.3 c.9: "Ar. quod contra pactum licitum non debet quis venire."

INTELLEXIMUS   JL 13950   1 Comp 1.21.11   X —
(e) C.27 q.2 c.20: "Ar. quod cum in aliquo rescripto aliquid precipitur . . . semper debet intelligi secundum quod recte fieri potest."

INTER CETERA SOLLICITUDINI   JL 12254   1 Comp 3.3.4   X —
(e) D.32 c.3: "Dicitur quod clerici coniugati debent carere beneficio ecclesiastico"; D.32 c.6: "Alex. III."

INTER CETERA   JL 14073   1 Comp 2.20.28   X 2.28.2
(e) C.2 q.1 c.10: see CUM B. IUVENIS.

IUDEI VEL SARACENI   —   1 Comp 5.5.5   X 5.6.5
(e) D.54 c.13: "Conversatio est prohibita cum iudeo . . . ut in concilio Romano (c.26)."

IUVENIS   JL 9655   1 Comp 4.1.18   X 4.1.3
(e) D.14 c.2: "Si vero neutra pars dubietatis ab evangelicis vel sanctorum patrum decretis vel mandatis dissentit id quod certius est tenere debemus."

LATOR PRESENTIUM   JL 14216   1 Comp 5.10.10   X 5.12.9
(e) D.50 c.39: "Omnis ludus inde prohibitus clerico. . . . Sed in alio extra videtur excusari."

LICET   —   1 Comp 1.4.15   X 1.6.6
(e) D.63 c.35: "In electione pape . . . statutum est . . . in concilio Romano (c.1)."

LICET DE BENIGNITATE   JL 14068   1 Comp 3.23.11   X 3.30.11
(e) C.16 q.1 p.c.41: see DILECTUS.

LICET PRETER SOLITUM   JL 14091   1 Comp 4.4.3   X 4.4.3
(e) D.34 p.c.6: "Sed numquid episcopus potest cum tali [sc. matrimonialiter coniuncto in sacro ordine] dispensare? Credo quod sic in tolerando sed non in promovendo"; D.8 c.2: "Alex. III"; D.23 c.5 = 1 Comp 2.13.14 = X 2.20.14; D.49 c.1 = 1 Comp 1.21.1 = X 1.20.1; D.50 c.39 = 1 Comp 5.10.8 = X 5.12.7; D.55 c.13 = 1 Comp 2.1.16 = X 2.1.4; D.61 c.16 = 1 Comp 2.18.6 = X 2.26.4.

LICET UNIVERSIS   JL 13974   2 Comp 5.4.2   X 5.6.8
(e) D.54 c.13: "Conversatio est prohibita cum iudeo"; D.86 c.24 = 2 Comp 2.2.1 = X 2.20.23.

LITTERAS   JL 9654   1 Comp 1.34.3   X 2.7.2
(e) C.15 q.4 c.2: "In causis debet prestari sacramentum de calumpnia . . . quamvis non iam passim fiat secundum canones."

(a)	(b)	(c)	(d)

LITTERAS TUAS — Po. 1560 — X —

(e) C.23 q.1 c.4: "Pendente causa matrimonii propter dubium licite videtur posse reddi debitum. . . . Tamen non usquequaque est observandum, ut in extra Innocentii III."

LITTERAS TUAS — JL 14008 — 1 Comp 1.5.2 — X 1.9.1

(e) De cons. D.4 c.107: "Mutationes [episcoporum] quandoque fieri possunt . . . sed non sine speciali licentia domini pape."

LITTERAS TUE FRATERNITATIS — JL 15734 — 1 Comp 4.20.5 — X 4.19.6

(e) C.28 q.1 c.5: "Quero ergo si illam post penitentiam maritus cogatur recipere . . . ? Urbanus III dicit quod non"; C.32 q.5 c.18 = 1 Comp 4.8.3 = X 4.8.3.

LITTERE — JL 14055 — 1 Comp 4.17.2 — X 4.16.1

(e) C.33 q.4 c.10: "[Alex.]: Interdictum ecclesie non dirimit matrimonium."

MAIORIBUS — — — 1 Comp 3.5.10 — X 3.5.8

(e) C.12 q.2 c.37: "In concilio Turonensi (c.1)."

MANIFESTUM — JL 5291 — 1 Comp 4.2.3 — X —

(e) C.30 q.2 a.c.1: "[Quidam] ad tale officium [coeundi] ante tale tempus reperiuntur idonei."

MEMINIMUS — JL 13162 — 1 Comp 3.5.14 — X 3.5.12

(e) C.1 q.2 c.1: "In consecratione episcopus exigat ut detur et nisi detur non consecret ecclesiam"; C.27 q.1 a.c.1: "Alex. III." = 1 Comp 4.6.6 = X 4.6.3; C.12 q.2 c.74 = 1 Comp 3.34.8 = X 3.39.8; C.17 q.2 c.1 = 1 Comp 4.5.3 = X 4.5.4; D.97 c.3: SCRIPTA = 1 Comp 2.15.2 = X 2.22.2; D.11 a.c.1: SIQUIS PAROCHIANORUM = 1 Comp 4.20.6 = X —.

MIRAMUR — JL 12666 — 1 Comp 2.4.3 — X —

(e) D.96 c.5: "Quid ergo si clericus convenit laicum? Nonne debet eum convenire nisi coram ecclesiastico iudice? Utique."

MONACHI — — — 1 Comp 3.24.1 — X —

(e) C.12 q.2 p.c.1: "De communi iure quilibet tenetur . . . sepeliri . . . ubi . . . habet domicilium"; C.12 q.2 p.c.7: "Contradicit Gregorius."

MONACHI — — — 1 Comp 3.30.2 — X 3.35.2

(e) C.16 q.1 a.c.1: "In concilio Romano (c.10)."

MULIERES — JL 13768 — 1 Comp 5.34.7 — X 5.39.6

(e) D.63 c.33: "Vasalli debent prestare sacramentum fidelitatis non solum ecclesie sed etiam prelato."

MULTORUM — JK 1293 — 1 Comp 5.5.3 — X 5.6.2

(e) D.54 p.c.12: "Christianus eripitur [iudeo] statim in libertatem nullo pretio dato."

(a)	(b)	(c)	(d)

NOBIS IN EMINENTI JL 10444 1 Comp 3.26.15 X —

(e) C.16 q.1 p.c.41: "Monachi sunt exempti a paratione decimarum. . . . Sed Adrianus restrinxit."

NON EST DUBIUM JL 13833 1 Comp 5.34.6 X 5.39.5

(e) D.21 c.1: "Sacrilegium committit quicumque inicit manus in . . . personam ecclesiasticam."

NON EST VOBIS SICUT ARBITRAMUR JL 12248 1 Comp 4.1.11 X 4.1.13

(e) C.16 q.7 c.19: "Non enim debent celebrari divina officia in . . . ecclesiis [donec que male facta sunt corrigantur]."

NON MAGNO OPERE — 1 Comp 3.37.2 X 3.50.2

(e) C.15 q.2 p.c.1: "Monachi non debeant exire claustrum . . . nisi hoc exposcat utilitas monasterii (Tours 1163, c.8)."

NON SATIS — 1 Comp 5.2.7 X 5.3.8

(e) D.8 c.5: "Ar. quod propter prolixitatem temporis quo quis moratur in crimine . . . non excusatur (Tours 1163, c.6)."

NON SINE MULTA JL 13976 — X —

(e) D.54 c.14: "Officia publica iudeis iniungantur."

NOS INSTITUTA JK 2536 1 Comp 3.24.3 X 3.28.1

(e) C.13 q.2 p.c.1: "Quilibet potest sibi eligere sepulturam"; C.13 q.2 p.c.7: "Secundum Leonem IV"; C.19 q.3 c.8: "Extra Leonis III."

NOS INTER ALIOS JL 13970 1 Comp 5.29.7 X 5.34.6

(e) C.2 q.1 c.17: "Non tamen dictabit iudex antequam sibi probetur crimen per confessionem rei"; C.2 q.6 p.c.39: "Alex."

NOSTI JL 12753 1 Comp 1.4.18 X 1.6.9

(e) D.63 c.10: see DIGNUM EST.

NULLA ECCLESIASTICA — 1 Comp 3.8.2 X 3.8.2

(e) D.70 c.1: "In concilio Romano (c.8)."

NULLI LICEAT — 1 Comp 3.11.4 X 3.13.5

(e) C.12 q.2 a.c.1: "Alienatio . . . comprehendit etiam emphiteosim perpetuam."

PERSONAS ECCLESIARUM JL 12253 1 Comp 5.16.3 X —

(e) D.19 c.3: "Episcopus non possit punire falsarios ante susceptum mandatum pape."

PERVENIT JL 14214 1 Comp 4.19.3 X —

(e) D.79 c.9: "Credo quod teneatur [papa] ei [uxori] reddere debitum."

PERVENIT AD AUDIENTIAM JL 14192 1 Comp 5.27.1 X 5.31.1

(e) C.2 q.1 c.12: "Nec suspendere sicut nec excommunicare potest episcopus clericum preter ordinem iudiciarium."

(a)	(b)	(c)	(d)

PERVENIT AD NOS QUOD CUM   JL 14313   1 Comp 2.20.15   X 2.28.13
PRESBITERI
(e) D.63 c.24: see EX LITTERIS QUAS; C.2 q.6 c.16: see AD AURES.

PERVENIT AD NOS QUOD CUM   JL 13794   1 Comp 4.8.1   X 4.8.1
QUIDAM
(e) D.11 a.c.1: "Generalis consuetudo est tamquam canon sive lex observanda."

PLACUIT UT SI QUISQUAM   —   1 Comp 2.18.1   X 2.26.1
(e) D.61 c.16: "Sicut enim ecclesia habetur acephala . . . non currit prescriptio contra eam."

PLURES   —   1 Comp 5.15.1   X 5.19.1
(e) C.10 q.2 c.2: "In concilio Turonensi (c.2)."

PRESBITERI   —   1 Comp 5.32.2   X 5.37.2
(e) C.16 q.1 p.c.41: see COMMISSE.

PRESBITERUM CUIUS DUOS   JL 8959   1 Comp 5.8.2   X 5.9.1
(e) C.17 q.4 c.21: "[Clerici] . . . possunt verberari . . . si non ferunt tonsuram vel habitum"; D.55 a.c.1 = 1 Comp 3.6.2 = X 3.6.2.

PRETEREA   JL 11865   1 Comp 3.28.1   X 3.32.1
(e) C.27 q.2 c.21: "Ipsa non profitente continentiam uxor potest . . . revocare [maritum] . . . ; Alex. dicit contra."

[PROPOSITUM   see CONSULTATIONIBUS]

QUA FRONTE   JL 14312   1 Comp 2.20.41   X 2.28.25
(e) D.16 c.9: "Nunc enim causa ecclesiastica non debet tractari nisi in ecclesia"; D.53 c.2: "Alexander."

QUAMVIS GRAVE   —   2 Comp 3.17.2   X 3.30.17
(e) C.16 q.7 a.c.1: "Laici auctoritate ecclesie sine peccato habere possunt feudatarium ius percipiendi decimas. Quare ergo sic prohibentur (Tours 1163, c.3)?"

QUAMVIS SIMUS   JL 14154   1 Comp 3.33.10   X 3.38.8
(e) C.16 q.7 c.26: "[Ius patronatus] possit donari . . . etiam sine consensu et auctoritate episcopi, quod Alexander innuit in illo decreto."

QUAMVIS SIMUS   JL 14156   1 Comp 1.2.3   X 1.3.3
(e) D.18 c.7: "Ar. quod cum una constitutio per aliam immutatur in secunda debet fieri mentio de prima"; D.25 c.1 = 1 Comp 1.21.7 = X 1.29.6; D.50 c.7 = 1 Comp 2.13.13; D.77 c.7 = 1 Comp 3.33.10 = X 3.38.8; C.2 q.6 c.18: "Alex."

QUANDO
(e) D.75 c.7: see EX ORDINE ROMANO.

(a)	(b)	(c)	(d)

QUANTO GALLICANA   JL 11925   1 Comp 5.4.3   X 5.3.3

(e) D.37 c.12: "Turpe lucrum est et peccatum mortale si quis accipit pecuniam ut det alicui licentiam docendi."

QUERELAM   JL 13165   1 Comp 5.2.14   X 5.3.15

(e) C.16 q.7 c.26: see AD AURES.

QUESITUM   JL 13583   1 Comp 1.23.2   X —

(e) D.63 c.24: "Ante appellationem non est excommunicatus, post excommunicari non potest"; C.2 q.6 c.18: "Alex. III."

QUESITUM   JL 15176   —   X —

(e) C.27 q.2 c.45 §3: "Sponsa remanebit cum secundo si ab eo est cognita. . . . Papa Lucius fuit in hac opinione."

QUESIVISTI   JL 13830   1 Comp 2.20.2   X —

(e) C.3 q.5 c.9: "Dicit Alexander de sublatione appellationis que si ponitur in medio non refertur ad sequentia."

QUIA IN OMNIBUS   —   1 Comp 5.15.5   X 5.19.3

(e) C.1 q.3 c.2: see DE HOC AUTEM.

QUIA IN QUIBUSDAM   —   1 Comp 3.33.4   X 3.38.3

(e) D.70 c.2: see QUONIAM ENORMIS.

QUI IN VIVORUM   [WH 804]   1 Comp 3.8.1   X 3.8.1

(e) C.9 q.1 c.5: "Non licet [episcoporum adhuc viventium sedes invadere]."

QUIDAM INTRAVIT   JL 14061   1 Comp 3.28.3   X 3.32.3

(e) C.7 q.1 c.42: "Ergo coniugatus qui sine consensu uxoris intravit . . . redditus . . . ea mortua debet redire ad monasterium . . . Alexander tamen dicit contrarium in extra."

QUOD A PREDECESSORE   —   1 Comp 5.7.2   X 5.8.1

(e) C.7 q.1 c.5: "Ar. quod intrusus . . . non potest disponere de rebus ecclesie . . . , in concilio Romano (c.2)."

QUOD SUPER HIS   JL 13869   1 Comp 1.9.5   X —

(e) D.31 c.4: see VENIENS; D.56 c.8: "Alex. III."

QUONIAM ABBAS   JL 14175   1 Comp 1.21.19   X 1.29.14

(e) C.18 q.2 c.27: "Si vero . . . [aliquid] exprimatur [ab aliquo] intuitu ecclesie non sic [i.e. morte illius] expirat."

QUONIAM ENORMIS   —   1 Comp 5.3.3   X 5.4.3

(e) D.70 c.2: "Nullus ad tempus debet institui in aliqua ecclesia (Tours 1163, c.5)."

QUONIAM IN QUIBUSDAM   —   1 Comp 3.33.4   X 3.38.3

(e) D.70 c.2: see QUONIAM ENORMIS; D.63 c.36: "In concilio Romano (c.17)."

[QUONIAM LICET   see SUPER HOC QUOD A NOBIS]

(a)	(b)	(c)	(d)

QUONIAM SACRIS   JL 13815   1 Comp 1.9.12   X 1.17.10

(e) C.7 q.1 c.14: see EA QUE HONESTATIS.

REFERENTE   JL 14168   1 Comp 3.5.9   X 3.5.7

(e) C.16 q.1 c.48: "Alex."; C.21 q.1 c.1: "[Episcopus] non cogitur . . . restituere [prebendam]."

RELATUM   JL 13803   1 Comp 5.23.3   X 5.27.3

(e) D.50 c.10: "Si clericus excommunicatus . . . officium celebravit perpetuo est deponendus."

RELATUM   JL 4269   1 Comp 3.24.4   X 3.28.2

(e) C.13 q.2 p.c.7: "Secundum Leonem IV"; C.19 q.3 c.8: "Extra Leonis."

RELATUM EST AURIBUS   JL 13885   1 Comp 3.5.7   X —

(e) C.7 q.1 c.14: "In genere licita est talis promissio [beneficii vel ecclesie] sc. que primo vacaverit."

RELATUM EST AURIBUS NOSTRIS   JL 12412   1 Comp 3.33.14   X —

(e) C.16 q.7 c.26: "Patronus non potest condere ius patronatus alicui ecclesie . . . , quod Alexander III videtur comprobare in illo extra."

RELIGIOSI   JL 14169   —   X —

(e) C.35 q.8 a.c.1: "Fit et talis dispensatio in coniunctione consanguineorum quandoque causa scandali."

REPREHENSIBILIS   —   1 Comp 2.20.42   X 2.28.26

(e) D.84 c.2: "Ubi quis vult fugere disciplinam . . . non est audienda appellatio . . . ; ar. in concilio Romano (c.6)."

REQUISIVIT   JL 14114   1 Comp 1.9.1   X 1.13.1

(e) C.7 q.1 c.45: "Si vero abrenuntiat loco et omni officio episcopali non potest nec debet episcopalia exercere. . . . Alex. III in extra."

REQUISIVIT   JL 15165   1 Comp 4.1.12   X 4.1.17

(e) C.27 q.2 c.33: "Lucius etiam III . . . dicit quod nullus est cogendus ducere sponsam de futuro."

SANE DE CLERICIS   JL 13946   1 Comp 3.3.3   X 3.3.2

(e) D.31 c.1: "Etsi aliquis nunc contrahit in minoribus ordinibus statim est repellendus ab omni ecclesiastico beneficio"; D.34 c.11: "Alex. III"; D.53 c.2 = 1 Comp 3.27.9 = X 3.31.9.

SANE NOS QUIA   JL 13835   1 Comp 1.21.16   X 1.29.11

(e) D.21 c.4: "Sive quis ex arbitrio sive ex delegatione cognoscat maior est in illa causa illis quorum tractat."

SANE SUPER HOC   JL 13948   1 Comp 1.6.2   X 1.11.2

(e) D.36 c.2: "Si ordinat aliquem . . . in tempore prohibito . . . nisi sit papa debet

(a)	(b)	(c)	(d)

privari ex toto potestate ordinandi"; C.1 q.3 c.4: "Alex. III" = 1 Comp 1.6.3 = X 1.11.3.

[SCRIPTA   see MEMINIMUS]

SI PERFODIENS FUR   —   1 Comp 5.10.5   X 5.12.3

(e) C.14 q.4 c.12: "Prosequitur illam permissionem de fure occidendo in illo extra."

SI QUA   JK 2812   1 Comp 4.12.1   X 4.12.1

(e) C.30 q.3 a.c.1: "Arrogatio impedit [matrimonium] ad tempus."

SI QUANDO   JL 14074   1 Comp 1.2.5   X 1.3.5

(e) D.81 c.15: "Si non obediunt [episcopi] causam domino pape debent rescribere."

SI QUI TESTIUM   JL 13926   1 Comp 2.13.24   X 2.20.8

(e) C.3 q.9 c.15: "Si tamen testes non possunt adesse . . . debet iudex ad eos mittere."

[SI QUIS PAROCHIANORUM   see MEMINIMUS]

SI SACERDOS   JL 14030   1 Comp 1.23.6   X 1.31.2

(e) D.33 c.7: "Ubi vero est ambiguitas persone . . . sed factum est certum precise danda est sententia et in genere, ut in extra quod habetur vi q.ii."

SICUT AIT   —   1 Comp 5.6.6   X 5.7.8

(e) C.1 q.1 a.c.1: "Simoniaci sint feriendi . . . aliquando . . . omnium bonorum spoliatione."

SICUT DIGNUM   JL 12180   1 Comp 5.10.7   X 5.12.6

(e) D.1 c.7: "Non peccat vim vi quis repellit si observat tria predicta, ut in extra"; D.45 a.c.1: "Alex."

SICUT EX LITTERIS   JL 14139   1 Comp 2.15.3   X —

(e) D.19 c.3: see PERSONAS; C.3 q.1 a.c.1 = 1 Comp 2.9.1 = X 2.13.2.

SICUT IUDEIS   JL 13973   2 Comp 5.4.3   X 5.6.9

(e) C.17 q.4 c.35: "Sub defensione Romane Ecclesie suscepti sunt iudei."

SICUT ROMANA   JL 12293   1 Comp 1.21.6   X 1.29.5

(e) D.8 c.1: "Ar. quod ubi quis negat aliquid negare debet et eius consecutionem"; D.23 c.6 = 1 Comp 1.2.1 = X 1.3.1; C.2 q.6 p.c.39: "Alex." = 1 Comp 2.20.13 = X 2.28.12; C.27 q.2 p.c.26 = 1 Comp 4.4.5.

SIGNIFICASTI   JL 14107   1 Comp 4.20.4   X 4.19.4

(e) C.7 q.1 c.19: "Non cogitur [vir] illam [adulteram] recipere nec illa potest eum repetere."

SIGNIFICASTI   JL 14027   1 Comp 4.4.8   X —

(e) C.27 q.2 c.51: "Dicit Alex. quod si post desponsationem de futuro sequeretur commixtio carnalis statim presumitur quod sit ibi matrimonium."

(a)	(b)	(c)	(d)

SIGNIFICAVIT NOBIS   JL 12378   1 Comp 2.20.24   X —

(e) C.2 q.2 c.3: "Potest iudicari ab eo a quo appellaverit si suus iudex sit excepto eo crimine super quo appellaverit."

SIGNIFICAVIT NOBIS O.   JL 13937   1 Comp 4.7.2   X 4.7.2

(e) C.29 q.2 c.5: "Coactus iurare quandam in uxorem postea sponte cognovit eam nec potest eam postea dimittere."

SIQUIS CONTRA SUAM   —   —   X —

(e) D.63 c.10: "In extra cap. Cartag. concilii (c.13)."

SIQUIS SANE PUERUM IN AQUA TER   JL 14200   2 Comp 5.20.1   X 3.42.1

(e) De cons. D.4 c.82: "Alex. III."

SOLLICITUDINI   JL 14235   1 Comp 4.1.5   X 4.16.3

(e) C.33 q.4 c.10: see LITTERE.

STATUIMUS   JL 14191   1 Comp 1.27.2   X 1.36.2

(e) C.16 q.7 c.7: "Sed numquid transactio [spiritualium] . . . est licita? . . . Sic inter ecclesiam et ecclesiam."

SUGGESTUM   JL 13870   1 Comp 2.20.20   X 2.28.15

(e) C.16 q.1 p.c.41: see COMMISSE.

SUPER EO QUOD A NOBIS   JL 14152   1 Comp 2.20.34   X —

(e) D.99 a.c.1: "In causis enim ecclesiasticis in minima etiam causa appellatur ad papam"; C.2 q.6 a.c.1: "Alex."

SUPER HOC QUOD A NOBIS   JL 13773   1 Comp 4.7.3   X 4.7.3

(e) C.27 q.2 p.c.30: "Si ergo quis cognoscit aliquam suo uxori attinentem in primo vel in secundo gradu . . . et est manifestum perpetuo est separandus ab uxore"; C.34 q.1/2 c.4: "Alex." = QUONIAM LICET = 1 Comp 4.8.2 = X 4.8.2.

SUPER ILLO   JL 14075   1 Comp 4.16.2   X —

(e) C.33 q.1 p.c.4: "Nec propter maleficium nec propter frigiditatem debeat quis separari."

TANTA   —   1 Comp 5.2.16   X 5.3.7

(e) C.6 q.1 a.c.1: "In crimine simonie et servi et infames et criminosi . . . admittuntur."

TANTA   JL 13917   1 Comp 4.18.6   X 4.17.6

(e) C.29 q.1 c.5: "Sed quero . . . an filii nati antequam iste cognosceret eius conditionem sint legitimi."

TESTES   JL 13925   1 Comp 2.14.6   X —

(e) C.2 q.6 c.38: "Nec prefate decretales dicunt neminem esse cogendum sed dicunt quod ecclesia Romana neminem consuevit cogere."

(a)	(b)	(c)	(d)

TRANSMISSE   JL 14086   1 Comp 4.18.3   X 4.17.3

(e) D.87 c.9: "Si quis aliquid iuris habet in hoc puero . . . simplici verbo eius non credetur."

TREUGAS   —   1 Comp 1.24.1   X 1.34.1

(e) D.89 c.11: "In novo concilio (c.21)."

UT NEMO PRESBITERORUM   JK 27   1 Comp 3.2.2   X —

(e) D.32 c.10: "Si vero consenserint [episcopi] pretio vel precibus deponendi sunt."

UNIVERSALIS   JL 14267   1 Comp 3.3.2   X —

(e) C.1 q.1 c.21: "Ar. quod electio et alienatio et investitura et huiusmodi ita confirmantur ex censura sequente sicut ex precedente"; C.1 q.2 c.9: "Alex."

VENIENS   JL 13995   1 Comp 1.9.6   X 1.17.5

(e) D.31 c.4: "Ar. quod clericus non debet habere ecclesiam quam pater eius habuit nullo medio."

VIDETUR NOBIS   JK 384   1 Comp 4.17.1   X 4.18.3

(e) C.33 q.4 c.10: "In extra Celestini"; C.3 q.5 a.c.1: "Excipiuntur duo casus in quibus indifferenter domestici admittuntur."

VIDETUR TIBI

(e) C.3 q.5 a.c.1: see VIDETUR NOBIS.

VIDUAS AUTEM   —   1 Comp 3.27.6   X 3.31.4

(e) C.20 q.1 c.4: "Nil enim refert an dictis vel factis quis consentiat."

VIGILANTI   JL 14186   1 Comp 2.18.7   X 2.26.5

(e) C.14 q.5 c.1: "Iure poli tenetur [rem alienatam] . . . reddere si vult salvari."

VOLUMUS   JL 6611   1 Comp 3.24.2   X —

(e) C.13 q.2 p.c.1: "Causa . . . maioris religionis licet cuique mutare sepulturam suam"; C.13 q.2 p.c.7: "Hoc dicit Pascalis."

Two Recensions of *Continuatio Prima*?

In chapter II we discussed the peculiar relationship between Bazianus and the *Continuatio* by examining some of the numerous references of the text to "bar." and noted that the transmission of the references in the surviving manuscript tradition is often inconsistent. MS Montecassino 396 in particular contains far more material from Bazianus than any of the remaining testimonies. This poses the question, do these textual fluctuations represent mere interpolations or did they arise from a systematic attempt to revise *Continuatio prima?*

As an appropriate testing ground for supposedly different versions of the work, it is convenient to concentrate on the *Cause hereticorum* (C.23–26), more precisely, on the section from C.23 q.4 c.34 to C.26. Since the *Continuatio* became the standard supplement for the missing portions of Huguccio's *Summa,* it is there that the manuscript basis, with up to twelve copies, is sufficient for critical comparisons.

A careful scrutiny of MS Montecassino, with its suspicious amount of inserted Bazianus material, yields six passages omitted either partly or altogether from the rest of the testimonies:[1]

1. C.23 q.5 c.43 s.v. *per primam indictionem*

1 Quilibet annus usque ad xv dicebatur indictio. Hec
  computatio introducta fuit a Romanis quibus primo
  quinquennio solvebatur aurum, secundo argentum, tertio
  es. Et postea incipiebant a capite. Bar. dicit quod primo
5 es, secundo argentum, tertio aurum.

MSS MC 150b, P1 51ra, B 314vb, LLS 315va, V 249vb, Fes., P2 274rb, L 243rb
1 xv] annum *add.* P1 dicebatur] dicebant Fes. vocatur P1   3 quinquennio] anno *add.* P1   4–5 Bar. . . . aurum] *add.* MC

---

1. See above, chapter II, nn.85–99. For the manuscripts used in this appendix, abbreviations will be used as follows: A: Admont, Stiftsbibl. 7;   B: Bamberg, Staatsbibl. Can. 41;   Fes.: Florence, Bibl. Laurenziana Fes. 126;   LLS: Lons-le-Saunier, Arch. Dép. 12.F.16;   MC: Montecassino, Bibl. Abbaziale 396;   P1: Paris, B.N. lat. 1539–7;   P2: Paris, B.N. lat. 3892;   V: Vatican City, Bibl. Apost. lat. 2280;   L: Leipzig, Univ. bibl. 985;   F: Florence, Bibl. Laur. S. Croce I sin. 4.

2. C.23 q.8 c.4 s.v. *Quicumque in bello iniusto*

1 Quale fuit inter Bononienses et Imolenses. Idem est et
in laico. Unde sepeliri non debet quia in bello iniusto
moritur. Presumitur enim de eius impenitentia qui
deprehensus est in re illicita, puta in rebus Veneris
5 professus est adulter. Et quicumque in peccato moritur
non debet cum sollempnitate scilicet cum psalmis nec in
cimiterio sepeliri, ut in novo concilio FELICIS, QUONIAM
IN QUIBUSDAM [Lat. III c.15, 17]. Asinina tamen sepultura
conceditur ei, puta in agro vel in via. Quod hodie fieri
10 debet de militibus qui moriuntur in tirociniis. Et ita
contrarium solvitur supra, e. q.v Placet [c.12]. Bas.
dicit quod clerici in minoribus positi et arma possunt
movere et milites fieri, sicut et matrimonia contrahere,
non obstante quod dicitur xx q.iii Eos [c.3] etc.
15 Illud intelligit de maioribus ordinibus. Item ar. quod
negatur eis in hoc capitulum oratio et oblatio intelligit
quoad frequentationem, ut lxxxviii c. ult. [c.14]. Hoc
autem dicit quia conceditur hic sepultura. Nam quomodo
concorderetur istud sine illis? Nullomodo, ut xcv
20 Illud [c.3]. Item ad hoc inducit ut "quibus vivis
communicamus" etc. Extra autem et alia omnia que tales
sepultura privant intelligit ad terrorem dicta. Sed
quid si penituerint in fine et de hoc constat vel per
testes vel per signa? Non videtur quod propter hoc
25 debea⟨n⟩t sepeliri nisi propinqui eorum pro eis
satisfaciant, ut in extra FELICIS [Lat. III, c.15],
MONACHI [1 Comp 3.24.1]. Sed contrarium est xxvi q.vi
Qui recedunt [c.7]. Preterea communicamus eis vivis,
ergo mortuis communicare debemus.

MSS MC 153b–154a, P1 51vb, LLS 316va, V 250vb, Fes., P2 273ra, B 316ra, L
245ra, F 287ra
2 quia] qui P1, L   3 enim de eius] enim eiusdem LLS, V, Fes., P2   4 puta in
rebus Veneris] puta in lege veteri LLS, P2 in lege veteris Fes. in lege vetus V   6
scilicet] *om.* P1, B   10 in tirociniis] in torneamentis P1, LLS, V, Fes., P2, B, F in
latrociniis *et add. in marg.* vel in tirociniis L   11–22 Bas. . . . dicta] *add.* MC   28
Preterea] non *add.* LLS, V, Fes., P2 nonne *add.* P1, B, L, F   29 ergo] et *add.* P1, B, L

3. C.23 q.8 c.28 s.v. *petenda*

1 precibus. Et dico si non confugerunt ad ecclesiam, ut
supra e. q.v Reos [c.7]. Si autem ad ecclesiam
confugerunt, defendere et vitam eius conservare tenetur,
ut xvii q. iiii Reum [c.9], excepto latrone publico.
5 Item secundum Baz. quando iniuste ad mortem ducitur,
ecclesia per subditos suos debet eum defendere armis.

MSS MC 155b, P1 52rb, LLS 317rb, V 251ra, Fes., P2 275va, B 317ra, L 246rb
1 Et] hoc *add*. P1, B, F idem *add*. L   1 confugerunt] confugerent P1 confugiunt
B, LLS, V, Fes., P2, F   3 vitam eius] eis vitam LLS, V, Fes., P2, L, F   5–6 Item
. . . armis] *add*. MC

4. C.23 q.8 c.32 s.v. *consultis*

1   Forte consuli debent quando incertum est que pena imponi
     debeat vel propter diversitatem penarum vel delicti vel
     personarum. Sed numquid episcopi possunt consulere
     principibus ut aliquem puniant ultimo supplicio? Minime,
5   nisi fuerit incorrigibilis. Possunt tamen consulere ut
     faciat quod iustitia dictet. Baz. dicit quod debet dicere
     prelatus et consulere ne eum interficiat, licet sit
     decapitandus. Potest ergo dicere: "Est occidendus
     secundum leges." Et potest rogare et consulere ne eum
10   interficiat. Vel melius dicas quod postquam aliquis egit
     penitentiam de aliquo crimine et dampnum restituit, non
     licet principibus ipsum punire episcopis inconsultis.

MSS MC 156b, P1 52va, LLS 317vb, V 251rb, Fes., P2 275vb, B 317rb, L 246va–
b, F 288ra
     1–2 imponi] *om*. P2 (*aliquot spatio intermisso*) imponi debeat] pena impetu V im-
petu LLS imponi deponit Fes.   6 dictet] dictat B, P1, LLS, V, Fes., P2, L, F   6–
10 Baz. . . . interficiat] *add*. MC   10 Vel melius] Vel in melius *add*. LLS, V, Fes.,
P2

5. C.24 q.2 a.c.1 s.v. *Quod autem*

1   Queritur an quis debeat excommunicari post mortem. Ad
     quod dicendum est quod non regulariter quia crimina morte
     extinguuntur. Excipiuntur quedam, ut siquis accusaretur de
     scismate vel heresi potest excommunicari post mortem, ut
5   infra, e. Sane profertur [c.6]. Similiter in crimine lese
     maiestatis et sacrilegii et aliis quibusdam secundum
     leges. Sed utrum pro his excommunicari vel dampnari debeat
     aliquis post mortem dubium est secundum canones. Si
     queratur de aliis peccatis an idem fieri possit,
10   dicimus quod refert utrum occulta sint an notoria. Pro
     nullo occulto potest aliquis accusari vel dampnari post
     mortem. Si vero notorium sit dampnari potest ** Hoc negat
     Baz. Dicit enim quod nec accusari nec dampnari potest. Et
     est orandum pro eo etsi non prosint ei orationes. Melius
15   est enim superesse his quibus nec obsunt nec prosunt quam
     deesse quibus prosunt, ut xiii q.ii Non estimemus
     [c.15]. Quod enim fit pro omnibus, pro singulis fit, ut de
     con. di.v Non mediocriter [c.24]. Quod autem obicitur sibi
     xxiii q.⟨v⟩ Placet [c.12] dicit esse illum specialem casum

20 et in tali in ipso facto inferri sententiam ** et expelli
a cimiterio fidelium. Non enim potest habere communionem
vel aliam veniam ab ecclesia quam superstes non quesivit.

MSS MC 162b–163a, P1 54va, LLS 320ra–b, V 252vb-253ra, Fes., P2 277vb–278ra, A, B 319vb, L 250va, F 290ra
1–2 Ad quod dicendum] Ad credendum V, A, P2 Et credendum Fes., LLS   2 est] *om.* P1   3 extinguuntur] ut *add.* P1, Fes., F ut xxiii di. Quorundam [c.14] *add.* V, A, P2, LLS accusaretur] accusetur V, A, P2, LLS, Fes., F excusetur L vel] de *add.* P1   5 lese] *om.* MC, L   7 debeat] iubeatur LLS, V, Fes., P2, A, B, F valeat L   10 dicimus] dicitur V, A, Fes., P2, LLS dic B quod] *om.* P1   12–20 Hoc negat . . . sententiam] *add.* MC *duobus asteristicis et initio et in fine glossae appositis.*

6. C.25 q.2 p.c.25 s.v. *nulli aliquid derogatur*

1 Aliud est enim lucrum non capere, aliud suum amittere.
Glosa Cardinalis. Bar. non approbat.

MSS MC 173a, P1 57va, LLS, V, Fes., A, P2, B 324ra, F 293rb
1 enim est *tr.* A, P2, LLS, B suum] *om.* B non *add.* V, Fes., LLS, P2 amittere] admittere MC, A ut in ff. qui in frau. cre. (Dig.42.8) l.vi Pretor, l.iiii Generalis *add.* V, Fes., LLS, B, F   2 Glosa] Glosam P1, Fes., F Glosa . . . approbat] *om.* P2, A, V approbat] illam *add.* B

The critical apparatus of the six texts just quoted indicates that MS Montecassino (MC) contains a version of the *Continuatio* decidedly different from that to be found in the remaining manuscripts. In five cases, MC alone includes the Bazianus material. There remains, on the other hand, only one instance (number 6) where the variants cross the line separating MC from the rest of the testimonies. Of course, none of these references to Bazianus can claim to be authentic. They not only lack a coherent textual tradition, but also reveal their spurious nature in that they are often badly integrated into the original. The way in which these Bazianus glosses intruded is nowhere more manifest than at C.24 q.2 a.c.1 (number 5), where a gloss of considerable length completely disrupts a formerly intact sentence. Realizing that the argument's flow was thoroughly disturbed, the scribe (or a reader?) of MC marked with asterisks the beginning and the end of the interpolation.

One might therefore tend to conclude that MC, owing to its great proportion of later added texts, is the more corrupted and lesser testimony compared to the other ones. Nothing, however, could be more misleading. As a matter of fact, it would be hard to arrive at a readable version of *Continuatio prima* without taking constant recourse to MC. Only P1 can rival the quality of its text, whereas the variants common to LLS, B, A, V, P2, Fes., F and L reveal their inferior quality. Despite its greater susceptibility to nonauthentic materials from Bazianus, MC rather presents the more polished version.[2]

2. To be sure, the present account does not document Bazianus material in the other MSS, which also contain a number of similarly interpolated passages. An ex-

There can be no doubt that the Continuator had himself a keen interest in Bazianus's teachings. After all, many of the references to "bar" had been included in the work from the beginning. Besides the six instances just quoted, the collations of C.23 q.4 c.34–C.26 confirm as authentic eight other texts mentioning opinions held by Bazianus.[3] What, then, is the most plausible scenario for the genesis of the *Continuatio*? Most likely, the Continuator drafted his commentary under the direct influence of Bazianus's lectures. When he had finished, he (or another student using it) continued to attend Bazianus's classes, and occasionally wrote the master's opinions into the margin. These added remarks gradually entered the text itself. The scribe of MC was apparently anxious not only to copy the body of text, but also to include the marginal glosses. Not so the copyist from whom most of the other testimonies derived.

Granted the overall superiority of MC and P1, it remains an open question if MC represents a recension of its own. To examine this problem, it is convenient to widen the scope of our evaluation.

a) C.25 q.2 c.25 s.v. *parrochie vice*

In 1914, six years after having established that the *Continuatio* was composed during the pontificate of Urban III (1185–87), Franz Gillmann called attention to the comment on *parrochie vice*. In the Vatican manuscript (V), he had discovered the reference to a decretal issued by Pope Celestine III on June 17, 1193.[4] Naturally, the papal letter represented a challenge for Gillmann's proposed date. But since another copy of the *Continuatio* in MS Bamberg, Can. 41 (B), omitted the passage, he felt entitled to dismiss its appearance in V as an interpolation. Later scholarship did not question Gillmann's preference of B's version, until the case was re-opened by Luigi Prosdocimi in 1955. The reading in V, he pointed out, received support from two other testimonies, Florence, Bibl. Laur. S. Croce (F), and Florence, Bibl.

---

ample is C.25 q.1 a.c.1 s.v. *Sancta Romana ecclesia* (in fine), where, following the brief remark of the *Continuatio*: "Valet ergo privilegium a papa concessum quousque ab alio successore suo revocetur" (Montecassino 396, p. 169b; Paris, B.N. lat. 15397, fol. 56va), the MSS LLS, V, Fes., A, P2, and B, report this gloss: "Basianus tamen distinguit. Si in secundo privilegio fiat mentio de primo, derogatur ei, ar. in extra QUAMVIS (JL 14156). Secus si mentio non fiat. Vel aliter, si dominus papa ad nullius petitionem, quod raro aut numquam fit, concessit alicui privilegium, illi per aliud privilegium non potest derogari. Secus si in petitionem alicuius concessum sit, ut C. de pet. bon. sub. [Cod.10.12], l.i et ii"; another instance appears in MS B (fol. 323va), at C.25 q.1 p.c.16 §1 s.v. *prescriptione*: "Bar. dicit: Quando ita circumvenit imperatorem ut minor xiiii annis posset condere testamentum, rescriptum impetravit sive in ⟨fraude facti⟩ sive in fraude tacendi. Etiam quando pretermisit circumstantias rei que a testibus proferri non debent. Quia omnem veritatem que tangit negotium dicere debent, ut iiii q. ix Hortamur [c.20]; iiii q iii. Item lege sola [c.3 §32]."

3. See the references listed above, chap. II, nn.136, 142, 148–51.

4. F. Gillmann, "Die Abfassungszeit," 247n.; for his earlier articles on the *Continuatio*, see chap. II, n.113 above.

Laur. Fes. 126 (Fes.).[5] This meant that a date later than 1185/87 could not be ruled out. But since Prosdocimi passed no definitive judgment on the matter, it is appropriate to take up the argument once again:

FIRST VERSION

Ad tempus suspendit
dignitatem episcopalem
huius ecclesie, non abstulit.
Mandat ergo ut ministrentur
5 ei officia divina tamquam
parrochie quia non habet
episcopium proprium. Quilibet
enim istorum episcoporum
visitator est, non proprius
10 episcopus, ut dicitur in fine
capituli. Et quilibet potest
clericos ordinare, causas
terminare, vel illi duo simul
si maiora sint negotia,
15

20

vel alter eorum si minora.
Ita tamen quod se non
impediant, nec eget alter
25 alterius licentia, cum ita
expressum est in forma
visitationis. Similiter
videtur sequi si causa sit
aliquibus delegata: unus
30 consensu aliorum possit
cognoscere.
Sed ibi necessarius est
specialis sensus quod non
est hic. Sed numquid uterque
35 visitatorum habebit plenam
potestatem instituendi vel
assignandi prebendas? An
simul hoc facere debebit?
Responsio: Prout eis
40 iniunctum est facient.

SECOND VERSION

Ad tempus suspendit
dignitatem episcopalem hoc
ius ecclesie, non abstulit.
Mandat ergo ut ministrentur
officia Dei natam quam
parrochie quia non sit
episcopium proprium. Quilibet
enim episcoporum istorum
visitator est, non proprius
episcopus, ut dicitur in fine
esset. Et quilibet potest
clericos ordinare
pre illi duo simul
si maiora sint negotia.
Non videtur verum cum sint
iudices delegati, nec in fine
mandati additum sit ut si
alter non potest ad ecclesiam ire
alter nichilominus exequatur,
ut extra ⟨ce⟩lesti., de of.
iu. de. cap. ⟨ii⟩.
Vel alter eorum si minora
sint. Ita tamen quod sese non
impediant, nec alter alterius
indiget licentia, cum ita
expressum est in forma
visitationis. Similiter
videtur quod si causa sit
aliquibus delegata, unus
consensu aliorum possit
cognoscere.
Sed ibi necessarius est
specialis sensus quod non
est hic. Sed numquid uterque
visitatorum habebit plenam
potestatem instituendi vel
assignandi prebendas? An
simul hoc facere debebunt?
Responsio: Prout eis
iniunctum est facerent.

5. L. Prosdocimi, "La Summa Decretorum," 367 n.36.

MSS MC 173a, P1 57va, B 324ra.

6 habet] habebat P1   12–13 causas] causam B terminare] possunt *add.* B   14 sint] *om.* B   22 minora] sint *add.* B   23 se] sese B   24–25 nec eget alter alterius] donec alter alterius indigeat B   28 sequi] quod *add.* P1   33 sensus] consensus P1   34 uterque] istorum *add.* P1   38 debebit] debebunt P1 debuerunt B

MSS V 255rb, Fes. 124ra, LLS 324ra, P2 280va, A 332vb, F 293rb.

5 Dei natam quam] Dei tamquam Fes. divina tamquam F   11 esset] *om.* A   13 pre] vel F pre illi duo] *om.* Fes.   20–31 ut extra . . . cognoscere] *om.* A, P2   21 cap. ⟨ii⟩] *om.* F

The text not only confirms our previous grouping of the manuscripts, but also adds some details. To begin with, the readings of B suggest that it may be closer to the superior version of the *Continuatio* in MC and P1 than any of the other testimonies. Concerning the second, larger family of witnesses, there further seems to emerge a subdivision that sets A and P2 apart from the rest of its members. Both P2 and A omit a long passage (lines 20–31), which the other representatives of the second version had separated from the originally preceding text (lines 11–14) through an interpolated gloss (lines 15–21). Also, there is an overall agreement between A and P2 with regard to the excerpts printed above (numbers 5–6), which once (number 6) resulted in their unanimous omission of a reference to Bazianus. The connection between P2 and A appears especially close.

Again, the collations reveal the inferior textual quality of the second version. Confusion seems to have crept in when an interpolator supplied a gloss (lines 15–21) partly opposing the Continuator's view. His rather crude intervention was most likely an attempt to update the comment according to the decretal of Celestine cited at the end. The phrase "alter nihilominus exequatur" echoes the papal letter.[6] For the same reason, it is possible that the paragraph beginning "Non videtur verum . . ." (lines 15ff.) originally did not include the reference to "extra . . ." (lines 20–21), which would make P2 and A represent the earlier form. But leaving aside chronological considerations, the present example offers additional evidence of the low level of textual accuracy typical of the second version. Take, for instance, the nonsensical "pre illi duo" (line 13) which most of its representatives failed to emend. Or the obvious mistake occurring when an unfortunate copyist transcribed what must have been an abbreviated "d'natamq" as "Dei natam quam" instead of the correct "divina tamquam" (line 5) in MC and P1. Finally, the second version misread "capituli" as "esset" (line 11), which throws a dubious light on the orthography of its archetype.

Most important, however, are the chronological clues to be derived from C.25 q.2 c.25. The passage attests to the great difficulties of the second version in integrating the gloss on Celestine's new legislation of 1193 (lines 15–

6. Lines 19–20, "extra . . . de of. iu. de. cap. ⟨ii⟩," certainly refer to the decretal PRUDENTIAM TUAM of Pope Celestine III (17 June 1193) = JL 17019 = 2 Comp 1.12.3 = X 1.29.21.

20). At the same time, it proves that the manipulation occurred after that date. The explicit reference to the decretal (lines 20–21), moreover, would not likely have been included until after the appearance of the *Collectio Gilberti* in 1201.[7] These findings certainly question the assumption that the second version represents a recension in the proper sense. There is, moreover, a second excerpt from the *Continuatio* providing evidence to that effect.

7. According to W. Holtzmann, *Studies,* 329 (index), the first systematic collection that included Celestine's letter under the title "De of⟨ficio⟩ iu⟨dicis⟩ del⟨egati⟩" was that of Gilbertus (ca. 1201/2), ed. R. Heckel, "Die Dekretalensammlungen des Gilbertus und Alanus nach den Weingartener Handschriften," ZRG Kan. Abt. 29 (1940), 187 = 1.13.2. If we accept the alternative reading "cap. ⟨ult.⟩" as correct, the date of the insertion has to be postponed by still another decade, because Celestine's letter became the final item of "De officio et potestate iudicis delegati" only with the publication of *Compilatio secunda* in 1211. In addition, most copies of the *Continuatio* refer to two other *extravagantes* that must derive from older decretal collections. The first was added from the so-called *Bambergensis*-group (before 1191) to C.25 q.1 a.c.1 s.v. *Sancta Romana ecclesia* (printed above n.2), where the MSS LLS, Fes., and B continue after the words "in extra: QUAMVIS," with: "item de of. et pot. iu. del. CETERUM." The decretal cited, CETERUM, had formed part of the papal letter QUAMVIS (JL 14156), and figured under the title "de of." etc. only in *Collectio Bambergensis* 33.9, and its derivatives, *Collectio Casselana* 42.9, and *Collectio Lipsiensis* 35.9 (cf. E. Friedberg, *Die Canones-Sammlungen zwischen Gratian und Bernhard von Pavia* [Leipzig, 1897]). In *Compilatio prima* (1191), the text instead was distributed under "De rescriptis," 1 Comp 1.2.3. Equally interesting is the second instance, first quoted by F. Gillmann, "Die Abfassungszeit" (1914), 247n.:

C.25 q.2 p.c.16 s.v. *non deprecantis affirmatione*

1 Simile in extra INTELLEXIMUS (JL 13950); supple
  'statuimus.' Vel convenit quod est in littera. In quadam
  dicitur decretali quod si inhibita est appellatio non
  possunt preces argui de mendatio. Sed quid est quod
5 in narratione iuris dicitur, cum dicat imperator: 'Omnia
  iura sunt in scrineis nostris'? Quod dicitur in decretali
  est iniquissimum.

MSS MC 172b, P1 57rb, V 255ra, Fes., A, B 323va, F   1–3 Simile . . . decretali] *om.* A   1 Simile] est *add.* V, Fes.   3 dicitur] *om.* V, Fes.   4 quod] *om.* V, Fes.   5 in narratione] de narratione V, Fes., B, F dicitur] *om.* V, Fes., B, F   6 sunt in scrineis nostris] in scrineis se habere, ut C. de testam. Omnium (Cod.6.23.23); et extra de of. iu. del. INTELLEXIMUS V, F in scrineis pectoris sui se habere, ut Cod. de testam. Omnium; et extra de of. iu. del. INTELLEXIMUS Fes., in serius se habere, ut C. de testam. Omni.; et in extra de of. iud. del., quantum ad incidentem questionem non quantum ad principale articulum A in serius se habere—iud. del. B   6 Quod dicitur in decretali] *om.* V, Fes. B et ex tunc de of. iu. del. INTELLEXIMUS *add.* A   7 est iniquissimum] nequissimum P1, *om.* B

MC and P1 confirm Gillmann's supposition that the reference in MSS Fes., V, B, and A to "de of. iu. del." (1 Comp 1.21.1) represents an intruded gloss (line 6).

b) C.26 q.2 c.11 s.v. *Licet pollutum*

We have seen so far that the textual tradition of the *Continuatio* is divided into two very distinct groups. Except perhaps for P1, none of them fully corresponds to the original version, since in both the flow of the argument is often disturbed by interpolations. After a careful study of the different readings, however, the version preserved in P1 and MC turns out to be much closer to the authentic draft, in quality as well as in time. It does not contain the above-mentioned decretal of 1193. The following text elaborates on the same chronological aspect.

FIRST VERSION	SECOND VERSION
Dic ergo in hac questione	Dic ergo in hac questione
quod sortes exquirere demones	quod sortes exquirere per
consulendo sive in	demones consulendo sive in
necessitate sive preter	necessitate sive preter
5 necessitatem prohibitum est	necessitatem prohibitum est
et immane peccatum. Si vero	et immane peccatum. Si vero
in grandi necessitate fusis	ingenti necessitate fusis
ad Deum precibus, facto	ad Deum precibus, facto
ieiunio sicut fecerunt	ieiunio sicut fecerunt
10 apostoli aliquis voluerit	apostoli aliquis noluerit
tale quid facere, non peccat.	tale quid facere, peccat.
Sicut episcopus huius	Sicut fecit episcopus
	Bononiensis (huius
civitatis dicitur fecisse in	predecessor) in
15 electione Antonini. Cum enim	electione Antonii. Cum enim
homines in electione	homines in electione
potestatis convenire non	potestatis convenire non
possent, episcopus scripsit	possent, episcopus scripsit
nomen ipsius Antonini in	nomen illius Antonii in
20 quadam carta, et in alia	quadam carta, et in alia
cuiusdam nomen probissimi	nomen cuiusdam probissimi
viri, et nomen tertii in	viri, et tertii nomen in
tertia carta. Et precepit	tertia carta a puero delata. Et ita
puero simplici ut ad se	populus elegit unam
25 afferret unam de cartulis	de scripturis illis, et
et ille potestas esset cuius	ita electus est Antonius,
nomen inveniretur in cartula	qui peroptime eo anno
a puero delata.	rexit civitatem.
Dicitur tamen quod in	Licet dicatur quod in
30 civitate regenda rector	civitate regenda rector
eligendus est non sorte	eligendus est arte
sed arte.	non sorte.

MSS P1, MC 174a   MSS V 255va, Fes. 124va–b, P2
23–27 carta . . . cartula] *om.* MC   281rb, LLS 324va, B 324va, A 333rb
                                     23 Et ita *om.* V   27 qui] *om.* B, V
                                     eo anno] *om.* B

Once again, the second, inferior version offers some rather inelegant variants (see especially lines 2, 8, 12). On the other hand, P1 emerges as the only copy that still preserves the original reading of lines 22–26, omitted by MC due to homoteleuton ("carta . . . cartula"). Considering that MC was also more susceptible to the intrusion of glosses of "bar.," P1 seems to attest to an earlier, and probably the earliest, stage of textual transmission. P1 further proves that the alternative report on the outcome of the consular election (lines 22–26) in the majority of testimonies is not authentic. The most important implications, however, derive from the variant reading of "predecessor" (line 13) in the second version. Awkwardly connected with the rest of the sentence, it suggests that a change of personnel in the Bolognese episcopate had taken place sometime between the draftings of the first and the later version. It would be hard to imagine otherwise how the "bishop of the city" (P1, MC), in the course of copying, could have become the "predecessor of the Bolognese bishop." Granting that, a look at the Bolognese annals reveals that the later version of the *Continuatio* must have come into being between 1187 and 1198, when the episcopal see of Bologna was occupied by Gerardus. According to the Continuator, Gerardus's "predecessor," Johannes (d. 13 Jan. 1187), had played a decisive role in electing Antoni(n)o dell'Andito to the office of the podestà in 1183.[8]

In sum, our collations show that the *Continuatio* has come down to us in two distinct traditions. Although each of them was subjected to the intrusion of foreign materials (especially from Bazianus's lectures), the version preserved in MS Paris 15397 and Montecassino is far more reliable than that to be found in the remaining copies. In fact, these trace back to what was probably a single, heavily corrupted exemplar (= [a]), which B seems to resemble very closely.[9] Later on, several references to *extravagantes* were added. They reveal that in some copies these manipulations had come to an end by 1193/1201 (A, P2), while in others the process went on until after 1201 (V, Fes., LLS, F). All in all, the findings rule out the possibility that we are confronted with a full revision of the first version. Still, they suggest that the examined manuscripts can be classified in the *stemma* shown in Figure 1.

8. For the dates given here, cf. P. B. Gams, *Series episcoporum ecclesiae catholicae* (Regensburg, 1873), 676; A. Hessel, *Geschichte,* 130 n.100, 131 n.4, 403 n.36; an English translation of the text (first version) has been given above, chap. II n.129.

9. The copy already carries the reference to *Compilatio prima* (n.7 above), while showing yet no sign of the intruded decretal of 1193 (text a). Moreover, it contains the reference to "predecessor" (text b after 1187).

STEMMA CODICUM

Accretions	MSS	Date
	Continuatio prima	1185/86
	P1	
a. Bazianus material	MC	
b. Text (b), lines 13–14	[a] —— B	1187–93
c. Text (a), lines 15–19	A, P2	1193–1201
d. Text (a), lines 20–21	F, V, FES., LLS	after 1201/11

FIGURE I

APPENDIX III

Dissensiones Dominorum in Huguccio's Summa

1. C.3 q.5 c.15 § 5 s.v. Hinc

Ex hoc capitulo aperte colligitur quod potest quis recusare
iudicem. Sed quidam legiste ut Pla., Bul., Jo.Ba. dicunt
quod ordinarius recusari non potest licet sit suspectus.
Sed potest peti quod alius ei associetur, ut in Aut. Ut
5 differentes iudi. § Si vero [Nov. 86 c.2]; et supra e. q.iii
Offeratur [p.c.4 § 5]. Sed hoc Aut. videtur pocius dicere
in contrarium. Sed dicunt quod partim loquitur de ordinario,
partim de delegato. Vel dicunt quod non loquitur nisi de
delegato. Delegatum vero dicunt posse recusari. Et ubicumque
10 lex dicit quod iudex potest recusari intelligunt "delegatus"
ut in premissa lege Iustiniani. Alii dicunt, ut Mar. et G.
quod tam ordinarius quam delegatus potest recusari. Et hec
est rei veritas. Nam et lex generaliter dicit quod quis
potest recusare iudicem. Et ratio quam lex subicit generalis
15 est sc. quia omnes lites debent procedere sine suspicione,
ut C. De iudiciis [Cod.3.1] Apertissimi [c.16], Cum specialis
[c.18]; et C. De iurisdict. o. iu. Nemo [Cod.3.13.4]; ubi
dicitur quod post litem contestatam non potest quis recusare
iudicem ordinarium. Ubi datur intelligi quod ante potest.

MSS Vatican, lat. 2280, fol. 132va (= V); Klagenfurt, xxix a.3, fol. 121va–b (=
KLA); Klosterneuburg 89, fol. 157ra (= KNB); Paris, B.N. lat. 15396, fol. 129rb (=
P); Munich, Staatsbibl. lat. 10247 (= M), fol. 120va.

ED.   1–16 ed. J. F. v. Schulte, Geschichte, 1.166 n.30;   2–3, 11–12 ed. L.
Fowler, " 'Recusatio iudicis' in canonist and civilian thought," SG 15 (1972), 719–
85 at 727 n.37;   13–15 ed. I. Perez de Heredia, Die Befangenheit des Richters im
kanonischen Recht (St. Ottilien, 1977), 9 n.9.

APP. CRIT.   2 p. bul. Io.b. V 7 partim loquitur] partim queritur KLA   11 G.]
Guar. KNB   11–12 ut in . . . delegatus] om. KLA.

APP. FONT.   2 Pla., Bul., Jo.Ba.] cf. nomina legistarum laudata a Dissensionum
collectionibus quae idem argumentum tractant, ed. G. Haenel, Dissensiones dominorum, 77: "Bul.," 149–50: "Al., B., Io.ba., Py."   11 Mar. et G.] Dissensionum
collectiones nomen Martini tantum confirmant, ed. G. Haenel, Dissensiones dominorum, 5, 77, 149–50, 344, 355–56; ed. V. Scialoja, "Nuova collezione," 336–37.
De eodem subiecto vide etiam Ordines iudiciarios a Johanne Baziano (ed. F. Patetta,
215b) nec non a Pilio (ed. L. Wahrmund, 40–42) confectos.

2. C.3 q.6 p.c.2 s.v. *exceptio fori*

Similiter exceptio procuratoria dilatoria est ut si reus
dicat "Non respondeo tibi quia dubito te esse procuratorem,"
vel "dico te non esse procuratorem." Ubi dicit se dubitare
illum esse procuratorem eque modo admittetur cautione
5 prestita. Ubi dicit illum non esse procuratorem eque modo
repellitur. Hoc Bulg. Pla. vero dicebat in electione rei
esse velletne eum repellere vel ad probationem eum cogere.
Sed Io.b. dicit electionem procuratoris esse velitne se
probare procuratorem esse an etiam cavere de rato.

MSS KNB, fol. 157vb; V, 133ra–b; P, 129vb; M, 121ra.
ED. 4–9 ed. J. F. v. Schulte, *Geschichte*, 1.166 n.30.
APP. CRIT. 4 eque modo] *om.* V, M admittetur] procurator *add.* KNB,
Schulte 6 p. [vero V
APP. FONT. 1–9 *Sumptum esse videtur ex Coll. Chis. 218,* ed. G. Haenel, *Dissensiones dominorum,* 131.

3. C.4 q.2/3 c.3 § 37 s.v. *honestioribus*

Item ex una parte discordant testes: Honestioribus licet
paucioribus credendum est, ut supra e. q. Si testes [c.3].
Quidam tamen iurisconsulti dixerunt in hoc casu omnes
repellendos. Sed Io.b. cum veritate legis dicit non esse
5 repellendos omnes sicut supra distinximus.

MSS KLA, fol. 128rb; V, 141ra; P, 137ra; M, 138ra.
APP. CRIT. 3 tamen] *om.* V omnes] esse *add.* P 4 repellendos] esse *add.* V
5 distinximus] distinxi V, M
APP. FONT. 3 Quidam] *quos Martinum Bulgarumque inter socios habuisse constat ex Dissensionum collectionibus,* ed. G. Haenel, *Dissensiones dominorum,* 230–31; ed. V. Scialoja, "Nuova collezione," 399–400. 4 Io.b.] *id quod Johannes Bazianus ipse expressit in Ordine suo iudiciario,* ed. F. Patetta, 238a; *itemque Pilius,* ed. L. Wahrmund, 102–3.

4. C.4 q.2/3 c.3 § 39 s.v. *omnibus in re propria*

Sed quid de venditore? Potest ferre testimonium in causa
civili pro emptore? Et dicit Io.b. quod non quia videtur
ferre testimonium pro se cum ipse videatur conveniri. Nihil
enim refert an conveniaris in propria persona an per aliam
5 mediam, ut patet in fideiussore et reo. Alii dicunt quod
sic. Quedam enim prohibentur in propria persona que non
prohibentur in aliena.

MSS KLA, fol. 128rb; V, 141ra; P, 137ra; M 138ra.
ED. 1–3 ed. J. F. v. Schulte, *Geschichte*, 1.166 n.30.
APP. CRIT. 2 videretur] V 3 testimonium] *om.* P, M

APP. FONT.   1–7 *Super hanc materiam* cf. Cod. 4.20.10.   2 Io.b.] *Teste Pilio,* ed. L. Wahrmund, 96, *Johannes Bazianus re vera fuit huius opinionis.*   5 Alii] *non inveni in operibus iurisconsultorum saeculi xii.*

5. C.10 q.2 c.2 § 6 s.v. *Perpetua*

i.e. duratura in persona primi et secundi heredis et viri
et uxoris si hoc nominatim convenit, ut in Aut. De non
alienandis aut per. § Emphiteosim autem [Nov.7 c.3]; hoc
dixit Mar. Io.b. et quidam alii dicunt melius "perpetua"
5 i.e. "duratura perpetuo" i.e. quamdiu pensio prestetur vel
parata sit prestari. Nec ipsi emphiteote vel eius heredi
potest dominus auferre dummodo paratus sit solvere
pensionem. Et hoc melius est. Sic enim vocabulum perpetui
exponitur in Instit. Locati et con. § Adeo [Inst.3.24.3];
10 sic enim dicitur excommunicatio "perpetua" i.e. quousque
quis perseverat in contumacia, ut i q.i Reperiuntur [c.7];
et x q.i Quia [c.13]; et xxvii q.i De viduis [c.7].

MSS KNB, fol. 189rb; KLA, 146rb; V, 165rb; P, 159vb; M, 148va.
APP. FONT.   1–9 *Eadem doctrina extat in quadam glossa anonyma* Codicis MS Monac. lat. 3509, fol. 160rb, *ad* Coll.9.3 § *Emphiteosis vero* (Nov.120 c.6): "i.e. in persona accipientis et heredis eius primi et secundi et viri et uxoris si hoc nominatim convenerit, ut supra, De non alienan. aut per. Vel aliter 'perpetuo,' id est ut quamdiu redditus sive pensio ecclesie prestetur neque ipsi emphiteotecario neque heredi eius alii ne cui imperator concessit liceat auferre, ut in Inst. De loc. et conduc."

6. C.10 q.2 c.2 § 10 s.v. *Sed melius*

Hoc non est de Aut. quia Authenticum dat his omnibus
actionem adversus eos qui alienaverunt, ut in Aut. t. De
non alienandis aut permut. § Si quis igitur emere [Nov.7
c.5]. Sed additum est a Guarnerio. *huiusmodi actiones* sc.
5 contra ipsos alienatores. *acceptori* rei ecclesiastice per
emptionem vel donationem vel pignorationem vel emphiteosim
citra formam legis. Vel ita: *actiones esse huiusmodi
acceptori* sc. emptori vel donatario vel creditori vel
emphiteote sic accipienti rem ecclesiasticam. In hoc
10 Martinus secutus est Guarnerium. Sed Bul. et Io.b. non.
Dicebat ergo Martinus quod huiusmodi emptor vel donatarius
vel creditor vel emphiteota si vel male fidei non habet
actionem adversus ecclesiam vel illum qui dedit, ut xvi
q.iii Universas [c.16 §4]. Si est bone fidei non habet
15 adversus ecclesiam sed adversus eum qui dedit, ut xii q.ii
Volaterane [c.25]. Sed melius dicitur quod sive sit bone
sive male fidei habet actionem, ut dicit Authenticum, non
adversus ecclesiam sed adversus eos qui alienaverunt. Nec
est curandum quod hic dicitur a Guarnerio. . . . Quidam vero

20 dicunt et male quod hoc habuit Guarnerius ex Authentico
sicut et premissa. Et dicunt hoc referri tantum ad
creditorem quasi dico quod creditor non habet actionem
adversus ecclesiam sed adversus datorem pignoris.

MSS KNB, fols. 189vb–190ra; V, 165vb; P, 160rb; M, 148vb.

ED.   1–4, 8–10 ed. F. Gillmann, AKKR 94 (1914) 441;   1–4, 8–23 ed. F.
Maassen, "Beiträge," 75–76;   9–19 ed. J. F. v. Schulte, *Geschichte*, 1.166 n.30.

APP. FONT.   1 Sed melius] Cf. *Summam Lips. ad loc. cit.*: "Quidam tamen dicunt hec esse verba Guarnerii" (MS Lips. 986, fol. 142ra).   1–4 *Glossa ut videtur
Irnerii (cum additamentis Martini?) invenitur in* MS Monac. lat. 22, fol. 5va, *ad* Cod.
1.2.14, *sic desinens:* "Sed melius dicitur omnino denegandas esse actiones huiusmodi
acceptori."   10–15 *Opinio Martini iterum apparet in glossa anonyma quae in* MS
Monac. lat. 3509, fol. 60ra, *ad* Auth. Coll.9.3 § *Si quis igitur emere* (Nov.7 c.5),
reperitur: "Quia accipit res suprafatas alienatoris titulo non gratuito rem quidem cum
omni medii temporis incremento restituat. At is qui dedit nullam habeat actionem
contra locum venerabilem sed adversus eum qui alienavit in donatione et rem quam
accepit cum suis accessionibus et cum omni causa restituit et aliud tantum."

7. C.16 q.3 a.c.1 s.v. *Quod autem prescriptione*

Prescriptio potest dici quelibet exceptio. Sed hic strictius
accipitur et describitur sic: Prescriptio est exceptio ex
tempore substantiam capiens que actioni personali vel
actioni in rem immobilem opponitur. Exceptio dictum est quia
5 prescriptione non dominium sed exceptio aquiritur secundum
Bulg., Pla., Io.b. Et isti dant utilem rei vendicationem si
quis post prescriptionem cadat a possessione. Mart. dat
directam quia dominium prescriptione asserit acquiri.

MSS KNB, fol. 243ra; V, 218va; P, 19rb; M, 190va.

ED.   1–4 L. Scavo-Lombardo, *La buona fede*, 66;   2–8 N. Vilain, "Prescription," 167 n.19;   4–8 J. F. v. Schulte, *Geschichte*, 1.166 n.30.

APP. FONT.   2–4 *Definitionem primo a Stephano Tornacensi*, ed. J. F. v. Schulte,
225, *inter canonistas divulgatam Huguccio cognovit ex Summa Johannis Faventini,*
MS Paris. lat. 14606, fol. 103va (= *Summa Lipsiensis*, MS Lips. 986, fol.
182vb);   4–9 *De hoc eodem argumento vide apparatum textus qui sequitur.*

Cf. C.16 q.3 p.c.15 § 1 s.v. *utiliter*

ut dicunt Bul., Pla., Io.b., quia prescriptione ut dicunt
non acquiritur dominium quamvis effectus dominii. Secundum
Mart. directo potest vendicare quia secundum eum dominium
acquiritur prescriptione.

MSS KNB, fol. 245vb; V, 220vb; M, 199rb.

ED.   1–4 ed. N. Vilain, "Prescription," 131 n.7.

APP. FONT.   1–4 *Versus qui repetunt dissensionem proximi excerpti* (supra,
vv.4–9) *sequuntur Summam Stephani*, ed. J. F. v. Schulte, 225, 228 (*ex qua verbotenus
Johannes Faventinus* [MS Paris. lat. 14606, fols. 103vb, 105rb], *et Summa Lipsiensis*
[MS Lips. 986, fols. 183rb, 185vb]), *nominibus Pla. nec non Io.b. insuper additis.*

Dissensionum collectiones nomina Martini Bulgarique tantum memorant, ed. G. Haenel, *Dissensiones dominorum,* 18–19, 89–90; ed. V. Scialoja, "Nuova collezione," 340; *item Tractatus qui dicitur De Prescriptionibus a* C. Gross, 265–66, *editus.*

8. C.30 q.5 c.11 s.v. *iudicantem oportet cuncta rimari*

Et dicunt quidam quod debet supplere de facto tantum, alii
de iure tantum, alii de utroque ut Pla. Quod magis credo.
Similiter hermoditio contracto iudex pro absente debet
allegare et eius partes implere, ut C. De appell. [Cod.7.42]
5 l. ult.; et C. De temporibus ap. [Cod.7.63] l.ii § ult.;
Idem credit Pla. iudicem debere facere quando mortuus
accusatur. Nam mortui absentia Dei repletur presentia. Cum
enim iudex iudicat quid aliud credi debeat quam Deum
iudicare in evangeliis coram positis presentem. Sic ergo
10 sive advocati sive litigatores minus dicant iudex ex officio
suo supplebit.

MSS KNB, fol. 297ra; V, 275rb; P, 78va–b; M, 246rb.
ED. K. W. Nörr, *Stellung des Richters,* 48.
APP. CRIT.   5 l.ii] l.i P, M
APP. FONT.   1–7 *Huguccio exscripsit ex Summa Sicardi, ad* C.3 q.7 (ed. K. W. Nörr, *Stellung des Richters,* 46), *addens nomen Placentini, ad quem et referunt Dissensionum collectiones,* ed. G. Haenel, *Dissensiones dominorum,* 268–69; ed. V. Scialoja, "Nuova collezione," 385–86, *Ordo qui dicitur Bambergensis,* ed. J. F. v. Schulte, 303, *nec non ipse Placentinus,* Summa Codicis (ed. Moguntiae, 1536) 76.

9. C.32 q.1 p.c.10 § 1 s.v. *reos facere*

Sed in hoc dissonant legiste. Quidam enim eorum dicunt quod
uxor numquam potest accusare virum de adulterio, alii dicunt
quod potest sed non iure mariti i.e. non sine pena talionis,
non sine inscriptione, non de suspicione. Sed maritus etiam
5 iure mariti accusat uxorem de adulterio sc. sine pena
talionis, quia si defecerit non patietur talionem, et sine
inscriptione et de sola suspicione. Sed hoc privilegium non
conceditur marito nisi infra lx utiles dies. Postea non
potest eam accusare nisi iure communi sicut quilibet alius.
10 Sunt et alia que dicuntur esse de iure mariti et spectare
ad privilegium mariti sc. ut in illis lx diebus preferatur
aliis in accusatione uxoris et quedam forte alia que non
tangunt locum istum. Io. vero Ba. de primis tribus que
dicuntur esse de iure mariti non assignat nisi unum sc.
15 quod maritus infra lx dies utiles accusat uxorem de
adulterio sine metu talionis. Sed debet inscribere, licet
non teneatur ad penam talionis. Non enim dicitur in lege
quod non teneatur inscribere, sed non tenetur vinculo
inscriptionis i.e. non vincitur inscriptione ad penam

20 talionis sicut alii inscribentes. Item posse accusare de
sola suspicione uxorem non est de iure mariti. Sed sic
intelligitur: Maritus potest accusare uxorem de sola
suspicione sine metu talionis usque ad lx dies utiles,
puta suspicatur crimen uxoris. Accusat eam. Deficit in
25 probatione. Non notatur de calumnia quod non contingeret
in alio. Et expresse dicit Io. ba. quod uxor secundum leges
non auditur de adulterio contra maritum. Sed quicquid leges
dicant, ego sequens mentem canonum dico quod uxor et
maritus in accusatione adulterii iudicantur ad non imparia;
30 ar. supra e. q. Si quis uxorem [c.4]; infra e. q.v Precepit
[c.19].

MSS KNB, fol. 302ra; V, 279vb; P, 83ra; M, 250va–b.
ED. G. Minnucci, *Capacità della donna*, 117 (*multis cum erroribus*).
APP. FONT.   13–20 *Idem dicit Johannes Bazianus in Ordine suo iudiciario*, ed.
F. Patetta, 228b.

10. C.35 q.9 a.c.1 s.v. *unde queritur*

Sed queret aliquis a quo debeat retractari sententia usque
ad xx annos vel postea quandocumque. . . . Et nota idem esse
in falsis testibus quod in falsis instrumentis. Placentinus
tamen dicit quod non retractatur sententia lata propter
5 falsos testes nisi corrupti fuerint pecunia. Sed Io.b.
dicit quod sic. Pla. utitur hac ratione, quia lex dicit
quod sententia lata propter testes corruptos pecunia est
revocanda nec invenitur alibi expressum quod si fuerint
corrupti precibus vel alio modo sententia debeat revocari,
10 ar. ff. De re iudi. Divus Adrianus [Dig.42.1.33]. Sed Io.b.
respondet et dicit quod hoc non nocet quia subauditur
'maxime.' Idem enim esset etsi non pecunia sed precibus vel
alio modo corrupti essent. Et hoc tali argumento quia ex
falsis instrumentis sententia lata revocatur, ut C. t. Si
15 ex falsis instrumentis [Cod.7.58], ll.ii et iii. Sed
appellatione instrumenti et testes continentur, ut ff. De
fide instrum. [Dig.22.4], l.i. Ergo sententia lata propter
testes falsos sive pecunia sive precibus sive alio modo erit
revocanda. Vel potest dici quod nomine pecunie intelliguntur
20 preces, obsequia, et quicquid est quo testes corrumpuntur.

MSS KNB, fol. 330vb; V, 324va; P, 108va; M, 277vb.
APP. FONT. *Sumptum esse videtur ex Dissensionum*, Coll. Chis. 218, ed. G. Haenel,
Dissensiones dominorum, 201.

BIBLIOGRAPHY

Manuscript Sources

Bernardus Parmensis. *Glossa ordinaria* (on X): Syracuse, New York, University Library Arents Coll. 1.

Boncompagno de Signa. *Quinque tabule salutationum*: MSS Munich, Staatsbibl. lat. 23499; Rome, Bibl. Vallicelliana C.40.

Compilatio tertia: MS Florence, Bibl. Naz. Conventi soppressi da ord. Vallombrosa 36 (325).

Evrardus Yprensis. *Summa decretalium questionum*: MS Reims, Bibl. de la Ville 689.

Glossae anteazonianae in Codicem: MS Munich, Staatsbibl. lat. 22, fols. 1–210.

Glossae anteazonianae in Novellas: MS Munich, Staatsbibl. lat. 3509, fols. 45–199.

Goffredus Tranensis. *Apparatus in X*: MS Paris, B.N. lat. 15402.

Honorius. Summa *De iure canonico tractaturus*: MS Laon, Bibl. municipale 371bis, fols. 83–170.

Hostiensis. *Lectura super X*: MSS Vienna, Österreichische Nationalbibl. lat. 2114 (first recension); Oxford, New College 205 (second recension).

Huguccio. *Summa decretorum*: MSS Admont, Stiftsbibl. 7; Florence, Bibl. Laur. Fesul. 125–26; Florence, Bibl. Laur. S. Croce i sin.4; Klagenfurt, Bischöfl. Bibl. xxix a.3; Klosterneuburg, Stiftsbibl. 89; Lons-le-Saunier, Arch. dép. 12 F.16; Munich, Staatsbibl. lat. 10247; Paris, B.N. lat. 3891, lat. 3892, lat. 15396–97; Vatican, Bibl. Apost. lat. 2280; Vienna, Ö.N.B. lat. 2061.

Huguccio Pisanus. *Derivationes*: MSS Berlin, Deutsche Staatsbibl. Hamilton 335; Berlin, Staatsbibl. lat. fol. 621; Florence, Bibl. Laur. Plut. xxvii sin. 5; Graz, Univ.bibl. 144 and 427; London, Brit. Mus. Addit. 18380; Lisbon, Bibl. Nac. Alcob. cccxc/277; Paris, B.N. lat. 15462; Vienna, Ö.N.B lat. 1454.

Huguccio (Pisanus?). *Summa artis grammatice*: MS Munich, Staatsbibl. lat. 18908.

Johannes Andreae. *Additiones* (on X): MSS Munich, Staatsbibl. lat. 6351 (first recension); Munich, Staatsbibl. lat. 15703 (second recension).

Johannes de Deo. *Summa super iv causis decretorum*: MS Vatican, Bibl. Apost. lat. 2280, fols. 371–388.

Johannes Faventinus. *Summa decretorum*: MSS Bamberg. Staatsbibl. Can. 37; Munich. Staatsbibl. lat. 14403; Paris. B.N. lat. 14606, fols. 1–166; Vatican, Bibl. Apost. Borgh. lat. 71.

Johannes Teutonicus. *Glossa ordinaria* (on the *Decretum*): MSS Admont, Stiftsbibl. 35; Vienna, Ö.N.B. lat. 2082.

Johannes Teutonicus. *Apparatus in Compilationem tertiam*: MS Munich, Staatsbibl. lat. 3879.

Laurentius Hispanus. *Reportatio lecture* (on the *Decretum*): MS Paris, B.N. lat. 15393 (third layer of glosses).

Laurentius Hispanus. *Apparatus in Compilationem tertiam*: MSS Admont, Stiftsbibl. 55, fols. 101ra–222ra; Karlsruhe, Landesbibl. Aug. xl, fols. 121ra–230va.

Note Atrebatenses: MS Arras, Bibl. munic. 271, fols. 149–60.

Servus appellatur (on 3 Comp): MS Paris, B.N. lat. 3967.

Sicardus Cremonensis. *Summa decretorum*: MSS Munich, Staatsbibl. lat. 4555 and lat. 8013.

Simon de Bisignano. *Summa decretorum*: MSS Augsburg, Stadtbibl. 1, fols. 1–72; Bamberg, Staatsbibl. Can 38, fols. 2–54.

Summa *Antiquitate et tempore*: MS Göttingen, Staats- und Univ. bibl. 2 Jurid. 159.

Summa *Aschaffenburg Perg. 26*: MS Aschaffenburg, Hof- und Stiftsbibl. Perg. 26, fols. 218–27.

Summa Casinensis ("Continuatio prima"): MSS Admont, Stiftsbibl. 7, fols. 325–33; Florence, Bibl. Laur. Fesul. 126, fols. 109–25; Leipzig, Univ. Bibl. 985, fols. 234ra–54rb; Lons-le-Saunier, Arch. dép. 12.F.16, fols. 313–25; Montecassino, Bibl. Abbaz. 396, pp. 113–90; Paris, B.N. lat. 15396, fols. 100ra–107ra, lat. 15397, fols. 2ra–vb and fols. 46vb–58rb; Vatican, Bibl. Apost. lat. 2280, fols. 248–56.

Summa *Iuditiorum instrumenta*: MS Munich, Staatsbibl. lat. 16084, fols. 28–29.

Summa Lipsiensis ("Omnis qui iuste"): MSS Leipzig, Univ. bibl. 986; Rouen, Bibl. munic. 743.

Summa Monacensis ("Inperatorie maiestati"): MS Munich, Staatsbibl. lat. 16084, fols. 1–9, 11–16, 18–27.

Summa *Paris 15397*: MS Paris, B.N. lat. 15397, fols. 172ra–183va.

Summa Reginensis: MS Vatican, Bibl. Apost. Reg. lat. 1061, fols. 1–48.

Summa *Reverentia sacrorum canonum*: MS Erfurt, Stadtbibl. Amplon. qu. 117, fols. 116–40.

Summa *Sicut vetus testamentum*: MS Florence, Bibl. Naz. Conventi soppressi da ord. G iv 1736, fols. 1–64.

Summa *Tractaturus magister*: MS Paris, B.N. lat. 15994.

Tancredus. *Glossa ordinaria* (on 3 Comp): MS Vatican, Bibl. Apost. lat. 2509.

Ugolinus de Sesso. *De recusatione iudicum*: MS Barcelona, ACA S. Cugat 55, fols. 140ra–va.

Vincentius Hispanus. *Apparatus in Compilationem tertiam*: MS Karlsruhe, Landesbibl. Aug. xl, fols. 121–230.

Printed Primary Sources

Carmina medii aevi posterioris Latina 2.1, ed. H. Walther (Göttingen, 1963).

Chronicon Estense, ed. L. Muratori, RIS 15 (Milan, 1729).

Corpus iuris civilis, ed. P. Krüger, T. Mommsen, R. Schöll, and W. Kroll (3 vols.; Berlin, 1872–95).

Decretales Gregorii IX, ed. E. Friedberg, *Corpus iuris canonici* 2 (Leipzig, 1881).

Dissensiones dominorum, ed. G. Haenel (Leipzig, 1834); ed. V. Scialoja, *Scritti giuridici* 2 (Rome, 1934) 327–413.

Egidius Spiritalis de Perusio. *Libellus contra infideles et inobedientes et rebelles Sancte Romane Ecclesie ac summo pontifici*, ed. R. Scholz, *Unbekannte kirchenpolitische Streitschriften* (Rome, 1914).

Franciscus Petrarca (?). *Chronica delle vite de' pontefici et imperatori Romani* (Venice, 1507, 1534); also printed as *Libro degli Inperadori et pontefici* (Hain 12809; Florence, 1478).

Franciscus Pipinus. *Chronicon*, ed. L. Muratori, RIS 9 (Milan, 1726).

Friderici I diplomata (for the years 1152–67), ed. H. Appelt, MGH DD 10.1–2 (Hanover, 1975–79).

Gratianus. *Concordia discordantium canonum sive Decretum*, ed. E. Friedberg, *Corpus iuris canonici* 1 (Leipzig, 1879).

Guilelmus Durantis. *Speculum iudiciale* (Lyons, 1521).

Hostiensis. *Lectura super X* (Strasbourg, 1512).

Huguccio. *Agiographia*, ed. G. Cremascoli, *Uguccione da Pisa: Liber de dubio accentu. Agiographia. Expositio de symbolo apostolorum* (Spoleto, 1978) 137–74.

Huguccio. *Expositio de symbolo apostolorum*, ed. ibid., 227–55; ed. N. Häring, "Zwei Kommentare von Huguccio, Bischof von Ferrara," SG 19 (1976) 365–398.

Huguccio. *Summa decretorum* (on C.27 q.2), ed. J. Roman, RHD 27 (1903) 745–805.

Huguccio Pisanus. *Liber de dubio accentu*, ed. G. Cremascoli, *Uguccione da Pisa*, 65–87.

Isidorus Hispalensis. *Etymologiarum libri xx*, ed. W. Lindsay (Oxford, 1911).

Johannes Andreae. *Adnotationes super Speculum Durantis* (Lyons, 1521).

Johannes Bazianus. *Libellus de ordine iudiciorum*, ed. F. Patetta, *Bibliotheca iuridica Medii Aevi* 2 (Bologna, 1892) 213a–223a.

Johannes Diaconus. *Descriptio ecclesie Lateranensis*, PL 78.1379–92.

———. *Liber de sanctis sanctorum*, ed. R. Valentini and G. Zucchetti. *Codice topografico della città di Roma* 3 (Rome, 1946) 325–73.

Ordo anonymus, ed. C. Gross. *Incerti auctoris ordo iudiciarius, pars summae legum et tractatus de prescriptionibus* (Innsbruck, 1870) 87–158.

Ordo Bambergensis, ed. J. F. v. Schulte. *SB Vienna* 70 (1872) 285–326.
Ordo Invocato Christi Domine. See Pilius.
Osbern of Gloucester. *Panormia*, ed. A. Mai. *Classicorum auctorum e Vaticanis codicibus editorum* 8 (Rome, 1836).
Papias. *Elementarium doctrinae rudimentum. Litera A* 1, ed. V. De Angelis (Milan, 1977).
Paucapalea. *Summa decreti*, ed. J. F. v. Schulte, *Die Summa des Paucapalea über das Decretum Gratiani* (Giessen, 1890).
Pilius, *Ordo iudiciarius*, ed. L. Wahrmund, *Quellen zur Geschichte des römisch-kanonischen Zivilprocesses im Mittelalter* 5.1 (Heidelberg, 1931).
Placentinus. *Summa Codicis* (Mainz, 1536).
Ranieri Sardo. *Cronaca di Pisa*, ed. O. Banti (Fonti per la storia d'Italia 99; Rome, 1963).
Regestum Pisanum, ed. N. Caturegli (Regesta chartarum Italiae 24; Rome, 1938).
Registrum Innocentii III, ed. O. Hageneder and A. Haidacher, *Die Register Innozenz' III.: 1. Pontifikatsjahr 1198–1199* (Graz/Cologne, 1964); ed. O. Hageneder, W. Maleczek, and A. Strnad, 2. *Pontifikatsjahr 1199–1200* (Rome/Vienna, 1979).
Riccobaldus Ferrariensis. *Compendium Romanae historiae*, ed. A. Hankey (Fonti per la storia d'Italia 108; Rome, 1984).
Riccobaldus Ferrariensis. *Compilatio chronologica, Pomerium, Historia pontificum Romanorum*, ed. L. Muratori, RIS 9 (Milan, 1726).
Rufinus. *Summa decretorum*, ed. H. Singer, *Rufinus von Bologna, 'Summa Decretorum'* (Paderborn, 1902).
Salimbene Parmensis. *Chronica*, ed. O. Holder-Egger, MGH SS 32 (Hanover, 1905/11); F. Bernini (Scrittori d'Italia 187; Bari, 1942); G. Scalia (Scrittori d'Italia 232–33; Bari, 1966).
Stephanus Tornacensis. *Summa decreti*, ed. J. F. v. Schulte, *Die Summa des Stephanus Tornacensis über das Decretum Gratiani* (Giessen, 1891).
Summa Coloniensis. ed. S. Kuttner and G. Fransen, *Summa "Elegantius de iure divino" seu Coloniensis* (MIC A.1.1: New York, 1969; MIC A.1.2–4: Vatican City, 1981–90).
Summa *Fecit Moyses tabernaculum*, ed. (in part) J. F. v. Schulte, *Die Summa des Stephanus Tornacensis*, 259–81.
Summa Parisiensis, ed. T. P. Mc Laughlin, *The "Summa Parisiensis" on the Decretum Gratiani* (Toronto, 1952).
Tholomaeus Lucensis. *Historia ecclesiastica*, ed. L. Muratori, RIS 11 (Milan, 1727).
Thomas Diplovatatius. *Liber de claris iuris consultis* 2, ed. H. Kantorowicz, F. Schulz, and G. Rabotti, SG 10 (1968).
Tractatus de prescriptionibus, ed. *Incerti auctoris ordo iudiciarus, pars summae legum et tractatus de prescriptionibus*, ed. C. Gross (Innsbruck, 1870).
Ugolinus de Sesso. *De recusatione iudicum*, ed. G. Martinez, in "Tres lec-

ciones del siglo xii del estudio general de Palencia," AHDE 61 (1991) 391–
449, at 412–17.
Vacarius. *Liber pauperum,* ed. F. de Zulueta (London, 1927).

Secondary Sources

Abellán, R. *El fin y la significación sacramental del matrimonio desde S. Anselmo hasta Guillermo de Auxerre* (Granada, 1939).
Albisetti, A. *Contributo allo studio del matrimonio putativo in diritto canonico. Violenza e buona fede* (Milan, 1980).
Anciaux, P. *La théologie du sacrement de pénitence au xiie siècle* (Louvain/ Gembloux, 1949).
Austin, H. "The sources of Uguccione's illustrative quotations," *Medievalia et Humanistica* 4 (1946) 104–6.
Baldwin, J. W. "The intellectual preparation for the canon of 1215 against ordeals," *Speculum* 36 (1961) 613–36.
———. *Masters, merchants, and princes: The social views of Peter Chanter and his circle* (Princeton, 1970).
Barotti, L. *Serie dei vescovi ed arcivescovi di Ferrara* (Ferrara, 1781).
Bellini, P. *L'obbligazione da promessa con ogetto temporale nel sistema canonistico classico, con particolare riferimento ai secoli xii e xiii* (Milan, 1964).
———. *Denunciatio evangelica e denunciatio iudicialis privata. Un capitolo di storia disciplinare della chiesa* (Milan, 1986); revised from idem, *L'obbligazione da promessa,* 195–256, 393–516.
Belloni, A. "Baziano, cioè Giovanni Baziano, legista e canonista del secolo xii," TRG 57 (1989) 69–85.
Benson, R. *The bishop-elect. A study in medieval ecclesiastical office* (Princeton, 1968).
———. "Review of S. Chodorow," *Speculum* 50 (1975) 97–106.
Benson, R., and G. Constable (eds.). *Renaissance and renewal in the twelfth century* (Cambridge, Mass., 1982).
Bernal-Palácios, A. *La "Concordia utriusque iuris" de Pascipoverus* (Valencia, 1980).
Bernini, F. "Che cosa vide e raccontò di Ferrara il cronista Salimbene da Parma?" *Rivista di Ferrara* 4 (1934) 28–35.
Bertram, M. "Die Abdankung Papst Coelestins V. (1294) und die Kanonisten," ZRG Kan. Abt. 56 (1970) 1–101.
Bertram, M., and M. Duynstee, "Casus legum sive suffragia monachorum," TRG 51 (1983) 326–69.
Blumenthal, U. *The Investiture Controversy. Church and monarchy from the ninth to the twelfth century* (Philadelphia, 1988).
Borchard, K. "Archbishop Gerard of Ravenna and Bishop John of Faenza," *Proceedings San Diego* (Vatican City, 1992) 572–92, at 584–92.
Boyle, L. "The beginnings of legal studies at Oxford," *Viator* 14 (1983) 107–31.

Brundage, J. *Law, sex, and Christian society in medieval Europe* (Chicago, 1987).

Burns, J. *The Cambridge history of medieval political thought, c. 350–c. 1450* (Cambridge, 1988).

Bursill-Hall, G. *A census of medieval Latin grammatical manuscripts* (Stuttgart, 1981).

Bursill-Hall, G., ed. *The history of grammar in the Middle Ages* (Amsterdam, 1980).

Braunfels, W., ed. *Lexikon der christlichen Ikonographie 5–8: Ikonographie der Heiligen* (Freiburg/B., 1973–76).

Brundage, J. *Medieval canon law and the crusader* (Madison/Milwaukee/London, 1969).

Brys, J. *De dispensatione in iure canonico, praesertim apud decretistas et decretalistas usque ad saeculum decimum quartum* (Bruges/Wetteren, 1925).

Cantelar-Rodríguez, F. *El matrimonio de herejes. Bifurcación del impedimentum disparis cultus y divorcio por herejía* (Salamanca, 1972).

Capitani, O., ed. *L'Università di Bologna: personaggi, momenti e luoghi dalle origini al xvi secolo* (Bologna, 1987).

Caron, P. *"Aequitas Romana," "Misericordia patristica" ed "Epicheia Aristotelica" nella dottrina dell'"Aequitas canonica"* (Milan, 1971).

Catalano, G. "Contributo alla biografia di Uguccione da Pisa," *Il diritto ecclesiastico* 65 (1954) 3–67.

———. *Impero, regni e sacerdozio nel pensiero di Uguccio da Pisa* (Milan, 1959).

Chodorow, S. *Christian political theory and church politics in the midtwelfth century: The ecclesiology of Gratian's Decretum* (Berkeley/Los Angeles/London, 1972).

Coing, H., ed. *Handbuch der Quellen und Literatur der neueren europäischen Privatrechtsgeschichte 1: Mittelalter, 1100–1500* (Munich, 1973).

Condorelli, M. *I fondamenti giuridici della tolleranza religiosa nell'elaborazione canonistica dei secoli xii–xiv* (Milan, 1960).

Conrat, M. *Die Epitome "Exactis regibus"* (Berlin, 1884).

Cortese, E. "Per la storia di una teoria dell'arcivescovo Mosè di Ravenna (m. 1154) sulla proprietà ecclesiastica," *Proceedings Salamanca* (Vatican City, 1980) 117–55.

Couvreur, G. *Les pauvres ont-ils des droits? Recherches sur le vol en cas d'extrême nécessité depuis Gratien (1140) jusqu'à Guillaume d'Auxerre (m. 1231)* (Analecta Gregoriana 111; Rome, 1961).

Cremascoli, G. "Uguccione da Pisa: saggio bibliografico," *Aevum* 42 (1968) 123–68.

de Marco, M. "Review of G. Cremascoli (ed.), *Uguccione da Pisa*," *Rivista di cultura classica e medievale* 21/22 (1978/79) 209–11.

de Sousa Costa, A. "John de Deo," *NCE* 7 (1967) 996.

del Re, N. *I codici Vaticani della "Summa decretorum" di Uguccione da Pisa* (Rome, 1938).

Delisle, L. *Le cabinet des manuscrits de la Bibliothèque Nationale* 2 (Paris, 1874).

Diehl, P. "'Ad abolendam' (X 5.7.9) and imperial legislation against heresy," BMCL 19 (1989) 1–11.

Dolcini, C. *Velut aurora surgente: Pepo, il vescovo Pietro e le origini dello Studium Bolognese* (Rome, 1987).

Erdö, P. *L'ufficio del primate nella canonistica da Graziano ad Uguccione da Pisa* (Rome, 1986); first in *Apollinaris* 54 (1981) 357–98, 55 (1982) 165–93.

Evenepoel, W. "La délimitation de l'année liturgique dans les premiers siècles de la Chrétienté occidentale," RHE 83 (1988) 601–16.

Fowler, L. "Innocent uselessness in civilian and canonist thought," ZRG Kan. Abt. 58 (1972) 107–65.

———. "'Recusatio iudicis' in canonist and civilian thought," SG 15 (1972) 719–85.

Fransen, G. "Manuscrits canoniques conservés en Espagne," RHE 48 (1953) 232–33, 49 (1954) 153.

———. "'Utrumque ius' dans les 'Questiones Andegavenses,'" *Études d'histoire dédiées à Gabriel Le Bras* (Paris, 1965) 2.897–911.

Fried, J. *Über die Entstehung des Juristenstandes im 12. Jahrhundert* (Cologne/Vienna, 1974).

Friedberg, E. *Die Canones-Sammlungen zwischen Gratian und Bernhard von Pavia* (Leipzig, 1897; repr. Graz, 1956).

Galgano, S. "Violenza nel consenso e matrimonio putativo," *Rivista di diritto civile* 13 (1921) 209–27, 438–94.

Gams, P. *Series episcoporum ecclesiae catholicae* (Regensburg, 1873).

Ganzer, K. "Zur Beschränkung der Bischofswahl auf die Domkapitel in Theorie und Praxis des 12. und 13. Jahrhunderts," ZRG Kan. Abt. 57 (1971) 22–82.

Garcia y Garcia, A. "Canonistica Hispanica iv," BMCL 1 (1971) 70–73.

———. "La canonística Ibérica (1150–1250) en la investigación reciente," BMCL 11 (1981) 41–75.

Gastaldelli, F. "Le 'Sententiae' di Pietro Lombardo e l' 'Expositio de symbolo apostolorum' di Uguccione da Pisa," *Salesianum* 39 (1977) 318–21.

Génestal, R. *Le privilegium fori en France du Décret de Gratien à la fin du xive siècle* (2 vols.; Paris, 1921–24).

Gilchrist, J. "The medieval canon law on unfree persons: Gratian and the decretist doctrines," SG 19 (1976) 271–301.

Gillmann, F. *Paucapalea und "Paleae" bei Huguccio* (Mainz, 1908); revised from AKKR 88 (1908) 466–79; reprinted in R. Weigand (ed.), *Schriften Franz Gillmann* 1, n.14.

———. "Die simonistische Papstwahl nach Huguccio," AKKR 89 (1909) 606–11.

———. *Die Siebenzahl der Sakramente bei den Glossatoren des gratianischen Dekrets* (Mainz, 1909).

———. "Die Designation des Nachfolgers durch den Papst nach dem Urteil der Dekretglossatoren des zwölften Jahrhunderts," AKKR 90 (1910) 407–17.

———. "Zur Geschichte der Ausdrücke 'irregularis' und 'irregularitas,'" AKKR 91 (1911) 49–86.

———. "Review," AKKR 92 (1912) 365–68.

———. "Weibliche Kleriker nach dem Urteil der Frühscholastik," AKKR 93 (1913) 239–53.

———. "Die Abfassungszeit der Dekretsumme Huguccios," AKKR 94 (1914) 233–51 = R. Weigand (ed.), *Schriften Franz Gillmann* 1, n.8.

———. *Die Notwendigkeit der Intention auf Seiten des Spenders und des Empfängers der Sakramente nach der Anschauung der Frühscholastik* (Mainz, 1916).

———. *Zur Lehre der Scholastik vom Spender der Firmung und des Weihesakraments* (Paderborn, 1920).

———. *Spender und äußeres Zeichen der Bischofsweihe nach Huguccio* (Paderborn, 1922).

———. "Zur scholastischen Auslegung von Mt. 16.18," AKKR 104 (1924) 41–53.

———. "Die Dekretsumme des Codex Stuttgart, Hist Fol. 419," AKKR 107 (1927) 192–250 = R. Weigand, *Schriften Franz Gillmann* 1, n.12.

———. "Die 'anni discretionis' im Kanon 'Omnis utriusque sexus' (c.21 conc. Lat. IV)," AKKR 108 (1928) 556–617.

———. "Clave non errante?" AKKR 110 (1930) 451–65.

———. *Des Johannes Galensis Apparat zur Compilatio III in der UB Erlangen (Cod. 349). Mit einem Anhang: Zur Inventarisierung der kanonistischen Handschriften aus der Zeit von Gratian bis Gregor IX.* (Mainz, 1938); of which the *Anhang* 54–94, has been reprinted in R. Weigand (ed.), *Schriften Franz Gillmann* 1, n.16.

Gouron, A. *La science juridique française aux xie et xiie siècles: Diffusion du droit de Justinien et influences canoniques jusqu'à Gratien* (IRMAe I, 4 d-e; Milan, 1978).

———. "Un école ou des écoles? Sur les canonistes français (vers 1150–vers 1210)," *Proceedings Berkeley* (Vatican City, 1985) 223–40.

———. "Sur les sources civilistes et la datation des sommes de Rufin et d'Étienne de Tournai," BMCL 16 (1986) 55–70.

———. "A la convergence des deux droits: Jean Bassien, Bazianus et maître Jean," TRE 59 (1991) 319–32.

Gross, C. *Das Recht an der Pfründe* (Graz, 1887).

Gründel, J. *Die Lehre von den Umständen der menschlichen Handlung im Mittelalter* (Münster/W., 1963).

Hageneder, O. "Das päpstliche Recht zur Fürstenabsetzung: Seine kanonistische Grundlegung," AHP 1 (1963) 53–95.

———. "Der Häresiebegriff bei den Juristen des 12. und 13. Jahrhunderts," in *The concept of heresy in the Middle Ages,* ed. W. Lourdeaux and D. Verhelst (Louvain/The Hague, 1976) 42–102.

Hartmann, W., and K. Pennington. *History of medieval canon law* 2 (Washington, to appear).

Heckel, R. "Die Dekretalensammlungen des Gilbertus und Alanus nach den Weingartener Handschriften," ZRG Kan. Abt. 29 (1940) 116–357.

Hehl, E. *Kirche und Krieg im 12. Jahrhundert. Studien zu kanonischem Recht und politischer Wirklichkeit* (Stuttgart, 1980).

Heitmeyer, H. *Sakramentenspendung bei Häretikern und Simonisten nach Huguccio* (Analecta Gregoriana 132; Rome, 1964).

Hessel, A. *Geschichte der Stadt Bologna von 1116 bis 1280* (Berlin, 1910); Italian version ed. G. Fasoli, *Storia della città di Bologna (1116–1280)* (Bologna, 1975).

Heyer, F. "Namen und Titel des gratianischen Dekrets," AKKR 94 (1914) 507–22.

Heywood, W. *A history of Pisa* (Cambridge, 1921).

Hödl, L. *Die Geschichte der scholastischen Literatur und die Theologie der Schlüsselgewalt I: Die scholastische Literatur und die Theologie der Schlüsselgewalt von ihren Anfängen bis zur Summa aurea des Wilhelm von Auxerre* (Münster/W., 1960).

Höhl, N. *Die Glossen des Johannes Faventinus zur Pars i des Decretum Gratiani: Eine literargeschichtliche Untersuchung* (thesis; Würzburg, 1987).

———. "Wer war Johannes Faventinus? Neue Erkenntnisse zu Leben und Werk eines der bedeutendsten Dekretisten des 12. Jahrhunderts," *Proceedings San Diego* (Vatican City, 1992) 189–203.

Holböck, F. *Der eucharistische und der mystische Leib Christi* (Rome, 1941).

Holtzmann, W. *Studies in the collections of twelfth-century decretals,* ed. C. Cheney and M. Cheney (MIC B-3; Vatican City, 1979).

Huizing, P. "The earliest development of excommunication latae sententiae by Gratian and the earliest decretists," SG 3 (1955) 277–320.

Hunt, R. "The 'lost' preface to the 'Liber derivationum' of Osbern of Gloucester," *Medieval and Renaissance studies* 4 (1952) 267–82 = G. Bursill-Hall (ed.), *The history,* 151–66.

Hussarek Ritter von Henlein, M. *Die bedingte Eheschliessung. Eine kanonistische Studie* (Vienna, 1892).

Imkamp, W. *Das Kirchenbild Innozenz' III.* (Stuttgart, 1983).

Juncker, J. "Die Summa des Simon von Bisignano und seine Glossen," ZRG Kan. Abt. 15 (1926) 326–84.

Kalb, H. *Studien zur Summa Stephans von Tournai* (Innsbruck, 1983).

———. "Bemerkungen zum Verhältnis von Theologie und Kanonistik am Beispiel Rufins und Stephans von Tournai," ZRG Kan. Abt. 72 (1986) 338–48.

Kehr, P. *Italia pontificia* 5 (Berlin, 1910).

Kempf, F. *Papsttum und Kaisertum bei Innocenz III. Die geistigen und rechtlichen Grundlagen seiner Thronstreitpolitik* (Miscellanea historiae pontificiae 19; Rome, 1954).

Kneepkens, H. *Het "Iudicium constructionis": Het leerstuck van de constructio in de 2de helft van de 12de eeuw* (Nimjegen, 1987).

Knox, R. "The problem of academic language in Rufinus and Stephan," *Proceedings Berkeley* (MIC C 7; Vatican City, 1985) 109–23.

Kristeller, P. *Iter Italicum* 4 (Leiden/London, 1989).

Kurtscheid, B. *Das Beichtsiegel in seiner geschichtlichen Entwicklung* (Freiburg, 1912).

Kuttner, S. *Kanonistische Schuldlehre von Gratian bis auf die Dekretalen Gregors IX.* (Studi e testi 64; Vatican City, 1935).

———. "Ecclesia de occultis non iudicat. Problemata ex doctrina poenali decretistarum et decretalistarum a Gratiano usque ad Gregorium PP. IX." *Acta congressus iuridici internationalis, Romae 1934* 3 (Rome, 1936) 225–46.

———. *Repertorium der Kanonistik (1140–1234)* (Studi e testi 71; Vatican City, 1937).

———. "Bernardus Compostellanus Antiquus: A study in the glossators of the canon law," *Traditio* 1 (1943) 277–340 = idem, *Gratian* n. vii (with "Retractationes").

———. "Papst Honorius und das Studium des Zivilrechts," ed. E. v. Caemmerer, *Festschrift für Martin Wolff* (Tübingen, 1952) 79–101 = S. Kuttner, *The history,* n. x (with "Retractationes").

———. "New studies on the Roman law in Gratian's Decretum," *Seminar* 11 (1953) 12–48 = idem, *Gratian,* n. iv (with "Retractationes").

———. "Additional notes on the Roman law in Gratian," *Seminar* 12 (1954) 68–74 = idem, *Gratian,* n. v (with "Retractationes").

———. "Pope Lucius III and the bigamous archbishop of Palermo," in *Medieval studies presented to Aubrey Gwynn, S.J.,* ed. J. Watt et al. (Dublin, 1961) 409–54 = S. Kuttner, *The history,* n. viii (with "Retractationes").

———. "Johannes Teutonicus," NDB 10 (1974) 71–73.

———. *The history of ideas and doctrines of canon law in the Middle Ages* (London, 1980).

———. "Universal pope or servant of God's servants," RDC 31 (1981) 109–50 = S. Kuttner, *Studies,* n. viii (with "Retractationes").

———. "Raymond of Peñafort as an editor," BMCL 12 (1982) 65–80 = S. Kuttner, *Studies,* n. xii.

———. "The revival of jurisprudence," in *Renaissance and renewal,* ed. R. Benson and G. Constable, 299–323 = S. Kuttner, *Studies,* n. iii (with "Retractationes").

———. *Gratian and the schools of canon law (1140–1234)* (London, 1983).

———. *Studies in the history of medieval canon law* (Aldershot, 1990).

Kuttner, S., and R. Elze, eds. *A catalogue of canon and Roman law manuscripts in the Vatican library* 1/2 (Studi e testi 322/28; Vatican City, 1986/87).

Kuttner, S., and E. Rathbone. "Anglo-Norman canonists of the twelfth century," *Traditio* 7 (1949/51) 279–358 = S. Kuttner, *Gratian* n. viii (with "Retractationes").

Landau, P. *Die Entstehung des kanonischen Infamiebegriffs von Gratian bis zur Glossa ordinaria* (Cologne/Graz, 1966).

———. "Hadrians Dekretale 'Dignum est' (X 4.9.1) und die Eheschließung

Unfreier in der Diskussion des 12. und 13. Jahrhunderts," SG 12 (1967) 511–53.

———. "Ursprünge und Entwicklung des Verbotes doppelter Strafverfolgung wegen desselben Verbrechens in der Geschichte des kanonischen Rechts," ZRG Kan. Abt. 56 (1970) 124–56.

———. *Ius patronatus. Studien zur Entwicklung des Patronats im Dekretalenrecht und der Kanonistik des 12. und 13. Jahrhunderts* (Cologne/Vienna, 1975).

———. "Die Entstehung der systematischen Dekretalensammlungen und die europäische Kanonistik des 12. Jahrhunderts." ZRG Kan. Abt. 65 (1979) 120–48.

———. "Quellen und Bedeutung des gratianischen Dekrets," SDHI 52 (1986) 218–35.

———. "Gratian (von Bologna)," TRE 14 (1986) 124–30.

———. "Die 'Duae leges' im kanonischen Recht des 12. Jahrhunderts." In P. Landau, *Officium und libertas Christiana* (Munich, 1991) 55–96.

———. "Frei und Unfrei in der Kanonistik des 12. und 13. Jahrhunderts am Beispiel der Ordination Unfreier," in *Die abendländische Freiheit vom 10. zum 14. Jahrhundert,* ed. J. Fried (Sigmaringen, 1991) 177–96.

———. "Vorgratianische Kanonessammlungen bei Dekretisten und in frühen Dekretalensammlungen." *Proceedings San Diego* (Vatican City, 1992) 93–116.

Landgraf, A. "Diritto canonico e teologia nel secolo dodicesimo," SG 1 (1953) 373–407.

———. *Dogmengeschichte der Frühscholastik* 1–4 (Regensburg, 1952–56).

Le Bras, G., ed. *Histoire du droit et des institutions de l'Église en Occident 7: L'âge classique (1140–1378). Sources et théorie du droit* (Paris, 1965).

Lefebvre, C. "L'aequitas canonica," in G. Le Bras, ed., *Histoire,* 406–20.

———. "Formation du droit canonique," in G. Le Bras, ed., *Histoire,* 167–74.

Legendre, P. *La pénétration du droit romain dans le droit canonique classique de Gratien à Innocent IV (1140–1254)* (Paris, 1964).

———. "Le droit romain, modèle et langage: De la signification de l'Utrumque Ius," in *Études dédiées à Gabriel Le Bras* (Paris, 1965) 2.918–25 = idem, *Écrits juridiques du Moyen Age occidental* (London, 1988) n. viii.

Lehnherr, T. "Der Begriff 'executio' in der Summa Decretorum des Huguccio," AKKR 150 (1981) 5–44, 361–420.

———. "Der Einschub in die Huguccio-Handschrift der Kapitelsbibliothek von Verona," AKKR 153 (1984) 56–76.

———. *Die Exkommunikationsgewalt der Häretiker bei Gratian und den Dekretisten bis zur Glossa Ordinaria des Johannes Teutonicus* (St. Ottilien, 1987).

Leonardi, C. "La vita e l'opera di Uguccione Pisano decretista," SG 4 (1956–57) 37–120.

Limone, O. "Il 'Liber de dubio accentu' (Cod. Ambr. E 12 inf.) falsamente attribuito ad Uguccione da Pisa," *Studi medievali* 25 (1984) 317–91.

Lindner, D. *Die Lehre vom Privileg nach Gratian und den Glossatoren des CIC* ([Altötting] 1917).

Liotta, F. "Baisio, Guido da," DBI 5 (1963) 294–97.

———. *La continenza dei chierici nel pensiero canonistico classico da Graziano a Gregorio IX* (Milan, 1971).

Maassen, F. "Beiträge zur Geschichte der juristischen Literatur des Mittelalters, insbesondere der Decretisten-Literatur des 12. Jahrhunderts," *SB Vienna* 24 (1857) 1–84.

Maccarone, M. "Sacramentalità e indissolubilità del matrimonio nella dottrina di Innocenzo III," *Lateranum* 44 (1978) 449–514.

McLaughlin, T. "The teachings of the canonists on usury (xii, xiii, and xiv centuries)," *Medieval studies* 1 (1939) 81–147, 2 (1940) 1–22.

Maffei, D. "Fra Cremona, Montpellier e Palencia: Ricerche su Ugolino de Sesso," *Rivista internazionale di diritto commune* 1 (1990) 9–30; also in REDC 47 (1990) 34–51.

Maisonneuve, H. *Etudes sur les origines de l'inquisition* (Paris, 1960).

Marigo, A. "De Huguccionis Pisani Derivationum latinitate earumque prologo," *Archivum Romanicum* 11 (1927) 97–106.

———. *I codici manoscritti delle "Derivationes" di Uguccione Pisano* (Rome, 1936).

Mayali, L. "The concept of discretionary punishment in medieval jurisprudence." *Studia in honorem eminentissimi cardinalis Alphonsi M. Stickler,* ed. R. Card. Castillo Lara (Rome, 1992) 299–315.

Mercati, S. "Sul luogo e sulla data della composizione delle 'Derivationes' di Uguccione da Pisa," *Aevum* 33 (1959) 490–94.

Miethaner-Vent, K. "Das Alphabet in der mittelalterlichen Lexikographie." In *La lexicographie au moyen âge,* ed. C. Buridant (Lille, 1986) 83–112.

Minnucci, G. *La capacità della donna nel processo canonistico classico: Da Graziano a Uguccione da Pisa* (Milan, 1989).

Mochi Onory, S. *Fonti canonistiche dell'idea moderna dello stato* (Milan, 1951).

Möhring, H. *Saladin und der dritte Kreuzzug* (Wiesbaden, 1980).

Motzenbäcker, R. *Die Rechtsvermutung im kanonischen Recht* (Munich, 1958).

Moynihan, P. *Papal immunity and liability in the writings of the medieval canonists* (Analecta Gregoriana 120; Rome, 1961).

Muldoon, J. "Extra ecclesiam non est imperium. The canonists and the legitimacy of secular power," SG 9 (1966) 551–80.

Müller, H. *Der Anteil der Laien an der Bischofswahl. Ein Beitrag zur Geschichte der Kanonistik von Gratian bis Gregor IX.* (Amsterdam, 1977).

Müller, W. "Lucretia and the medieval canonists," BMCL 19 (1989) 13–32.

———. "Huguccio of Pisa: Canonist, bishop, and grammarian?" *Viator* 22 (1991) 121–52.

Munier, C. "Droit canonique et droit romain d'après Gratien et les décrétistes," *Etudes d'histoire du droit canonique dédiées à Gabriel Le Bras* (Paris, 1965) 2.943–54 = C. Munier, *Vie conciliaire et collections canoniques en Occident, ive–xiie siècles* (London, 1987) n.6.

Murray, A. *Reason and society* (Oxford, 1978).

Muratori, L. *Antiquitates Italicae medii aevi* 5 (Milan, 1741).

Neumeyer, K. *Die gemeinrechtliche Entwicklung des internationalen Privat- und Strafrechts bis Bartolus* 1–2 (Munich, 1901–16).

Noonan, J. "Gratian slept here: The changing identity of the father of the systematic study of canon law," *Traditio* 35 (1979) 145–72.

Nörr, K. *Zur Stellung des Richters im gelehrten Prozeß der Frühzeit: "Iudex secundum allegata non secundum conscientiam iudicat"* (Munich, 1967).

————. "Die kanonistische Literatur," ed. H. Coing, *Handbuch* 365–75.

Onclin, W. "La contribution du Décret de Gratien et des décrétistes à la solution des conflits des lois," SG 2 (1954) 115–50.

Orlandi, G. "Review of G. Cremascoli, *Uguccione da Pisa*," *Aevum* 53 (1978) 397–98.

Ouy, G., and V. Gerz-van Buren, *Le catalogue de la bibliothèque de l'abbaye de Saint-Victor de Paris de Claude de Grandrue* (Paris, 1983).

Pacaut, M. *Alexandre III. Etude sur la conception du pouvoir pontifical dans sa pensée et dans son oeuvre* (Paris, 1956).

Padoa Schioppa, A. "Sul principio della rappresentanza diretta nel diritto canonico classico," *Proceedings Toronto* (Vatican City, 1976) 107–31.

Pakter, W. *Medieval canon law and the Jews* (Ebelsbach, 1988).

Pennington, K. "The legal education of Pope Innocent III," BMCL 4 (1974) 70–77.

————. *Pope and bishops. The papal monarchy in the twelfth and thirteenth centuries* (Philadelphia, 1984).

————. "Huguccio of Pisa," DMA 6 (1985) 327–28.

————. "Review of W. Imkamp, *Kirchenbild*," ZRG Kan. Abt. 72 (1986) 417–21.

————. "Johannes Teutonicus (Semeca, Zemeke)," DMA 7 (1986) 121–22.

————. "An earlier recension of the 'Lectura super X' of Cardinal Hostiensis," BMCL 17 (1987) 77–90.

————. "Johannes Andreae's 'Additiones' to the Decretals of Gregory IX," ZRG Kan. Abt. 74 (1988) 328–47.

————. "Law, legislative authority, and theory of government," in J. Burns, ed., *The Cambridge history*, 424–53.

Perez de Heredia y Valle, I. *Die Befangenheit des Richters im kanonischen Recht* (St. Ottilien, 1977).

Peters, E. *The shadow king. Rex inutilis in medieval law and literature, 754–1327* (Princeton, 1970).

Petersohn, J. "Das Präskriptionsrecht der Römischen Kirche und der Konstanzer Vertrag," in K. Herbers, H. Kortüm, and C. Servatius, eds., *Ex ipsis rerum documentis. Beiträge zur Mediävistik. Festschrift für H. Zimmermann zum 65. Geburtstag* (Sigmaringen, 1991) 307–15.

Philippart, G. *Les légendiers latins et autres manuscrits hagiographiques* (Typologie des sources du moyen âge occidental 24–25; Turnhout, 1977).

Piergiovanni, V. *La punibilità degli innocenti nel diritto canonico dell'età classica I: La discussione del problema in Graziano e nella decretalistica* (Milan, 1971).

————. "La lesa maestà nella canonistica fino ad Uguccione," *Materiali per una storia della cultura giuridica* 2 (1972) 55–88.

Portemer, J. *Etudes sur les "Differentie iuris civilis et canonici" au temps du droit classique de l'église* (Paris, 1946).

Post, G. "Copyists' errors and the problem of papal dispensations 'contra statutum generale ecclesiae' or 'contra statum generalem ecclesiae' according to the decretists and decretalists, ca. 1150–1234," SG 9 (1966) 359–405.

Powell, J. "Honorius III's 'Sermo de dedicatione ecclesie Lateranensis' and the historical-liturgical traditions of the Lateran," AHP 21 (1983) 195–209.

Prosdocimi, L. "La 'Summa Decretorum' di Uguccione da Pisa," SG 3 (1955) 349–74.

————. "I manoscritti della 'Summa Decretorum' di Uguccione da Pisa: Iter Germanicum," SG 7 (1959) 251–72.

Rambaud, J. "Le legs de l'ancien droit: Gratien. Le legs de droit romain," in G. Le Bras, ed., *Histoire du droit,* 119–29.

Raming, I. *Der Ausschluß der Frau vom priesterlichen Amt. Gottgewollte Tradition oder Diskriminierung?* (Cologne/Vienna, 1973); English trans. by N. Adams, *The exclusion of women from the priesthood* (Metuchen, N.J., 1976).

Reuter, T., and G. Silagi. *Wortkonkordanz zum Decretum Gratiani* (MGH—Hilfsmittel 10.1–5; Munich, 1990).

Rigaudière, A. "Regnum et civitas chez les décrétistes et les premiers décrétalistes (1150 env.–1250 env.)." *Théologie et droit dans la science politique de l'état moderne* (Collection de l'Ecole française de Rome 147; Rome, 1991) 117–53.

Rink, O. "Die Lehre von der Interpellation beim Paulinischen Privileg in der Kirchenrechtsschule von Bologna, 1140–1234," *Traditio* 8 (1952) 306–65.

Ríos-Fernández, M. "El primado del Romano pontífice nel pensamiento de Huguccio de Pisa decretista," *Compostellanum* 6 (1961) 47–97, 7 (1962) 97–149, 8 (1963) 65–99, 11 (1966) 29–67.

Roussier, J. *Le fondement de l'obligation contractuelle dans le droit classique de l'église* (Paris, 1933).

Russell, F. *The just war in the Middle Ages* (Cambridge, 1975).

Sarti, M. *De claris archigymnasii Bononiensis professoribus* 1–2 (Bologna, 1769–72), ed. M. Fattorini; second ed. by C. Albicinius and C. Malagola (Bologna, 1888–96).

Savioli, L. *Annales Bolognesi* 2.1 (Bassano, 1789).

Scavo-Lombardo, M. *Il concetto di buona fede nel diritto canonico* (Rome, 1944).

Scharnagl, A. *Das feierliche Gelübde als Ehehindernis* (Freiburg, 1908) 153–56.

Schizzerotto, G. "Uguccione da Pisa," *Enciclopedia dantesca* 5 (1976) 800–802.

Schmitz, H. *Appellatio extraiudicalis. Entwicklungslinien einer kirchlichen*

Gerichtsbarkeit über die Verwaltung im Zeitalter der klassischen Kanonistik (1140–1348) (Munich, 1970).

Schulte, J. F. v. *Geschichte der Quellen und Literatur des canonischen Rechts von Gratian bis auf die Gegenwart* 1 (Stuttgart, 1875).

Sguicciarini, D. *Il privilegio paolino in un testo inedito di Uguccione da Pisa* (Rome, 1973).

Soetermeer, F. "Une catégorie de commentaires peu connue. Les 'commenta' ou 'lecturae' inédites des précurseurs d'Odofrède," *Rivista internazionale di diritto commune* 2 (1991) 47–67.

Somerville, R. "Pope Innocent II and the study of Roman law," *Revue des études islamiques* 44 (1976) 105–14 = idem, *Papacy, councils, and canon law in the 11th–12th centuries* (Aldershot, 1990) n. 4.

Sot, M. *Gesta abbatum. Gesta episcoporum* (Typologie des sources du moyen âge occidental 37; Turnhout, 1981).

Stenger, R. "The episcopacy as an ordo according to the medieval canonists," *Medieval studies* 29 (1967) 67–112.

Stickler, A. "Der Schwerterbegriff bei Huguccio," *Ephemerides iuris canonici* 3 (1947) 201–42.

———. "Sacerdotium et Regnum nei decretisti e primi decretalisti. Considerazioni metodologiche di ricerca e testi," *Salesianum* 15 (1953) 575–612.

———. "Imperator vicarius papae. Die Lehren der französisch-deutschen Dekretistenschule des 12. und beginnenden 13. Jahrhunderts über die Beziehung zwischen Papst und Kaiser," *MIÖG* 62 (1954) 165–212.

———. "Decretisti Bolognesi dimenticati," *SG* 3 (1955) 375–410; revised version of "Vergessene Bologneser Dekretisten," *Salesianum* 4 (1952) 481–503.

———. "Decretistica Germanica adaucta," *Traditio* 12 (1956) 593–605.

———. "Problemi di ricerca e di edizione per Uguccione da Pisa e nella decretistica classica," *Bibliothèque de la Revue d'histoire ecclésiastique* 33 (1959) 111–28.

———. "Huguccio," *LThK* 5 (1960) 521–22.

———. "Uguccio de Pise," *DDC* 7 (1965) 1355–62.

———. "Il canonista Laurentius Hispanus," *SG* 9 (1966) 461–550.

———. "Hugh (Huguccio)," *NCE* 5 (1967) 200–201.

———. "La 'sollicitudo omnium ecclesiarum' nella canonistica classica," in G. Ercole and A. Stickler, eds., *Communione interecclesiale: collegialità—primato—ecumenismo* (Communio 13; Rome, 1972) 2.547–86.

———. "Die Ekklesiologie des Dekretisten Huguccio von Pisa," *Proceedings Berkeley* (Vatican City, 1985) 333–49.

Tanon, L. "Etude de litterature canonique: Rufin et Huguccio," *Nouvelle revue historique de droit français et étranger* 13 (1889) 681–728.

Teetaert, A. *La confession aux laiques dans l'église latine depuis le viiie jusqu'au xive siècle* (Wetteren/Bruges/Paris, 1926).

Thurston, D., and D. Attwater, eds. *Butler's lives of the saints* (4 vols; New York, 1956).

Tierney, B. "Some recent work on the political theories of the medieval canonists," *Traditio* 10 (1954) 594–625 = idem, *Church law* n. i.

———. *Foundations of the conciliar theory. The contribution of the medieval canonists from Gratian to the Great Schism* (Cambridge, 1955).

———. "Pope and council: Some new decretist texts," *Medieval studies* 19 (1957) 197–218 = idem, *Church law*, n. ii.

———. *The origins of papal infallibility 1150–1350* (Leiden/London, 1972); repr., with a "postscript" (Leiden/London, 1988).

———. "'Only the truth has authority': The problem of 'Reception' in the decretists and in Johannes of Turrecremata," in K. Pennington and R. Somerville, eds., *Law, church and society. Essays in honor of Stephan Kuttner* (Philadelphia, 1977) 69–96 = B. Tierney, *Church law*, n. xiv.

———. *Church law and constitutional thought in the Middle Ages* (London, 1979).

———. "Origins of natural rights language: texts and contexts, 1150–1250," *History of political thought* 10 (1989) 615–46.

Tiraboschi, G. *Storia dell'augusta Badia di S. Silvestro di Nonantola, aggiuntovi il codice diplomatico della medesima* 1–2 (Modena, 1785–86).

Van de Wouw, H. "Notes on the Aschaffenburg manuscript Perg. 26," BMCL 3 (1973) 97–107.

———. "Guido de Baysio," LMA 4 (1989) 1774.

Van Hove, A. "La territorialité et la personnalité des lois en droit canonique depuis Gratien (vers 1140) jusqu'à Jean d'Andreae (m. 1348)," RHD 3 (1922) 277–332.

———. "Droit justinien et droit canonique depuis le Décret de Gratien," *Miscellanea van der Essen* (Brussels, 1948) 1.257–71.

Vetulani, A. "Gratien et le droit romain," RHDFE 24–25 (1947–48) 11–48; repr., with "addenda et corrigenda," in idem, *Sur Gratien et les décrétales*, ed. W. Uruszczak (Aldershot, 1990) n. 3.

———. "Trois manuscrits canoniques de la Bibliothèque Publique de Leningrad," SG 12 (1967) 195–201.

Vilain, N. "Préscription et bonne foi du Décret de Gratien (1140) à Jean d'André (m. 1348)," *Traditio* 14 (1958) 121–89.

Vodola, E. *Excommunication in the Middle Ages* (Berkeley/Los Angeles/London, 1986).

Watt, J. "The theory of papal monarchy in the thirteenth century: The contribution of the canonists," *Traditio* 20 (1964) 179–317; repr. separately (New York, 1965).

Weigand, R. *Die bedingte Eheschliessung im kanonischen Recht I: Die Entwicklung der bedingten Eheschliessung im kanonischen Recht. Ein Beitrag zur Geschichte der Kanonistik von Gratian bis Gregor IX.* (Munich, 1963).

———. "Die Lehre der Kanonisten des 12. und 13. Jahrhunderts von den Ehezwecken," SG 12 (1967) 445–78.

———. *Die Naturrechtslehre der Legisten und Dekretisten von Irnerius bis Accursius und von Gratian bis Johannes Teutonicus* (Munich, 1967).

———. "Die Rechtslehre der Scholastik bei den Dekretisten und Dekretalisten," *Ius canonicum* 16 (1976) 61–90; also in: *Persona y derecho* 4 (1977) 339–70.

————. "Bazianus und B-Glossen zum Dekret Gratians," SG 19 (1976) 453–96.

————. "Romanisierungstendenzen im frühen kanonischen Recht," ZRG Kan. Abt. 69 (1983) 200–49.

————. "Huguccio und der Glossenapparat 'Ordinaturus Magister,'" AKKR 154 (1985) 490–520.

————. "Die anglo-normannische Kanonistik in den letzten Jahrzehnten des 12. Jahrhunderts," *Proceedings Cambridge* (Vatican City, 1988) 249–63.

————. "Die Glossen des Johannes Faventinus zur Causa 1 des Dekrets und ihr Vorkommen in späteren Glossenapparaten," AKKR 157 (1988) 73–101.

————. "Die Durchsetzung des Konsensprinzips im kirchlichen Eherecht," ÖAKR 38 (1989) 301–14.

————. "Burchardauszüge in Dekrethandschriften und ihre Verwendung bei Rufin und als Paleae im Dekret Gratians," AKKR 158 (1989) 429–51.

————. "Paleae und andere Zusätze in Dekrethandschriften mit dem Glossenapparat 'Ordinaturus Magister,'" AKKR 159 (1990) 448–63.

————. "Huguccio von Pisa," LMA 5 (1990) 89–90.

————. "Frühe Kanonisten und ihre Karriere in der Kirche," ZRG Kan. Abt. 76 (1990) 131–58.

————. *Die Glossen zum Dekret Gratians. Studien zu den frühen Glossen und Glossenkompositionen* (SG 25–26; Rome, 1991).

————, ed. *Gesammelte Schriften zur klassischen Kanonistik von Franz Gillmann 1: Schriften zum Dekret Gratians und den Dekretisten* (Würzburg, 1988).

Weimar, P. "Die legistische Literatur der Glossatorenzeit," in H. Coing, ed., *Handbuch*, 129–60.

————. "Differentienliteratur," LMA 3 (1986) 1042–43.

————. "Dissensiones dominorum," LMA 3 (1986) 1120–21.

————, ed. *Die Renaissance der Wissenschaften im 12. Jahrhundert* (Zurich, 1981).

Weinzierl, K. *Die Restitutionslehre der Frühscholastik* (Munich, 1936).

————. "Das Zinsproblem im Dekret Gratians und in den Summen zum Dekret," SG 1 (1953) 549–76.

Weitzel, J. *Begriff und Erscheinungsformen der Simonie bei Gratian und den Dekretisten* (Munich, 1967).

Zeliauskas, A. *De excommunicatione vitiata apud glossatores, (1140–1350)* (Zurich, 1967).

Zulueta, F. de, and P. Stein. *The teaching of Roman law in England around 1200* (London, 1990).

INDEX OF REFERENCES TO MEDIEVAL
LEGAL COMMENTARIES

GENERAL INDEX

Huguccio: The Life, Works, and Thought of a Twelfth-Century Jurist
was composed in Sabon by Brevis Press, Bethany, Connecticut;
printed and bound by Thomson-Shore, Inc., Dexter, Michigan;
and designed and produced by Kachergis Book Design,
Pittsboro, North Carolina.